The Roots of African-American Identity

The Roots of African-American Identity

Memory and History in Free Antebellum Communities

ELIZABETH RAUH BETHEL

St. Martin's Press
New York

ISBN 0-312-21836-2 (paper)
ISBN 0-312-12860-6 (cloth)

Library of Congress Cataloging-in-Publication Data
Bethel, Elizabeth Rauh.
    Under the trees that we have planted : memory and history in the
Antebellum free African-American community / Elizabeth Rauh Bethel.
        p. cm.
    Includes bibliographical references and index.
    ISBN 0-312-12860-6
    1. Free Afro-Americans—History. 2. Afro-Americans—History—To
1863. 3. Afro-Americans—Race identity. 4. Afro-Americans—
Historiography. I. Title.
E185.18.B48 1997
973'.0496073—dc21   96-54636
                                                      CIP

Design by Acme Art, Inc.
First published in hardcover: 1997
10 9 8 7 6 5 4 3 2 1

CONTENTS

for
Lorenzo Johnson Greene

PREFACE

The Roots of African-American Identity spans the eight decades between the American Revolution and the Civil War and focuses on African Americans living in the nominally free northern and western states. Although the book is anchored in particular events and social structural processes, it is not a conventional narrative history. This is, rather, a series of essays arranged in a loosely chronological form. I beg the indulgence of the historians. My aim was to write about race, to explore the construction of a politicized racial identity, and to examine the ways in which a relatively small population of free African Americans living in the antebellum North reformulated their collective past and, as a result of that reformation, then perceived, understood, acted upon, and remembered particular events. My interest and emphasis is human agency and how a group of fundamentally marginalized people crafted a uniquely New World ethnic identity that informed popular African-American historical consciousness.

This is a book about the transition from individualized and autobiographical rememberings of particular events to corporate memory—the memories of families, of communities, and of generations that offer critical evaluation and reinterpretation to the individualized experience; and it is a book about how the collective representations around which that corporate memory revolved, and the popular historical consciousness that gives form and substance to all memory, fueled collective efforts to claim and live a promised but undelivered democratic freedom in the years between the American Revolution and the Civil War. The vision of freedom and historical consciousness crafted during the antebellum years by African Americans living in the free states of the North proved powerful and enduring. In an immediate sense, that vision and consciousness drove the National Convention Movement, the first civil rights movement in the United States, informed mass migrations to Haiti and Canada and a smaller migration to Africa, and, in a less immediate manner, shaped post-1865 African-American participation in Reconstruction, formed the spiritual and ideological foundation for the modern Pan-African movement, and provided the historical legacy for the civil rights movement of the 1960s.

On March 5, 1858, a festival at Boston's Faneuil Hall commemorated the anniversary of Crispus Attucks's death and protested the *Dred Scott* decision. I have used that festival as the vehicle to explore the connection between cultural memory and popular historical consciousness and to illustrate the crucial role opinion leaders play in the construction of both memory and consciousness. The occasion and the activities of that evening reflected a national African-American political agenda of considerable scope and vision that had been crafted over eight decades of collective struggle. William Cooper Nell, active in the anti-slavery movement and generally regarded as the first African-American historian, had fashioned a gathering rich in the iconography of African-American protest. Two martyred heroes—Crispus Attucks and Dred Scott—formed the centerpiece of the Festival. Their lives and deaths spanned the life of the nation. Attucks symbolized the promises for equality and freedom embedded in the American Revolution and Scott represented the tragic failure, the contemporary realities peoples of African descent faced in the United States. The Prologue examines the details of the Commemorative Festival, and through those details—especially the lives of the participants—poses the importance of generational memory as the foundation for historical consciousness.

Part I, "Fashioning a Moral Community, 1775-1800," takes as its focus the era of the First Emancipation, the ending of slavery in the Northern states, and explores the expectations African Americans living in the North held for full and unconditional inclusion in the life of the nation. Chapter 1, "'In the Bowels of a Free and Christian Country': Living in the Revolutionary Era," views those expectations through the experiences of Revolutionary War soldiers and in the fundamentally rural milieu of Revolutionary America. Emphasizing the discontinuity between the lived and the remembered past, this chapter focuses on the lives and circumstances of four African-American Revolutionary War soldiers: Quomony Quash, Cato Howe, Plato Turner, and Prince Goodwin. Implicit contrasts between William Cooper Nell, the patrician Bostonian, and the proletarian soldiers underscore the discontinuities between the lived and the remembered pasts. The chapter crafts a portrait of the social and political contours of race identity during the Revolutionary Era. Chapter 2, "'Sons and Daughters of Distress': A Theology of Liberation," examines the development of an explicitly African-American theology in the urban areas of the post-Revolutionary North. Taken together, the first and second chapters argue for an intersection of the physical and the spiritual in the creation of the moral community that would inform both corporate memory and collective action in subsequent decades.

Part II, "Environments of Memory, 1800-1835," focuses on two crucial events around which race identity and consciousness revolved for African Americans during the early decades of the nineteenth century: 1807-8 federal legislation prohibiting U.S. participation in the African slave trade, which seemed to African Americans to promise the ending of slavery in the United States as well as cultural reunification with a lost legacy; and the Haytian Revolution, which held forth a model of political agency and racial achievement denied to African Americans living in the United States. Chapter 3, "From Laws and Revolutions, Freedom *Lieux*," examines the process by which the historical event is lifted from the larger movement of history, seemingly frozen in time, and then transformed into a collective representation, a *lieu de memoire* that is only loosely connected to the original event. Chapter 4, "Africa Envisioned, Africa Found," extends this analysis into the particularistic domain of Africa, the lost homeland and the reclaimed legacy. Chapter 5, "Moral Community, Ethnic Identity, and Political Action" returns the focus to the U.S. milieu and to the 1829 Cincinnati Crisis as a catalytic event. The chapter demonstrates the power of race identity that has been crafted on a *lieu de memoire* to drive collective mobilization and political action.

Part III, "History and the Politics of Memory, 1835-1860," is anchored in the New World Diaspora, a time when an estimated 20 percent of the free African-American population left the United States to establish permanent homes in Canada, Haiti, or Africa. Chapter 6, "Haiti, Canada, and a Pan-African Vision," contrasts the Haytian and Canadian migrations and argues for the enduring power of the freedom *lieux*. African Americans had elevated Toussaint, the Haytian slave revolutionaries, and the events surrounding the creation of the island republic to a mythic stature. Haiti represented a model of race unity and political agency that contrasted sharply with their own circumstances. After 1820, many African Americans sought to translate the physical emancipation and spiritual reunification Haiti symbolized into personal action. Over subsequent decades approximately thirteen thousand African Americans migrated to Haiti. The migration, which forged new connections between Haiti and African Americans living in the United States, informed a popular historical consciousness firmly anchored in New World milieux of memory. In contrast, Canada offered not opportunity but sanctuary, and an estimated sixty thousand African-American refugees fled the United States for that sanctuary. African

Americans were concerned, even preoccupied, with emigration after 1835, and particularly with conditions in the Canadian refugee settlements. That preoccupation anticipated the drive for the cultural unification of people of color that has informed Pan-Africanism into the twentieth century. Chapter 7, "Biography, Narrative, and Memory: The Construction of a Popular Historical Consciousness," focuses on three texts published between 1840 and 1865 that employ established African-American themes to consciously reshape race identity and challenge two fundamental tenets of American racism, the inherent biological foundations of African inferiority and the moral rightness of the subordination of Africans: J. W. C. Pennington's *Text-Book of the Origins and History of the Colored People* (1841); William Cooper Nell's *Colored Patriots of the American Revolution* (1855); and William Wells Brown's *The Black Man: His Antecedents, His Achievements, and His Genius* (1863). Within these three productions memory has been transformed into an apparatus designed to serve specific political and ideological ends. While the *milieux de memoire* are varied—Africa, the American Revolution, transnational heroes—the *lieux de memoire* uniformly address American issues: full and unconditional citizenship; economic, political, and cultural equity and equality.

The Epilogue, "Emancipation, Reconstruction, and Empire-Building," focuses on two texts: William Still's, *The Underground Rail Road* (1873), and Frances Ellen Watkins Harper's *Iola Leroy* (1893). Both focus on Southern topics, Still on flights from slavery and Harper on African-American physical and cultural reunification in the South during Reconstruction. Considered as interrelated productions, these two texts illustrate the transition of African-American memory from a focus on personally lived experiences recounted in real time through autobiographical memory, to collective experiences recalled through constructed memory and told in historical time. An examination of that process illuminates how a people reshaped and politicized collective identity. The popular historical consciousness that resulted from this body of shared beliefs, myths, and images connected a New World past to an American present and validated a vision of the future that informed the African-American political agenda into the twentieth century.

The research for this book began in 1981 at the Parting Ways Museum in Plymouth, Massachusetts, when Marjorie Anderson, then the director of the museum, first introduced me to the four obscure Revolutionary War soldiers—Quomony Quash, Cato Howe, Plato Turner, and Prince Goodwin—who form the centerpiece of Chapter 1,

"'In the Bowels of a Free and Christian Country,' Living in the Revolutionary Era." For that introduction I remain most grateful. In a project that has spanned so many years, I have incurred enormous debts, both intellectual and personal. In many cases there is an overlap between the two categories. The process began that year when Rhett Jones, Donald M. Scott, and Lorenzo Johnson Green guided my work for the museum. They were generous and gracious to this sociologist who had wandered onto the historian's terrain. During that year Professor Green and I formed an intellectual friendship deeper than any I have experienced before or after. He guided me in my initial forays through the material in chapters 2 and 3, "'Sons and Daughters of Distress': A Theology of Liberation," and "From Laws and Revolutions, Freedom *Lieux*"; and shortly before his death he told me to write this book. I hope he is satisfied with my work.

In 1983 I received a fellowship to support study and research at the Newberry Library. There I enjoyed the intellectual support and the hospitality of Richard Brown as I worked my way through the delights of the Newberry, material related to the development of African-American communities in the Old Northwest and to the Canadian migration. For four years, from 1985 through 1989, Donald Scott, sharing his near-encyclopedic knowledge of archival resources, guided me from one repository of Americana to the next: The American Antiquarian Society (1985, 1986), The W. E. B. DuBois Institute at Harvard University (1986), The Boston Public Library (1986), The Rhode Island Historical Society (1986), The New Bedford Historical Society and Whaling Museum (1986), The Library Company of Philadelphia (1987), The Historical Society of Pennsylvania (1987), and The Schomburg Center of the New York Public Library (1988). I was supported during this period by fellowships from the National Endowment for the Humanities, The Rockefeller Foundation, The American Antiquarian Society (Peterson Fellowship), and the Historical Society of Pennsylvania. During this period of research the essays that have become chapters began to take form as I grappled with the distinction between the mass migrations to Haiti, the African west coast, and Canada, and with the forces that fueled those migrations. Throughout that time I was blessed to work with archivists and librarians whose bibliographic skill and knowledge far surpassed mine and without whose support and guidance this book would lack substance. For their enthusiasm and their thoughtful assistance, I am particularly indebted to: Nancy Burkett, Georgia Barnhill, Keith Arbor, Phil Lapsansky, Howard Dodson, Diana Lachatanere, and Betty Gubert.

From 1987 through 1990 I participated in the Memory and History Working Group at the DuBois Institute, Harvard University, and it was during that time, guided and encouraged by my colleagues in the working group, that I began to organize the body of material around the theme of memory, collective representations, and popular historical consciousness. Randall Burkett shared his understandings and insights about African-American clergy with me, and in dialogue with him I revisited and reinterpreted the African migration. Nathan Huggins urged me not to overlook nor to underestimate the National Convention Movement. His imprint on chapter 5, Moral Community, Ethnic Identity, and Political Action, is clear. I refined my perspective on the African material that eventually became chapter 4, Africa Envisioned, Africa Found, during 1989, when I was fortunate to attend Leonard Thompson's NEH Summer Seminar on Political Mythology. Professor Thompson and my colleagues in the seminar were enormously helpful in my efforts to bring order to a massive amount of data. The material in chapter 7, Biography, Narrative, and Memory: The Construction of a Popular Historical Consciousness, and the Epilogue, Emancipation, Reconstruction, and Empire-Building, has grown from a series of lectures I gave in India during the first half of 1990. There, in settings far removed from my familiar environment, I was forced to make fresh sense of William Cooper Nell, William Wells Brown, William Still, and Frances Ellen Watkins Harper. I am grateful to my students and Indian colleagues for their questions and their demands for intellectual integrity. Conversations with Professors Sundarum and Jayalakshmi at the University of Madras, Professor Rita Ray at Osmania University, and Professor Shankar at Bharathidasan University were especially crucial in shaping my thinking on the politicization of race identity.

My students have been an ongoing source of critical support as I have worked my way through various pieces of the argument that is now this book: The participants in my 1984 and 1986 NEH Seminars for School Teachers, "Autobiography and African-American Identity," at the Rhode Island Black Heritage Society were certainly critical consumers and colleagues. The students at Lander University who over the past decade have enrolled in my African-American Communities course always have demanded that the argument not just be pretty, but also makes sense; the participants in my seminar "Memory and Sociological Methodology," sponsored by the United States Educational Foundation in India and held at the University of Madras in 1990, offered rich insights into the ways in which ethnic identity shapes politics and collective action. Several of my colleagues merit special mention: Marvin Cann, Genevieve Fabre, Patricia Evridge Hill, Bettie Horne, Terry Lancaster, Nellie McKay, Lynda Penland, Samrendra Singh, Rowena Stewart, Meredith Uttley, and Friederike Wiedemann. For various reasons I am very grateful to each of you. Friends, in and out of the academy, have sustained me at various times: Dorinda Beaumont, while I was working at the Schomburg; Nancy DeRoche and Mary Bennett, as I traveled up and down the East Coast between Lander and Harvard; Joan Scott, whose ability to combine friendship with intellectual criticism continues to enrich my life; Mike and Sue Monaghan, whose "midnight specials" at their swimming pool have been important to my late-night productivity. At St. Martin's Press, Jennifer Farthing, Maura Burnett, and Alan Bradshaw have imposed their skills, wit and professionalism on the process required to transform a manuscript into a book.

Lander University is a small, four-year liberal arts institution. It is a university grounded in teaching, not research. Yet it has proved itself, again, as able and willing to accommodate this scholar-at-work. I am grateful for the sabbatical I received in 1995 that provided the time I needed to complete a final full draft of the manuscript. I am grateful, too, for the skill and the enthusiasm of the librarians. Without the assistance of Dan Lee, Betty Williams, and Susan Going this book would not have been completed.

Ann Crawley has again endured the disruption of our life with her unfailing good grace and good humor. Thank you.

The Revolution Remembered: The Fifth of March, 1858

*The colored people of the United States have no destiny
separate from that of the nation of which they form an
integral part. . . . If we, born in America, cannot live upon
the same soil in terms of equality . . . then the fundamental
theory of the American Republic fails, and falls to the
ground.*

—William Cooper Nell, 1860[1]

DURING LATE FEBRUARY 1858, a broadside prepared by William Cooper
Nell appeared in Boston announcing that a Commemorative Festival
would be held at Faneuil Hall on Friday, March 5, 1858. The date marked
two important events for African Americans: On March 5, 1770, Crispus
Attucks, a fugitive from slavery, had been the first American to die in the
Revolution, during the Boston Massacre; and on March 5, 1857, the
United States Supreme Court had declared that African Americans had
no rights that white Americans were bound to respect when it rendered
its decision regarding Dred Scott's freedom suit. Crispus Attucks symbolized a lost American heritage, and Dred Scott represented the failed
possibilities, the tragic contemporary realities for people of African
descent in the United States.[2]

Following a pattern of public celebrations and rituals well established in nineteenth-century America, and reflecting increasingly focused
demands for civil equality among African Americans living in the
Northern states, the Commemorative Festival welded the two historical
moments into a public celebratory rite that simultaneously claimed for
African Americans the civic legacy of the Revolution and protested the

persistence of slavery in the nation they had helped to create. This rite would be repeated annually from 1858 through 1865, when slavery was at last ended in the United States.

On March 5, the day of the Festival, an invitation to "The Great Faneuil Hall Meeting" appeared in William Lloyd Garrison's anti-slavery newspaper, *The Liberator,* over the signature of John T. Hilton:

> Friends of freedom, awake! and come to the meeting to be held in Faneuil Hall, on Friday evening, March 5th. . . . Yea, rally and commemorate the massacre of 1770, when Attucks fell, and bled for Liberty! Come, listen to the eloquence of Phillips, Parker, and Remond! Come to the charms of music—participate in the refreshments—and view the relics of by-gone days!
>
> Come one, come all! Rock the Cradle of Freedom, and render this an occasion to be remembered.
>
> John T. Hilton[3]

John T. Hilton was well known to the Bostonians who read *The Liberator.* A veteran of the Revolutionary War, a founding member of the General Coloured Association of Massachusetts, a civil rights organization established by "some of the most progressive Negroes of Boston" in 1828 (five years before William Lloyd Garrison established the American Anti-Slavery Society and popularized the anti-slavery cause in the United States), Hilton had been an acknowledged and respected leader within Boston's African-American community and a consistent advocate of full and unconditional civil rights for African Americans for more than half a century when he affixed his name to the invitation printed in *The Liberator.* In addition to his military service during the Revolution, Hilton had supported David Walker during the 1820s; he had joined with William C. Nell, John S. Rock, and Benjamin Roberts— men thirty years his junior—in the battle to desegregate the Boston public schools during the 1840s and 1850s; he had been among those who sought during the 1850s to erect a monument in Boston to memorialize Crispus Attucks, the fallen hero of the Boston Massacre.[4] With few of his generation still alive, Hilton's personal history of civil rights activism forged an important symbolic link between the autobiographically remembered past that the Festival memorialized and the circumstances of the lived present that the Festival protested. Hilton's imprimatur lent enormous credence to this public ritual that recalled and reconstructed the Revolution through an explicit vocabulary of political protest. Within the ritual of the Festival, the remembered heroic past was joined with the tragedy of the lived present, and the fused imagery that resulted traced the cultural and political geography of African-American identity at mid-century.

The Commemorative Festival of 1858 had been crafted from well-established nineteenth-century cultural traditions surrounding public ceremony and celebration. In an age when literacy was limited and mass communication media primitive, the ritual and oratory embedded in public gatherings contained deep political and cultural significance for Americans of both European and African descent. Parades, processions, and festivals—common forms of ceremony and ritual—provided opportunities for people to publicly proclaim a collective identity and also served to strengthen and solidify the boundaries of class and ethnicity that buttressed and circumscribed American politics of self-interest. At the same time, for Americans of European ancestry, public celebrations of a common past—such as the Fourth of July—forged a collective national identity.[5] The constructed memories surrounding these events held social, political, and cultural significance for all the participants. Such was the case with the Commemorative Festival.

By the middle years of the nineteenth century, personal memories of the Revolution had for the most part been replaced by a public body of cultural myth that described the nation's beginnings. In that myth, the colonists who reluctantly had taken up arms against the British had been transformed from the "summer soldiers and sunshine patriots" Tom Paine had lambasted into men of heroic stature; and in the shift from real time to remembered time, the events that had marked the progress of the Revolution from tentative protest to intentional nation-building had become publicly fixed local holiday celebrations.[6] Yet, in the nation of twenty-nine million, three million African Americans had been excised from the public memory of a war in which many of their fathers and grandfathers had fought and some had died. At mid-century, neither the myth of the remembered past nor the lived reality of daily life acknowledged the vital presence of African Americans in a nation they had helped to create.

Despite this public betrayal, resonant personal memories of that Revolution had been preserved within African-American families and communities for three generations, and the unfulfilled promises of civic equality that circumscribed daily life contrasted dramatically with the civil liberties implicitly held forth by the remembered promise of the Revolutionary moment. William Cooper Nell—journalist and business agent, civil rights activist by avocation, son of a Revolutionary War veteran—sought to transform those autobiographical and fundamentally private legacies into a national, public consciousness.[7] Nell capitalized on the preserved memories of fathers and grandfathers who had directly exchanged enslavement for freedom by enlisting in the state militia or the Continental Army. The Commemorative Festival he organized joined together those autobiographical, family, and community memories with material documentation of the legacy of oppression and exclusion that paralleled the historical movement of those memories. The resulting festival, spanning eight decades of undelivered promises, served two interconnected purposes: it celebrated a lost African-American past, and it validated the contemporary demands of African Americans for full and unconditional inclusion in the civic life of the nation they had helped create.

MEMORY POLITICIZED

On the surface, the Commemorative Festival appeared typical of the anti-slavery meetings held in Boston and elsewhere throughout the Northern states during the antebellum years. William Lloyd Garrison, Theodore Parker, Wendell Phillips, John S. Rock, and Charles Lenox Remond were featured platform speakers. The gathering was held in Faneuil Hall, a place where abolitionists had been pressing their cause for more than a quarter of a century. Yet, this gathering differed in two crucial respects from other protests against and demands for an end to slavery. First, prominent white abolitionists did not share the evening's spotlight with one or two meticulously groomed and promoted professional fugitives. Rather, the whites—Garrison, Parker, and Phillips—had been invited to participate in an event organized and carried out by African Americans. Second, this event was not intended as an explicit protest against slavery. It had been designed specifically to revise and expand the myth of the nation's beginnings in such a fashion as to include African Americans; and in so doing, the Commemorative Festival drew on a long-standing African-American celebratory tradition as it constructed an historical validation for contemporary protests against injustice and demands for full and unconditional rights as American citizens.

In the years following the Revolutionary War, autobiographical vision and desire had intersected with the discontinuities explicit in the lived and then remembered moment. Crafted within a milieu of

disappointment and disillusionment, events that symbolized the promised deliverance, identified at those intersections, then crystallized as
resonant *lieux de memoire*—empirical and symbolic sites—from which
African-American cultural memory developed.[8] Anticipating subsequent
movements among immigrants, working people, and women, the
African-American tension between a lost past and an uncertain future
forged a popular historical consciousness from those *lieux de memoire,*
moments in history "torn away from the movement of history."[9] Within
the boundaries of consciousness, movements driven by nationalism
aimed to reconcile the contradictions that derived from African ancestry
combined with New World nativity. Simultaneously, those movements
advanced African Americans' claims to physical, cultural, intellectual,
and spiritual autonomy and equality. By mid-century, within African-
American cultural memory a legacy of suffering contended with a vision
of the deliverance from that suffering, and public litanies of misery had
been eclipsed by an unrestrained collective demand for full inclusion in
the civic life of the nation and the cultural reunification of a people
fractured by New World enslavement.

Freedom festivals that recalled and signified these moments
anchored an African-American cultural map that had been expanded and
elaborated in the years between the Revolution and the Civil War. That
map differed in several important ways from the national calendar of
festivals and holidays white Americans celebrated. Among white Americans, public celebrations of the national calendar aimed from the earliest
years of the republic to fix the American collective consciousness on
specific moments in time and to invent from those moments a national
historical memory anchored in mythologized heroism. Gradually, local
celebrations of relatively localized moments, such as the Battle of Bunker
Hill celebrated annually in Boston for a time, were replaced by nationally
shared commemorations. In this manner, the Fourth of July became the
quintessential national freedom celebration for white Americans. During
the early years of the republic, the Fourth of July celebrations varied
enormously from place to place, ranging from pious, church-like
moments of public thanksgiving to rowdy events marked by "pomp and
parade . . . guns, bonfires and illuminations."[10] African-American
Revolutionary War veteran James Forten[11] described how heavily alco-
holized, public celebrations of national liberation became days of exile
for African Americans, when they "dare not be seen after twelve o' clock
. . . for no sooner do the fumes of that potent Devil, Liquor, mount into
the brain, than the poor black is assailed like the destroying Hyena or

the avaricious Wolf!"[12] Many must have shared the sentiment about the holiday Frederick Douglass[13] would express in 1860: "So long as slavery persists in the United States, Fourth of July celebrations serve only as a thin veil to cover up crimes which would disgrace a nation of savages."[14]

As a result, from the outset African Americans sought alternatives to the white Fourth of July celebrations from which they were symbolically and materially excluded, and they crafted freedom celebrations designed to reinvent and rearrange the national past.[15] From 1808 until the mid-1820s, many African Americans living in the northern states gathered to commemorate and celebrate the First of January. The date held dual significance in the African-American cultural calendar, since it was the anniversary both of Toussaint's declaration of the independent republic of Hayti and of the enactment of United States legislation prohibiting ships sailing under the nation's flag from participating in the African slave trade. For a time, Fourteenth of July celebrations marked the judicial ending of slavery in Massachusetts; and in New York State, African Americans celebrated the implementation in 1799 and 1817 of gradual emancipation legislation on July 5. From 1834, the year Great Britain abolished slavery in the British West Indies, until the 1865 general emancipation of slaves in the Southern United States, many African-American communities had celebrated British West Indies Emancipation Day on the First of August. Amid much pomp and parade, with carriaged processions of Revolutionary War veterans, members of benevolent and literary societies, and the committee on arrangements, entire communities made a public show of their "industry, integrity, [and] temperance." Women and children joined the parades, waving flags from the windows of omnibuses. Along waterways like the Hudson and Susquehanna rivers, chartered steamboats brought "large delegations from different localities" to common points of celebration like Geneva, New York and Harrisburg, Pennsylvania.[16] In a resonant declaration of Pan-African race unity, African-American communities made clear that the freedom of all descendants of Africa in the New World was a cause for great celebration.

Supported and reinforced by often elaborate rituals, focused always on the contradictions of slavery in a democratic society, these intentional and conscious rearrangements of the national calendar aimed to transform and reinvent the national past. While white festivals punctuated a consciously constructed and remembered collective national calendar, African-American celebrations fixed historical consciousness on moments that symbolized what could have been and should have been a common civic destiny and attempted to reconcile the fundamental paradox of an identity of self and consciousness of others that derived from African ancestry combined with residence in the New World. In both symbol and substance the 1858 Commemorative Festival reflected this legacy of freedom festivals.

In addition to the standard speeches by various luminaries of the anti-slavery movement, Nell had arranged an exhibition of "Emblems—Relics—Engravings—Documents . . . of Revolutionary and other Historic association," choral singing, and music "at intervals" by Bond's Quadrille Band. Tickets of admission could be bought for seventy-five cents at various abolitionist gathering places around Boston: Samuel S. Hanscom's periodicals shop on Cambridge; Bela Marsh's book shop on Bromfield; and the offices of *The Liberator* through Robert F. Wallcut, the paper's Boston agent. African-American women and men who were established and outspoken political activists, primarily professional, primarily free-born, dominated the evening's activities. They were people of privilege in their thirties and forties, people whose public behavior clearly was framed within a self-conscious identification with race. Many were relative newcomers to Boston, but others were Boston natives who traced their roots in the city's history back to the American Revolution. They had joined together in choral groups with names that proclaimed common heroes and shared politics: the Attucks Glee Club, the Bards of Freedom, and the Northern Singers shared the platform that night with John S. Rock and Charles L. Remond, the most dramatic and radicalized African-American orators of the period.

The seven-member Attucks Glee Club included two visual artists who would both gain national reputations and a future attorney and city judge, as well as a porter and a hairdresser who are otherwise relatively obscure. Edward Bannister had migrated from his native New Brunswick to Boston during the early 1850s, worked for a time as a hairdresser while he struggled to build his reputation as an artist, earned a solid reputation as a first-rate landscape painter, and was drawn into the anti-slavery movement and African-American city politics primarily through the interests and activities of his wife, Christiana Cartreaux.[17] William Simpson, a portrait artist, was a Buffalo native who had come to Boston with his companion, the white writer Matthew Wilson, in 1854. Although there is no evidence that Simpson lectured on the anti-slavery circuit, his work was known and admired by anti-slavery and civil rights activists. William Wells Brown described Simpson's portraits of John T. Hilton—"rich in depth of feeling" in full Masonic regalia—and the

Honorable Charles Sumner as "admired for their life-like appearance, as well as for the fine delineation that characterizes them."[18] The two artists stood on the platform at Faneuil Hall alongside the Ruffin brothers, George and James. George L. Ruffin, a future attorney and judge, was a newlywed in 1858 and working as a hairdresser. In 1853, his free-born parents had brought George and his seven brothers and sisters from Richmond, Virginia to Boston, a city they believed would be more hospitable to a free family of color than their Southern home had been. The elder Ruffins had chosen wisely; the family prospered in their new home. In 1858 George L. Ruffin married Josephine St. Pierre. Both the young Ruffins would enjoy long careers in public service and social reform that paralleled those of two lifelong abolitionist and social-reformer friends, Frederick Douglass and William Lloyd Garrison.[19]

John S. Rock—abolitionist, physician, dentist, attorney—delivered the first major address at the Festival. A relative newcomer to Boston— he had moved to the city from Philadelphia in 1853—Rock quickly had become involved in local anti-slavery and civil rights activities, meeting regularly with the Boston Vigilance Committee, providing medical care to sick fugitives who passed through Boston, and participating in the campaign to desegregate Boston's public schools. Rock maintained warm personal friendships with both Nell and Charles Lenox Remond, who would follow his remarks at the Festival with equally powerful oratory.[20]

Born in Salem, Massachusetts, Charles Lenox Remond had been actively involved in the anti-slavery and equal rights movements since 1838, when he was appointed the first African-American lecturer for the Massachusetts Anti-Slavery Society. The exceptionally well-known speaker had toured with other abolitionists through New England and the midwestern states and had been one of four Americans who represented the American Anti-Slavery Society at the 1840 World's Anti-Slavery Convention in London. With William Lloyd Garrison, Remond had refused to take his assigned seat on the floor of the convention when he learned that the American women delegates had been required to sit apart from the Convention proceedings, in a rear gallery of the auditorium. Remond and Garrison chose to sit with their women colleagues. Like John S. Rock, Remond had been involved in the campaign to desegregate the Boston public schools and, at the 1855 testimonial meeting honoring William Cooper Nell for his leadership in the campaign, Remond had proposed that African Americans should withhold the payment of their taxes until their civil rights—particularly the right to vote and serve on juries—were no longer denied them. Foreshadowing the twentieth-century Chicago and Harlem "Don't Buy Where You Can't Work" economic boycott of merchants and retail stores that discriminated in their employment practices, Remond urged a "No Privilege, No Pay" protest against state and local governments.[21] In 1858, Remond was at the pinnacle of his career: outspoken, flamboyant, and deeply respected and admired. His presence on the speaker's platform, like John Rock's, signaled a gathering deeply grounded in the traditions surrounding the anti-slavery and equal rights movements.

At a time when respectable women did not appear on public platforms, the anti-slavery movement provided both white and African-American women an avenue for public political participation that had not been previously available to them. The women who participated in the 1858 Festival were members of a feminist vanguard, women whose strong opposition to slavery proved more powerful than the prevailing norms mandating public silence on the issue. To be sure, during the 1830s the American Peace Society had encouraged women to become involved in "moral revolutions" and to support the ending of war through prayer, reading peace tracts, writing peace hymns, and inculcating appropriate values in their children, but women were actively discouraged from taking publicly visible actions on behalf of the peace cause. The earliest public activists in the anti-slavery movement were white Quaker and African-American women, the former drawing on a Quaker legacy that encouraged public participation of women in the affairs of the church and the latter drawn by race identity to the anti-slavery cause. Maria W. Stewart had lectured briefly in Boston on anti-slavery and racial uplift topics between 1831 and 1833, although her efforts had not been received very positively, and Sarah and Angelina Grimké would lead the brave women, white as well as African American, who risked their reputations and their physical safety to support the anti-slavery cause in public venues. A movement toward the equality of women within the public domain began in private parlors, but a groundswell of interest and concern as well as the popularity of early female abolitionist lecturers—the Grimké sisters, Maria Weston Chapman, Lydia Marie Child, Sarah Remond, and Frances Ellen Watkins—forged the inevitable link between the abolition of slavery and the rights of women.[22]

In addition to the two most well-known female participants at the 1858 Festival, Frances Ellen Watkins and Charlotte Forten, women appeared throughout the program and were publicly visible on the stage at Faneuil Hall, clearly transcending the "proper bounds of a Christian woman's conduct" and employing "unladylike methods" to support the anti-slavery cause.[23] The 1858 Festival provided an opportunity to both women and men to turn their literary and musical talents toward political ends. Watkins, whose anthem, "Freedom's Battle," had been composed especially for the occasion and was performed by the Attucks Glee Club, was a traveling representative with the State Anti-Slavery Society of Maine in 1858. She brought an impressive set of credentials to her contribution to the Festival. Born in 1825 to free parents in Baltimore, Maryland, orphaned at the age of three, and educated for a time in her uncle's private school in Baltimore, Watkins had been self-supporting since the age of thirteen. She had taught school before she went North, had joined the anti-slavery cause, and had published two volumes of poetry—*Forest Leaves* in 1846 and *Poems on Miscellaneous Subjects* in 1855. Garrison had written an introduction for the 1871 edition of *Poems.* She was a prolific writer; her essays on religion and abolition were published in various periodicals, including *The Anglo-African Magazine,* and after her debut as an anti-slavery lecturer in New Bedford—a place where other African Americans also entered the anti-slavery lecture circuit—Watkins began to speak regularly on behalf of the anti-slavery cause at a time when respectable women generally were discouraged from public speaking.[24] Watkins would continue to lead African-American protests against slavery, and after 1865, she condemned racism and denounced racial stereotypes. Her novel, *Iola Leroy, or Shadows Uplifted,* which would be published in 1893, challenged the political and cultural racism of the era by remembering slavery and Reconstruction through the lens of African-American experiences.

Like Watkins, Charlotte Forten had written an anthem for the Festival, a parody on "Red, White, and Blue" that was performed by the Northern Vocalists, an all-male quartet. Although the Philadelphian would be best remembered as a school teacher in the Carolina Sea Islands during Reconstruction, in 1858 Forten had been living in the home of Charles Lenox Remond for four years, sent north by her grandfather, James Forten, to obtain her education. Both the Forten household in Philadelphia and the Lenox household in Salem were vital intellectual, political, and cultural centers for the African-American intelligentsia, and Charlotte probably had been drawn in to participation in the Festival as a result of her residence at the Remond home.[25]

The occasion and the activities reflected a national African-American political agenda of considerable scope and vision. Shaped as much by the thought of Jupiter Hammon, the slave-orator of the Revolutionary Era,[26] as by the better-known slave-orator of the nineteenth century, Frederick Douglass, and as much by the middle class-uplift endeavors of Bostonian Nancy Gardner Prince[27] as by the grassroots resistance of Harriet Tubman,[28] that agenda had emerged from over eight decades of collective struggle. Transcending the factious and persistent debates regarding emigration to Africa or Hayti and withdrawal from the United States, a nation where slavery persisted unchallenged, versus the desirability of an integrated, biracial world that marked the public discourse among Martin Delany and Frederick Douglass, Charles Lenox Remond and Henry Highland Garnet, Nell, with his friends and colleagues, had fashioned a gathering rich in the iconography of African-American protest. Two martyred heroes stood at the center, their lives and deaths spanning the life of the nation.

MARTYRS AND HEROES

William Cooper Nell offered a keenly fashioned history lesson that evening. He began by reviving an abandoned local holiday that celebrated the beginnings of the Revolutionary War. The town of Boston had held an annual public celebration on the anniversary of the Boston Massacre—the night Attucks had died—on the fifth of March from 1770 until 1783, when it had been discontinued in favor of a Fourth of July celebration.[29] Nell transformed the meaning of that eighteenth-century town tradition by redefining the holiday, shrewdly centering Crispus Attucks in the already-popular cultural image of soldier-patriots engaged in an heroic battle. The story told through the symbolism of the Commemorative Festival became a metaphor for the nation's failure to make good the democratic promises of the Revolution to all her citizens.

Crispus Attucks had died on the night of the Boston Massacre. Like many of his countrymen who also would die in the coming war, Attucks's origins and the details of his life prior to the events on March 5, 1770, remain obscure. Whatever the details of his personal life may have been, African-American historians from Nell to Joseph T. Wilson, George Washington Williams, and Benjamin Quarles have kept his memory alive. Attucks has been described as a giant of a man, standing more than six feet tall and well-proportioned, "whose looks were enough to terrify any person." A mulatto, possibly part Indian, an escaped slave, probably coming to Boston from Framingham, Massachusetts, Attucks had been in his mid-forties in 1770. In the legend Nell constructed, Attucks led the charge that night, acting not as a misguided incendiary but as a "true patriot." Nell's narrative of the events began when Attucks heard the fire bell and left Thomas Simmons's victualling house to join the crowd gathering on King Street. He picked up a club from a handy woodpile and, brandishing it, he urged his comrades into battle, crying: "Be not afraid; they dare not fire: why do you hesitate, why do you not kill them, why not crush them at once?" William Cooper Nell portrayed Attucks as inspired by "the blessings of liberty, the horrors of slavery," as the historical centerpiece of the Commemorative Festival.[30] With the invented Attucks, Nell had elaborated a familiar element of African-American historical consciousness; a martyred hero whose loyalty and bravery had been repaid by the basest form of public neglect. He had been ignored and then forgotten by white Americans in official versions of the nation's beginnings.

Crispus Attucks had been recalled and canonized, however, by a number of African Americans during the 1850s and was not an unfamiliar figure to those who had gathered at Faneuil Hall on March 5, 1858. On public platforms, in print, and through personal appeals, the African-American elite had crafted and popularized Attucks as the quintessential African-American soldier-hero, a "true patriot" of the Revolutionary Era. On March 5, 1851, the eighty-first anniversary of Attucks's death, Nell, Charles Lenox Remond, Henry Weeden, Lewis Hayden, Frederick G. Barbados, Joshua B. Smith, and Lemuel Burr had presented a petition to the Massachusetts legislature requesting a $1500 apportionment to erect a monument to their martyred patriot. (That petition had been denied on the basis of a thinly supported assertion that Attucks had not been the first to fall in the exchange of fire.)

To be sure, the effort by African-American Bostonians to establish a public monument that would affix official recognition to Attucks's patriotism reflected a certain pride in a local hero and perhaps a broader formal historical consciousness surrounding Crispus Attucks. At the same time, more casual references to Attucks in contemporary anti-slavery writings, often linking his action to current protests against slavery, disclosed a popular consciousness that transcended formal recountings of the past. Following the acquittal of whites and African Americans tried for treason when they refused to assist in the attack against fugitive slaves at Christiana, Pennsylvania, an "Impartial Citizen" had editorialized in *The Liberator* that "the eternal truths for which Jefferson wrote, and Attucks bled . . . had not been utterly in vain."[31] In a speech delivered to the Massachusetts legislature in 1853, William J. Watkins had justified a petition seeking authorization to form an independent militia company invoking Attucks' military valor. That petition, signed by sixty-five African Americans, had asserted that those who objected to "an able-bodied colored [militia] company parading down State Street" had shut their eyes and closed their memories to "the noble Crispus Attucks."[32] In 1857, at a meeting held at Israel Church in Philadelphia to protest the *Dred Scott* decision, Charles Lenox Remond spoke in angry and bitter language, denouncing the United States and asserting that the freedom "bought with the blood of Crispus Attucks had been used to enslave and degrade colored men."[33] Linked to Thomas Jefferson, invoked to justify contemporary proposals for military mobilization of African Americans, joined with the liberation of the nation, Crispus Attucks had penetrated the popular historical consciousness of African Americans well before March 5, 1858.

Nell's concern with African-American military heroes, however, extended well beyond a single soldier, a single battle, and even a single war. In 1851 Nell had published *Services of Colored Americans in the Wars of 1776 and 1812,* a twenty-four page pamphlet that probably served as the preliminary study for his longer and more detailed *Colored Patriots of the American Revolution,* which was published in 1855. The pamphlet also anticipated the historical argument Nell employed to advance more explicit demands for the franchise in his 1860 pamphlet, *Property Qualifications or No Property Qualifications, A Few Facts on the Record of Patriotic Services of Colored Men of New York, During the Wars of 1776-1812. Colored Patriots,* an extensive state-by-state inventory of the soldiers among his father's generation, had established Nell as "the first Negro historian of consequence."[34] Yet Nell's reconstruction of the past always aimed to establish historical significance in terms of contemporary political issues. In *Colored Patriots* and again in the Commemorative Festival, Attucks symbolized thousands of anonymous African Americans who had fought in the Revolution; and by evoking recurring images of individual heroism and patriotic acts countered by national betrayal, Nell grafted a redefined memory of the Revolution onto the increasingly vocal calls for full and unconditional citizenship that issued from African-American conventions, newspapers, and public rhetoric during the middle decades of the nineteenth century.[35]

Nell well understood that in the symbolism of mid-nineteenth-century American political mythology, military service denoted respectability, commanded respect, and conferred citizenship. Those public trademarks of the middle classes had been denied African Americans irrespective of education, intelligence, occupation, wealth, or any other objective indicator of social standing. While "the Orator's voice and the Author's pen," he had written in the Author's Preface of *Colored Patriots,* detailed the activities and achievements of African Americans in education and the ministry, "a combination of circumstances has veiled from the public eye a narration of those military services which are generally conceded as passports to the honorable and lasting notice of Americans."[36] He did not need to elaborate on the "combination of circumstances" that had prevented the presentation of a just view of historical events. African Americans knew and understood those circumstances all too well. Those who had responded to his call had come to Faneuil Hall that Friday night to celebrate a collective heritage as well as to protest a collective fate. Crispus Attucks symbolized that heritage and Dred Scott represented the tragic contemporary realities for people of African descent in America.

Dred Scott had been born a slave in Southampton County, Virginia around 1795. In 1827, when Scott was thirty-three, his master, Peter Blow, took him to St. Louis. Blow died in 1831 and in the settlement of his estate Scott was assigned to Blow's daughter, Elizabeth. Two years later Elizabeth sold Scott to John Emerson, a white army physician. Emerson then took Scott as his body servant to Fort Armstrong, in Illinois, and to Fort Snelling, in Wisconsin Territory, during 1836 and 1837. In these locations slavery was forbidden by the 1820 Missouri Compromise, but Emerson nonetheless held Scott as a slave. The two returned to Missouri sometime in 1838; and Emerson assigned Scott to Colonel Henry Bainbridge as a body servant. When Emerson died in 1843, Scott, who had tried to buy his freedom, became the property of Emerson's widow, Irene. She then hired him out to various St. Louis families. Dred Scott, by this time in his mid-forties, was a married man with a family to support. He was frequently unemployed.

Irene Emerson eventually decided to quit the West and returned to Massachusetts in 1845 or 1846. She might have freed Scott, but instead, she abandoned him. Impoverished, Scott received some monetary support from Taylor and Henry Blow, grandsons of his original master. The two men financed Scott's 1847 suit for his own freedom and that of his family, which was filed in Missouri Circuit Court. The case dragged on until 1852, when Judge William Scott of the Missouri Supreme Court denied Scott's contention that he had gained his freedom as the result of residence in a "free" state. Irene Emerson then "sold" Scott to her brother, John F. A. Sanford, of New York, thereby transferring Scott's case to federal court. In 1857 the United States Supreme Court issued the infamous Taney Decision in which Roger B. Taney, the slaveholding Chief Justice of the United States Supreme Court, declared that African Americans had no rights that whites were bound to respect. African Americans had followed the case closely. The outcome held the potential to affirm a freedom many had claimed and trusted or to render that freedom capricious. While the five-to-four ruling by no means reflected a clear-cut interpretation of the law, it nonetheless had affirmed a deeply held commitment within the ruling white elite to maintain white supremacy. For Dred Scott, and by implication for all African Americans, there had been and there would be no protection under the law. Many must have felt the hollow victory when, two months after Taney delivered the Court's decision, Henry Blow "bought" Scott and his family and freed them. Scott worked for a year as a hotel porter in St. Louis and then died of tuberculosis, several months after the 1858 Commemorative Festival.[37]

Charles Lenox Remond had responded to the Taney Decision by calling for a revolution. The following year, speaking from the floor of the Convention of Colored Citizens of Massachusetts, in a thinly disguised condemnation of the moral suasionists, Remond declared that African Americans would "gain nothing by twaddling and temporizing" and demanded "something more than prayers" in the fight against oppression. Still, not all voices within the African-American elite joined Remond's call to arms against the growing oppression. At the same convention William Cooper Nell's more measured response offered an ideological bridge between the Garrisonian moral suasionists and those who were calling for more direct and confrontational strategies to end Southern slavery. Nell joined together "the names and services of Colored Americans in the wars of their country" with a "Protest against the Dred Scott Decision which denies them Citizenship." In a most deliberate fashion, Nell had fixed African-American public memory in the discontinuities of American ideology.[38] Crispus Attucks had sacrificed his life for the liberty of a nation that had denied Dred Scott his personal liberty.

FROM A LIVED TO A REMEMBERED PAST

Attucks had died a martyr in the cause of national freedom, and Scott had been martyred by the nation as he fought for his freedom. James Barbados, Primus Hall, Thomas Paul, John T. Hilton, and Nell's father, William G. Nell—Boston leaders of an earlier generation—probably would have responded to the *Dred Scott* decision by calling a mass meeting at the African Meeting House or in one of the African churches, as they had when they protested the American Colonization Society's African emigration program. Those racially separated gathering places had provided a protected terrain where African Americans claimed psychological as well as physical independence from white domination. But in 1858, when African Americans were faced with the political and civil crisis which the *Dred Scott* decision evoked, Faneuil Hall offered an explicit connection to the Revolutionary Era that the African Meeting House and the churches lacked.

Nell may have intended to recapture the precedent for racial equality that had been implicit in Crispus Attucks's burial. Attucks and Jonas Caldwell, a white who also had been killed that night, both "being strangers to the city," had been buried together from Faneuil Hall in 1770. The hearses carrying their coffins had joined those bearing the bodies of Samuel Maverick and Samuel Gray, two Boston residents who also had been killed during the Massacre. The two separate processions had converged at a junction in King Street and "marched in columns six deep . . . to the Middle Burying Ground," where the four fallen Revolutionaries were buried together in a single grave.[39] Or Nell may have intended that those who came to Faneuil Hall that evening recall it as the place where African-American Bostonians first had gathered for religious worship on Tuesday and Friday afternoons in 1789, before there had been a separate African Meeting House or African Church, and when sixteen-year-old Thomas Paul, who had recently come to the city from rural New Hampshire, had served as "exorter," interpreting the Scripture to those who gathered.

After 1830 the focus of the Faneuil Hall gatherings had changed. The struggle for equality now included white abolitionists. African Americans came to Faneuil Hall then for other purposes: in support of Garrison and the American Anti-Slavery Society rallies, and to protest against the growing number of kidnappings. The first of the statewide "Latimer meetings" were held there in 1842 in an effort to save George Latimer from being returned to slavery. Later the fates of others in like circumstances—George and Ellen Craft, and then Anthony Burns—had been of pressing concern.[40]

By the 1840s, the debate between the separatists and the integrationists had become as sharply articulated as it would be in the 1960s. Nell rejected the racial separatism that had characterized the public meetings and cultural texture of his father's generation. He envisioned, then worked to achieve, a world free from discrimination, a world in which among "the Anglo-Saxon, Teutonic, Celtic, and African . . . there exists perfect good feeling . . . and there is no apparent consciousness of a difference of race or condition."[41] The heroes and martyrs of the Commemorative Festival had sacrificed their lives in the pursuit of that goal. Nell and his colleagues intended to carry it forward.

THE EXHIBIT

The doors to Faneuil Hall opened at six o'clock that Friday evening, allowing the gathering crowd an opportunity to stroll about the hall, to see and to be seen, and to review the historical exhibit of "interesting relics and mementos of olden times" that Nell had collected and put on display at the base of the speakers' platform before the speakers were scheduled to begin. Some came early, perhaps to pay their respects to one or another of the speakers. Certainly Remond, Parker, Rock, and Garrison had large popular followings. But many black Bostonians probably came especially to "exchange congratulations" with Grand-mother Boston, aged 105, and eighty-eight-year-old Father Vassell, "a venerable man and woman who have come down to us from a former generation."[42]

As they examined the documents and artifacts and talked with the "living mementos" Nell had gathered, many African Americans must have felt that the exhibit did much to "present a just view of our origin," a view that many white Americans in the antebellum North, even those who readily condemned Southern slavery, preferred to overlook.[43] The exhibit, which spanned 150 years, reached out to a lost African homeland and cultural legacy through a single, undated fragment of Arabic sentences. Written by a North Carolina slave, those few sentences, probably unintelligible to most who viewed them that night, captured the essence of a common African heritage in which tribal distinctions and ancestral memory were blurred by New World enslavement.[44]

Four documents from the colonial period traced the gradual enslave-ment of African Americans in the North: The indenture papers of Sampson Negro, dated March 1700, told of an ambiguous moment in the history of African slavery in British North America, a time when not all Africans were slaves and the indenture system still offered some a reason to hope for eventual personal liberty. A bill of lading for the Negro Girl, Flora, consigned to one John Powell of Boston in 1718, signaled the immediate presence of the African slave trade in colonial Boston's harbor. Two local items, a bill of sale for a Negro boy and a horse, dated January 9, 1760, and John Gridley's receipt for five Black Men, dated April 3, 1770—one month after Crispus Attucks had died—made clear the grim fate of men and women who, on the eve of the Revolution, remained chattel property.

Two paintings depicted the active presence of African Americans in the Revolutionary War. *The Scene in State Street, March 5th, 1770* portrayed Crispus Attucks at the center of events during the Boston Massacre. Nell's promotional broadside had declared that Attucks, "in lifting his arm against Captain Preston, received two musket balls, one in each breast, and fell . . . the first Martyr in the American Revolution." *The Scene in State Street* provided visual verification of Nell's claim. A goblet and powder horn said to have belonged to Attucks, on display alongside the painting, provided the material evidence of this hero's life. In the second painting, *Washington Crossing the Delaware,* another patriot, Prince Whipple, could be plainly seen at the stroke oar, "quite prominent, near the Commander-in-Chief." Much later revisions of the nation's historical memory would recall and celebrate these and other moments of African-American military valor, but those who attended the 1858 Commemorative Festival could not have envisioned or anticipated those events or the transformation of consciousness that made them possible.

White commanders from General George Washington to Captain William Todd had hesitated to arm African Americans during the early stages of the war and did so only when they had no other options for maintaining a fighting force. By 1778 the need for manpower on the Continental Line overpowered racist fear and cultural convention, and military commanders were given the authority to arm the black soldiers who already carried muskets and rifles. Nell told that story, too, through a receipt for a gun and bayonet issued to a soldier named Newport Rhode Island on January 9, 1776. Rhode Island's arms receipt was set beside another military document that further traced his military career. A letter from Captain Perkins to Brigadier General Green, dated July 11, 1776, described the arrest of one Captain Whitmarch for abusing Newport Rhode Island while his regiment had been encamped at Long Island.

Additional documents elaborated the breadth of African-American military duties and services: William Todd's return of his artillery company, dated October 31, 1778, included a soldier named Negro Prince. In General Washington's own handwriting, an honorable discharge for Brister Baker from the Connecticut Regiment in June, 1783 bore silent witness to that soldier's faithful service. The flag Governor Hancock had presented to the Bucks of America, the black Boston regiment, in front of his Beacon Street mansion at the close of the war, recalled and acknowledged the honor and recognition accorded by an earlier generation of white Americans to the African-American soldiers who had fought to liberate the nation from British rule and oppression. Nell brought the exhibit into the present with two final documents. The first, a power of attorney signed by one Basil Garretson, seaman, told a story of resistance to exploitation. Garretson had served on board the private-armed schooner *Mammoth* out of Baltimore during the War of 1812. His "reputed master," J. C. Deshong of Baltimore, subsequently had claimed Garretson's prize money. Garretson had hired a lawyer to recover his money. While the outcome of Garretson's suit is not known, the sailor clearly had exercised one of the rights that whites were no longer bound to respect. He had challenged the legality of another man's seizure of money he had earned. Implicitly, that document also told of the erosion of the slave system in the mid-Atlantic and New England states in the decades following the end of the war.

Gradually—in some instances by legislative action or judicial decision, in other instances as the result of personal initiative—people like Garretson had gained some of the civil rights other Americans then enjoyed without question. Yet, slavery was a tenacious institution. Nell provided one final documentation of its continuing presence at mid-century. A bill of sale for the purchase of a slave by Colonel Titus, "of Kansas notoriety," dated August 1855, reminded everyone that Roger B. Taney prevailed: "Colored men have no rights that white men are bound to respect." Despite the honor and patriotism—evident prerequisites for citizenship—that African Americans had displayed for more than three quarters of a century, the nation denied their petition. Slavery persisted.

THE DISCOURSE[45]

Nell, ever the historian, opened the evening's round of speeches and entertainment by tracing the history of the Fifth of March celebration in Boston from its beginning in 1771 as a local festival to that moment in 1783 when Bostonians decided to discontinue their commemoration of the Boston Massacre in favor of the Fourth of July as their celebration of the nation's beginnings. Nell justified the revival of the holiday in blunt language, citing "the alarming spread of despotism in these United

States" in general, and in particular, "the annihilation of the Citizenship of Colored Americans by the Dred Scott decision." Nell believed that commemorating the martyrdom of Crispus Attucks and Dred Scott would heighten public awareness of the daily legal and moral contradictions African Americans endured.

John S. Rock—physician, dentist, orator, and anti-slavery activist—followed Nell to the speaker's podium. When Rock stepped forward to speak at Faneuil Hall that night he lived in a house on Southac Street, a few doors down from several members of the Attucks Glee Club—brothers George and James Ruffin, and George Washington, a porter.[46] He had an established reputation not only as a thoroughly competent physician and dentist but also as a fiery and persuasive orator and a tireless worker in the anti-slavery cause, and was as well known through his writings that had been published in Garrison's *Liberator* as he was through his oratory. He began by countering white charges of African-American cowardice, letting the cadence of his words carry the passion that drove them. Like Nell, John Rock believed that the historical record spoke for itself: "Our fathers fought nobly for freedom," he declared, "but they were not victorious. They fought for liberty but they got slavery." He guided his argument from past wars to the more immediate imagery of an impending war: "Sooner or later the clashing of arms will be heard in this country," he warned, and then "150,000 freemen capable of bearing arms, and not all cowards and fools, and three quarters of a million slaves, wild with the enthusiasm caused by the dawn of the glorious opportunity of being able to strike a genuine blow for freedom, will be a power that white men will be 'bound to respect.'"

A musical interlude followed Rock's stunning condemnation of Chief Justice Taney's remarks justifying the *Dred Scott* decision. The Bards of Freedom, a quartet composed of the Misses Hester and Phebe Whitest, Miss Arianna Cooley, and Mr. John Grimes, sang "Freedom's Battle," with piano accompaniment by Mrs. Adelaide V. Putnam, the wife of prominent Boston hairdresser George Putnam. Heavy with religious imagery, Watkins's anthem emphasized the moral foundations of the anti-slavery movement, "a high and holy mission, on the battle-fields of life." The kinship of race bound Watkins and many other black abolitionists to the slaves, and her anthem made repeated references to that kinship, forged in the sorrows of slavery: "See Oppression's heel of iron, grind a brother to the ground," the Bards of Freedom sang, and then, in the following verse, "On my blighted people's bosom, mountain loads of sorrow lay." Addressing those still enslaved as well as those who labored in the anti-slavery cause, Watkins's anthem concluded by urging trust and faith, "not in human might," but in the sure knowledge that "in the darkest conflict, God is on the side of right."

Theodore Parker, in the reversed role of token white abolitionist, followed the Bards of Freedom performance with brief remarks on the merits of the anti-slavery movement, and then the Festival returned to its African-American focus, with singing by the Attucks Glee Club and Mrs. Putnam again at the piano. The seven men—George Washington, a porter, Ira S. Gray and George L. Ruffin, hairdressers and barbers, William H. Simpson and Edward (Edwin) Bannister, both artists, and Thomas S. Boston (perhaps a kinsman of Grandmother Boston) and John F. Hott—sang "The Colored American Heroes of 1776," an anthem that recalled the honor and valor of African-American soldiers who had fought "side-by-side with Washington . . . and with great Warren bled and died." Like the Festival itself, the seven verse anthem linked the heroic past to the tragedy of the present in biting social criticism of "perfidy beyond compare:"

> Yet now that British rule has ceased,
>   And Independence has been gained,
> Judicial tyrants* have decreed
>   Such have no rights to be maintained!

———————
*See decision of the U.S. Supreme Court in the *Dred Scott* case.[47]

Leaving no room for doubt, the *Dred Scott* case was referenced to "judicial tyrants" in the printed Festival program.

Wendell Phillips followed the performance by the Attucks Glee Club. Like Parker, Phillips offered token comments on the heroism of African Americans in the Revolutionary War, but he also emphasized the importance of unity in the anti-slavery movement. Following those remarks, Nell returned to the podium to read a letter from Thomas Wentworth Higginson[48] lending his support to the evening's cause. Garrison followed Nell, briefly commenting on the merit of the Festival and, like Parker and Phillips, affirming the anti-slavery cause and upholding the moral-suasion strategy: "I believe God has called us all to peace—slaveholders as well as slaves," Garrison intoned. The work of the present, he argued, "is to disseminate light—to change public opinion—to plead every man with his neighbor—to insist upon justice—to demand equal rights—to crush slavery wherever it exists in the land."

Parker, Phillips, Higginson, and Garrison all condemned slavery as immoral and illegal, and they uniformly called for continued support for the anti-slavery movement. Despite their strong opposition to slavery, however, the white abolitionists set limits on their support for their African-American colleagues. None of the white abolitionists even implicitly supported the claims to full and unconditional citizenship Nell and his colleagues advanced through the martyrdom of Crispus Attucks. To be sure, Parker, Phillips, Higginson, and Garrison were deeply moral men and their anti-slavery politics were not capricious. Yet, like most white Americans at mid-century, the four were seemingly unable to countenance the ideas that Nell and his colleagues envisioned; full and unconditional equality and the eradication of racially set political, economic, educational, and social barriers. Nell may have issued their invitations to participate with some ambivalence, and although all of the white abolitionists spoke within consistently predictable frameworks, their remarks must have been judged as weak and equivocal by some who were present in Faneuil Hall that night.[49]

The remarks by Garrison behind them, the festival participants settled back to enjoy another musical interlude. With Miss Amanda Scott "skillfully presiding at the piano," the Northern Vocalists, an all-male quartet, sang Charlotte L. Forten's parody on "Red, White, and Blue" that had been written especially for the occasion. Heavily laden with a teenager's sentiments, Forten's anthem drew the nation's flag into the evening's civil rights iconography. The Northern Vocalists sang:

> Oh, when shall each child of our Father,
> > Whatever his nation or hue,
> Be protected throughout thy dominions,
> > 'Neath the folds of the red, white and blue.

Like Rock, Charlotte Forten anticipated the coming war in her anthem, and she, too, promised that African Americans would readily rally to the Union's cause:

> With freedom, and hope and brave ardor,
> > We'd battle the miscreant crew,
> And proudly aloft raise our banners,
> > With cheers for the red, white and blue.[50]

Forten's anthem provided an apt transition for Charles Lenox Remond, often regarded as the most outspoken—and the most radical—of the African-American abolitionists. Remond began his remarks by boldly affirming "the right of the colored people to strike for their freedom, when the time shall come." Like Nell, Remond easily linked African Americans with the nation's beginnings: "Washington and Attucks opened the Revolution of the past," he asserted, bending the historical chronology to suit his rhetorical needs. Yet "the patriotism of the colored man in '76 has been repaid by the most base ingratitude, on the part of the white people of this country."

Shifting his focus to more immediate issues and placing himself squarely in the direct-confrontation anti-slavery camp, Remond characterized the 1851 shoot-out at Christiana, Pennsylvania, between the slavecatchers Gorish and his son and those who were helping a fugitive to escape as the opening of "the Revolution of the present."[51] Among the most radical of the African-American abolitionists, Remond declared that "the time has come for colored men to meet their enemies, not only in public debate, but in those places where their rights are considered and passed on," in legislative bodies and in courts of law. For Remond, the ballot and the gun were equally potent weapons in the revolution against "negrophobia." Declaring resistance against slavery and all forms of race prejudice to be "our right and duty," Remond proclaimed his intention to "spit upon the [Dred Scott] decision and defy Judge Taney, and all his associates and abettors." Chiding "colored men and colored women" for their lack of involvement in "the anti-slavery cause," Remond invoked a familiar slogan of the movement: "No Union With Slaveholders!" he declared, rejecting gradual emancipation schemes and invoking the controversial proposal then current in anti-slavery circles to withdraw from a nation where slavery persisted.

The report of the Festival proceedings that appeared in Garrison's *Liberator* indicated that with Remond's speech "this portion of the exercises" had been concluded. The printed program, however, promised a final performance by the Northern Vocalists: "Ho! for Kansas," a single verse that kept alive the dream of John Brown's Kansas and offered clear testimony of the presence of Free Soilers in Boston.

> Ho! for the Prairies wide and free;
>   Ho! for the Kansas Plain!
> Where men can live in liberty,
>   Free from the tyrant's chain.[52]

The myth of national beginnings William Cooper Nell constructed in 1858 offered a reformed version of the past, a version Nell and others of his generation consciously had fashioned to validate their demands for political and social inclusion. Like all myth-makers, Nell crafted his version of the historical past within the constraints and context of his own real time, drawing selectively from a body of shared beliefs, symbols, images and memories filtered through a century-long African-American tradition of protest and resistance against enslavement. The Commemorative Festival located two crucial points on an African-American cultural map fashioned from the collective pursuit of an elusive freedom: the first claimed African-American rights to citizenship as a legacy of already demonstrated patriotism; and the second linked past to present in the lives of two martyred African Americans.

The remembered past depicted in the 1858 Commemorative Festival differed from the lived moment it recalled in subtle detail of meaning, motive, and substance, for reconstructed, historical memory can never precisely replicate either the lived or the autobiographically remembered experience. Still, invention rather than replication had been the goal of the 1858 Festival, for the text of the Festival also had traced the African-American intellectual journey from an individually lived to a collectively remembered past—a journey that began during the eighteenth-century transition from slavery to freedom in the New England and mid-Atlantic states. The onset of that journey from ancestral memory located in unconsciously preserved skills, rituals, and habits to a consciously constructed and politically driven New World past coincided, not coincidentally, with the Revolutionary Era in the New World, and it spanned the decades between the Revolution and the Civil War, aiming to counter and to reconcile the paradox of African ancestry combined with New World nativity. From the outset, the journey anchored African-American efforts to claim and realize a homeland and to resolve the discontinuities of memory that paralleled the persistence of slavery and other violations of African Americans' civil rights in a democratic society.

Fashioning a Moral Community, 1775–1800

INTRODUCTION

During the decades surrounding the Revolution, African Americans living in New England and the mid-Atlantic states anticipated the ending of slavery well before the individual states enacted legislation abolishing the institution. While some waited for the inevitable legal and judicial decisions that did eventually end their bondage, others were not able or willing to wait, and took action on their own behalf. Driven, perhaps, by milieux of memory that transcended autobiography, they capitalized on the erosion of the structural supports for slavery that preceded the First Emancipation and either bought themselves or simply walked away from masters who were becoming increasingly ambivalent about owning slaves. Many exchanged military service during the Revolutionary War for their freedom. In this manner individual initiatives of various sorts combined with state-by-state legislative actions and judicial decisions and, in a gradual fashion, between 1777 and 1820 slavery ceased to exist in the Northern states.

During this time of transition from slavery to freedom, African Americans claimed their autonomy in both physical and cultural spaces. Some established stable homes in stable places, often in the towns and villages where they had been slaves. Others defined physical freedom differently, not in terms of the right to settlement that white colonists automatically enjoyed, but in terms of the right to move about without restriction or limitation. Yet physical freedom alone proved incomplete. Freedom also surely included the right to worship in dignity and the right to an identity that incorporated memories of a lost homeland and imaginings of life freely lived. Claims to spiritual and psychological autonomy were inevitable parallels to physical freedom.

In areas where African Americans were spatially concentrated—in cities, along waterways, and on the Atlantic seaboard—physical freedom brought challenges and opportunities for constructing a distinctive creolized culture. This emerging culture drew on collective representations distilled from diverse traditions and legacies: From the Enlightenment, the natural-rights philosophy that had fueled political revolutions in both Europe and the New World now provided the intellectual apparatus that guided citizen petitions demanding an end to slavery and calling for full and unconditional inclusion in the national civic culture. Superimposed on the natural-rights philosophy, a synthetic ethnic heritage forged from a combination of racial oppression and generational and autobiographical memories of New World experiences informed a racially anchored identity that African Americans proclaimed through the names of churches, schools, meeting halls, and mutual-aid societies. In a world where some were free but others still enslaved, these organizations formed the infrastructure of an emerging moral community organized around two interconnected values: race unity and racial uplift. In Boston, New York, Philadelphia, and the coastal area extending from Providence, Rhode Island to Plymouth, Massachusetts, Africans and their descendants framed collective expectations about life in a "free" society. Those expectations, in turn, guided the strategies and tactics African Americans employed during the decades following the Revolution to claim for themselves the democratic promises that were implicit in the era.

To pose the introspective question *Who am I?* presupposes some attention to related matters of identity: *Where have I been? With whom am I connected? What are the nature of those connections?* For African Americans living in the Northern states during the years of the gradual, or First Emancipation, there were no quick and ready answers. Even for those who entered into that period already free, establishing logical connections between personal and collective identity posed clearly troublesome dilemmas. The expectations for full and unconditional inclusion in the life of the nation that African Americans held during the final decades of the eighteenth century were never fulfilled, and as a result a concern with matters related to racial distinction and discrimination, ranging from domestic slavery and the slave trade to local community relations, preoccupied many at the onset of the nineteenth century. Torn away from an ancestral past, African Americans constructed, preserved, and celebrated a mythologized past. Prevented from exercising the full prerogatives of citizenship, and lacking the material and symbolic resources to develop viable pressure groups that might penetrate the formal machinery of politics, African Americans forged a cultural identity and an agenda for community action that blocked or at least softened the disadvantages of race. The infrastructures of African-American material communities revolved around helping each other and combating the seemingly impenetrable wall of American racism. Both had become defining features of African-American identity.

By mid-century, on the eve of a long-awaited second emancipation—the abolition of slavery in the Southern states—the details of this moment when African Americans first had claimed physical and psychological freedom had been eclipsed by the passage of time and the overwhelming prospect of the long battle against slavery finally won. William Cooper Nell had attempted to preserve the military service of his father's generation in *Colored Patriots of the American Revolution* (1855), his state-by-state inventory of the black soldiers of that era. But their steadfast loyalty to a fragile army had been largely forgotten in the national memory of the Revolutionary Era. Still, the legacy of the Revolutionary Era extends beyond the details of African-American military service. African-American responses to the First Emancipation—the strategies they devised to make real their limited and conditional freedom—are both the product and the producer of ancestral memory.

"In the Bowels of a Free and Christian Country": Living in the Revolutionary Era

master Spooner, sir.

I can't wright myself but I get somebody [to] make Pen and Ink [and] tell you I am well . . . I have been Traveling all over This Country . . . where there is nothing but Indians & torreys all of way but Soon as they hear we was Coming they all Run away and left there tents and all there artillery and most everything they Had then we come back to this place . . .

Tell my wife I well and want to see her ver much. I come see [her] one Day when we'll kill all Regulars

—Letter from a colored servant,
In camp at Loudens Ferry, 8 miles from Albany,
September 3, 1777[1]

WILLIAM COOPER NELL AND HIS CONTEMPORARIES had fashioned Crispus Attucks as a martyred hero in order to symbolize historical continuity in the African-American struggle for personal liberty in the United States. To be sure, in the Revolutionary Era that struggle had been a daily reality, and military service in the Patriot cause, particularly for African Americans living in New England, often carried implicit if not explicit promises of personal freedom. Certainly, many individuals seized that opportunity. Most, however, were neither martyrs nor heroes, and their soldiering represented not so much a commitment to the Patriot cause as a shrewd and calculated interpersonal exchange of bondage for freedom.

At the same time, the invented past of the 1858 Festival muted African Americans' understandings of personal freedom that had been forged during the Revolutionary Era. Inevitably, the invented past must mask the ways in which perceptions and definitions grounded in a particular historical moment and place will guide the actions people take to claim their freedom and reconcile contradictions in identity. Such was the case for the "colored servant" believed to have been Cato Howe of Plymouth, Massachusetts, writing to his "master," Ephriam Spooner,[2] from a Continental Army encampment near Albany in the fall of 1777, disclosing what must have been for most African-American soldiers the essence of that exchange: an autonomous future grounded in personal and family stability. Howe could not have anticipated that the freedom for which he and thousands of other African-American soldiers fought in the Revolutionary War would be limited and provisional. Nor could the young soldier have anticipated that physical freedom was only the first crucial dimension of a more encompassing freedom African Americans would demand and claim in the coming decades.

Little is known about Cato Howe's life prior to his first enlistment in the Continental Army in the spring months of 1775. Described in the enlistment documents as less than five feet tall and giving his occupation as a laborer, the nineteen-year-old must have seemed an unlikely defender of the Patriot cause. Still, Howe seems to have served his country well, as did the vast majority of the five thousand other African Americans who fought for the nation's independence from Great Britain. William Cooper Nell placed Howe among the African American soldiers who served under the command of Major John Pitcairn at the Battle of Bunker Hill. In a war fought primarily in the North until 1779, the majority, like Cato Howe, were Northerners. For most, military service held resonant personal ramifications, often the opportunity to gain personal freedom.[3] For all, in light of the prevailing official debates and public contradiction regarding the use of African-American soldiers, fighting for the freedom of the nation was a paradox.

From the outset of the war, the white colonists felt enormous ambivalence about enlisting African Americans in military service. Despite a decree by the Massachusetts Committee of Safety that "no slaves be admitted into this army upon any consideration whatsoever" after the battles at Lexington and Concord in April 1775, African Americans were routinely enlisted in the state militia.[4] In October 1775, with the call to arms among the patriots reaching a fevered pitch, representatives of the New England and Southern colonies met to coordinate strategy and policy. At that meeting all agreed to reject the enlistment of African Americans, slave or free.[5] As is so often the case in moments of national crisis, however, policy crafted to serve political ends did not serve the military exigencies of the moment. By the time that agreement had been struck, Washington already had provisionally enlisted free African Americans from Boston into the Continental Army, and Prince Hall, a young, free-born Barbadian immigrant to Boston, had petitioned the Boston Committee of Public Safety to enlist slaves in the defense of the city as a way of preparing for the freedom he believed would inevitably follow the war.[6] The petition did not receive a favorable hearing, but as the Committee for Public Safety and the elite in the Continental Army debated and set policy for the army, Cato Howe had been serving as a private in the Continental Line for several months, and Quomony Quash, also a Plymouth man, was on active duty as well.[7] Howe and Quash would return to Plymouth after the war; there they would test the "fundamental theory of the American republic" for which they had fought, and they would find that theory lacking. They would be unable to live on American soil "in terms of equality" with other Americans.[8]

Like Cato Howe, Quomony Quash first had enlisted in the militia as a teenager. The sixteen-year-old slave boy, son of Quashey and Phillis Quandey, first went to war with his master, Theophilus Cotton, in 1775, serving as Cotton's waiter, or body servant.[9] The two, master and slave, served together in Captain Nathaniel Goodwin's 1st Plymouth Regiment for eight months. The young teenager, his occupation given as "trade laborer," reenlisted for a three-year term in a regiment commanded by Cotton. By 1781 the circumstances surrounding the boy's military service had changed dramatically. His master, Theophilus Cotton, had filed a document of manumission with the Plymouth Notary Public that made clear the terms of Quash's second enlistment:

> in Consideration of my Negro Quomminy having Inlisted himself at my request into the Service of the Continant for three years, and upon his faithfully Serving the full time without departing therefrom, and my receiving the one half of the wages due for said Service, together with the bounty Given by the Town, do at his commincing twenty-one years of age, quit all pretentions to him as a Slave. . . . And I do allow said Quomminy out of the bounty Three hundred paper Dollars—old Emission, and five hard ones, with half of his Wages.[10]

Although Cotton died shortly after the manumission document was recorded, Quash kept the agreement, serving to the end of the war. He was stationed for a time at West Point and then sent to Rutland, in western Massachusetts, where he guarded prisoners. Like Cato Howe, Quomony Quash seems to have served his country well. He was discharged from the militia in 1783, his term of service completed, and at the age of twenty-four Quomony Quash had fulfilled his contract and earned his freedom.[11]

As Cato Howe and Quomony Quash shouldered arms and followed orders, both the British and Patriot generals, who understood the politics of slavery, manipulated it to their military advantage. On January 17, 1777, Governor John Dunmore offered immediate freedom to African-Americans "able and willing to bear arms for King George III." Tacitly acknowledging a prohibited reality, General George Washington responded by recommending, also on January 17, 1777, that African-American soldiers be reenlisted in the Continental Army.[12] Washington's motives for initiating the policy shift probably had been informed as much by realistic manpower needs as by a desire to neutralize Dunmore's appeal to African-American slaves. Reluctant to leave their homes, farms, and families unattended for protracted periods of time, many white colonists had preferred three-month enlistments to the longer two-year terms that provided a reliable fighting force. As a result, both the Continental Army and the various state militias were plagued by labor shortages throughout 1776. When Washington demanded reliable troops, the Continental Congress ordered states to fill their militia quotas "forthwith" in any way possible.[13] One of the men who stepped forward to fill the Plymouth quota was Plato Turner, "A Negro man of said Plimouth, mariner."[14] Born about 1744, Plato Turner first enlisted in the Continental Army in the spring of 1776, at the age of thirty-two. Like Cato Howe, Turner served for a time in Colonel John Bailey's 2nd Plymouth Regiment, and through a series of reenlistments, like Howe and Quash, he served to the end of the war and then returned to Plymouth.

Like many other "summer soldiers," Howe, Quash, and Turner apparently returned to Plymouth between enlistments, using those pauses in the war to conduct a variety of personal business. Clearly, the soldiers were planning their futures. In 1777, his second year of military service, Cato Howe married twenty-five-year-old Alathea, a woman from the Plymouth area. Their marriage would end with her death almost half a century later.[15] In addition to the private correspondence from a soldier to a master waiting at home, Howe executed at least one business transaction with Ephriam Spooner. On January 30, 1781, two years before his final discharge from the army, Howe apparently borrowed money from Spooner, for he deposited a promissory note with Spooner that stated simply: "Please pay to Mr. Elijah Cushing one hundred and fifty Dollars old emission and I will pay you the same."[16]

In the same month as his July 1779 reenlistment, thirty-five-year-old Plato Turner bought a house and the right to a small tract of unimproved land from Job Cushman, a white Plymouth resident, probably using his bounty money to pay Cushman. The fact that the deed transferring ownership from Cushman to Turner was signed by them in 1779 but not recorded at the Registry of Deeds until 1785 suggests that perhaps not all the conditions of the transaction were met until after Turner was discharged from the army in 1783.

While the details surrounding the lives of Howe, Quash, and Turner are vague, the circumstances that shaped their lives and destinies—like the death of Crispus Attucks—transcend individual experience and tell us a great deal about the ways in which African Americans envisioned, imagined, and acted upon opportunities for freedom during the Revolutionary Era. Cato Howe had addressed Ephriam Spooner as his "master," and while there is no record of either his enslavement or his manumission, the single fragment of correspondence and Spooner's loan of money to him suggest that Howe probably had been Spooner's slave at one time, and that in any case there was an enduring and reciprocal dimension to their relationship.

At the war's end, Howe would return to Plymouth where he and Alathea would settle alongside Plato Turner and Quomony Quash and their families at a place called The Parting Ways, on land that once had been the town's commonly held sheep pasture. It is in part from experiences and perceptions such as theirs, drawn through the filtered lens of generational memory, that William Cooper Nell's generation crafted the African-American historical consciousness of the 1850s.

Although no more than 10 percent of all Africans and their descendants in the United States lived in the Northern states between 1790 and 1820, the number of free African Americans living in these areas was disproportionately high. By the turn of the century 60 percent of the African Americans living in the Northern states were free, and by the 1820s slavery had been virtually eradicated in the North. Further, the spatial distribution of Africans and African Americans differed radically from the spatial distribution of white Americans in the nominally free Northern states. Although the bulk of the white population

lived in small towns and rural areas and over time expanded steadily
westward into the lands of the frontier, African Americans tended to
cluster along waterways, on the coast, and in urbanized areas. This
reversed settlement pattern tended to offset sparsity of numbers with
clusters of population density.[17] As a result, an ever-expanding nucleus
of free and newly freed people crystallized within a relatively small but
physically concentrated numerical minority. This demographic incon-
gruity held both social and cultural implications. During the final
decades of the eighteenth century, places like The Parting Ways lost their
appeal and many—probably the younger, the more ambitious, and the
more adventuresome—African Americans in the Northern states
migrated steadily from the countryside to cities. As is often the case in
great periods of population movement, less is known about those who
stayed than about those who migrated. The lives of Cato Howe, Plato
Turner, and Quomony Quash, however, tell an important story about
the limitations of freedom and about the social and cultural foundations
upon which those limitations were based.

A PLACE CALLED THE PARTING WAYS

A combination of motives and circumstances probably drew Cato Howe,
Plato Turner, and Quomony Quash separately to The Parting Ways in
the years following the Revolutionary War. When the war ended, the
newly created United States remained fundamentally a rural nation of
small farmers, and the prevailing popular vision of personal success
hinged on land ownership. While their ability to translate this vision into
personal reality may have been limited, the three soldiers must have
shared in that understanding of personal stability and security. All had
lived in the Plymouth area before the war and they probably knew about
The Parting Ways, a relatively vacant tract of land at the outskirts of
town where "the strolling poor," people who lacked legal inhabitancy in
a town and therefore were forced to wander from place to place in a more
or less perpetual state of homelessness, had lived from time to time over
the preceding decades.

At the close of the eighteenth century, the vast majority of the United
States population lived either in rural areas or small towns and villages,
and for most, daily life in these settings was centered in a rich fabric of
social relationships. Although many young male New Englanders would
respond to the diminished availability of land in the years after the
Revolution by joining the migration into the open lands of the Old

Northwest Territory, for others, returning to the place of their birth after the war held a degree of safety and familiarity.[18] For Howe, Turner, and Quash, as for other newly emancipated African Americans, the decision about where to live was complicated by matters related to race. Relationships with former masters and paternalistic whites were complex and the psychosocial dependencies of slavery and servitude enduring. As the three veterans returned to Plymouth, their personal circumstances were changed but their sense of home and family remained intact. The Parting Ways also held an appeal of availability, and the settlement that developed there, midway between the strolling poor and the comfortably middle class, at the perimeter of Plymouth social and economic life, became a metaphor for the lives of many newly emancipated African Americans in the young republic.

The town of Plymouth initially had laid out a three-square-mile tract of common grazing land for town residents' sheep on May 24, 1704. At Plymouth, as elsewhere, fluid and dynamic forces shaped human land-use patterns. To some degree, the destiny of the sheep pasture was shaped by location, climate, terrain, soil, and vegetation, but within those physical boundaries and limitations a thick cake of custom informed the interaction of people with the physical environment. In southeastern Massachusetts in the seventeenth and eighteenth centuries, English conventions surrounding the laying out of towns guided the initial allocations of land and the distinctions colonists made between common and privately held land.[19] Additionally, traditions surrounding popular claims on common lands persisted and combined as cultural memories with more immediate economic, demographic, and social pressures in southeastern Massachusetts to drive the transformation of the sheep pasture and other open lands in the area from public to private property by the middle decades of the eighteenth century.[20] Similar demographic and economic forces, at least in part, informed the historical memory of subsequent generations of African Americans.

Located along both sides of the Carver Road leading westward and inland from Plymouth toward the hamlet of Carver and on toward Bridgewater and Taunton, the sheep pasture lay only a short distance south of the fork in the road connecting Plymouth and Plympton.[21] While removed from the town, the pasture lay along a well-traveled road, and this location would figure prominently in the subsequent transformation of its use.

Over the years various townsfolk may have grazed sheep informally on the tract, but no evidence suggests the sheep pasture was used extensively for its designated purpose. Perhaps the thin, sandy soil did not produce sufficient pasturage to support sheep grazing, or perhaps an early interest in sheep husbandry waned as Plymouth residents turned increasingly to the sea and the maritime trades for their livelihood. Whatever the specific reasons may have been, more immediate demographic pressures were building in the area. A population expanding by natural increase throughout New England, and particularly in southeastern Massachusetts, resulted in a colonial baby boom. A maturing generation demanded homesites and farmland, for in this fundamentally rural society even people with other occupations maintained small subsistence farms. The land surrounding the sheep pasture, much of it still not granted by the town in the early years of the eighteenth century, offered likely opportunities for settlement to newly maturing men and women. Probably responding to these pressures, the Proprietors began to parcel out land grants in the area surrounding the sheep pasture. Two of these grants are particularly important to the development of The Parting Ways.

In 1707 the Town of Plymouth granted a twenty-six-acre tract of land abutting the sheep pasture to the Cushman family, and in 1711 the Proprietors laid out ten acres of land in the vicinity of the sheep pasture to Joseph Rickard.[22] Both Cushman and Rickard were descendants of *saints*—a term used to describe the pious members of the original Pilgrim inner congregation among the first settlers in Old Plymouth Colony—and, following established custom, both probably applied for land grants when they reached adulthood and were ready to establish households independent from their parents.[23] Both families would play a continuing role in the transformation of the sheep pasture after 1750. During the decades immediately preceding the onset of the Revolution, when previously stable status and social arrangements eroded, changes in the lives of a younger generation of colonists would parallel changes in the use of the sheep pasture.

Status conventions surrounding race also would shape the transformation of the sheep pasture. From the outset of European colonization, race figured differently in the social arrangements of southeastern Massachusetts than in either the Southern colonies or in neighboring Rhode Island. Although the Puritans who settled the region did not hold particularly progressive views on matters related to race, they placed a high priority on universal justice. Biblical, statute, and English common law weighed equally in shaping legal codes in colonial New England.[24] While the 1641 Massachusetts Bay Body of Liberties (subsequently adopted by the New England Confederation of Massachusetts Bay,

Connecticut, and Plymouth Colonies) legalized lifetime servitude for "lawfull captives taken in just warres, and such *strangers* as willingly selle themselves or are sold to us," enslavement did not automatically result in loss of civil liberties as it did elsewhere in the American colonies.[25] In both the Southern colonies and in Rhode Island, the intersection of economic ties to the African slave trade and efforts to establish a plantation economy reinforced racially fixed caste arrangements, but in the Plymouth area, where the economy was differently structured, the distinction between enslavement and indenture often blurred.[26] Still, colonists in the Plymouth area could not be described as racially enlightened. They had led the movement toward the enclosure and enslavement of the Wampanoag Indians during the seventeenth century, removing the more troublesome younger men in the tribe by shipping them to the West Indies for sale into slavery and assigning the others to designated reservations at the conclusion of King Philip's War. Additionally, slaveholding among the wealthy was relatively common during the eighteenth century, popularized in the region through the vigorous coasting trade with the Caribbean.[27]

At the same time, manumission, which was not prohibited by law in New England, also was relatively common, particularly on the death of a master; and an ongoing tradition of African and African-American land ownership that began in the early eighteenth century further masked the status distinctions surrounding race.[28] In 1711, the same year Joseph Rickard, a descendant of a Pilgrim *saint*, obtained the ten-acre grant of land abutting the Plymouth sheep pasture, Sash, an African, bought a two-and-one-half acre tract of land near Spruce Swamp.[29] In 1727, Cornish Cuffee—a free black man—bought half a lot from Joshua Forbes, the son of one of the town's original Proprietors.[30] In 1734, Susannah Edson conveyed two acres of land to Phebe, a woman Edson described in the deed as "the Daughter of my negro woman Sarah." That same year Scipio, "negro-man and servant of Samuel Kingman, Gentleman," purchased one and one-half acres of land bounded on one side by land "the widow Susannah Edson hath given by a deed of gift to Phebe, the Daughter of said Scipio."[31] Whatever motives may have informed Edson's and Kingman's transactions, the fact of the transactions makes quite clear that land ownership was not limited to European colonists, nor was it a privilege extended only to free Africans and their descendants. Scipio's deed plainly stipulates that he is a servant, and that he has the right to transmit the property to "his Heirs and assigns." Contradicting all the received historical knowledge about the boundaries between slave and free status, Scipio and Phebe, an enslaved father and his daughter, had become owners of land in colonial New England.

Eighteenth-century land ownership among Africans and African Americans may have reflected an informal extension of the spirit of Old Plymouth Colony legislation that had provided five-acre homesteads to indentured servants when they completed their term of service.[32] Certainly, the white Plymouth colonists lived within the constraints of a powerful sense of obligation and responsibility that would have informed such an extension. At the same time, however, there is no evidence of land grants by the town (as opposed to private gifts or outright purchases) to Africans or African Americans, and land ownership did not automatically confer either social or political equality for African Americans in the area. Nevertheless, the absence of rigid racial barriers and the conventions that facilitated relaxed interracial contact resulted in a social climate where Africans and their descendants "hovered on the fringes of full participation in social and economic life."[33] Still, the precedent had been established for land ownership, and over the next fifty years African Americans bought and sold tracts of varying sizes throughout southeastern Massachusetts, apparently living scattered among their white neighbors rather than in racially distinctive clusters, as was the more typical ecological arrangement in urban areas. Most purchased relatively small tracts, less than five acres, where they probably built houses and maintained subsistence gardens—stable homes in stable places.

By 1750 the effects of a building economic crisis in the colonies were being felt in a very personal fashion by some families in the rural Plymouth area. "Warnings out of town" (the colonial version of eviction, at a municipal level) increased throughout the area. Whole families were set adrift in a world where personal and family stability rested on legal "settlement" in a particular town. The numbers of poor and indigent who wandered from town to town but rarely were allowed to settle permanently had increased, for then, as now, towns avoided when possible the inflation of their poor rolls. The resulting pressures, both personal and collective, also figured in the transformation of the sheep pasture. For nearly a quarter of a century, from 1755 to 1779, impoverished and marginalized white colonists appropriated the Plymouth sheep pasture for their own use. They built rude homes there, cultivated the land, enclosed the space, and even operated a tavern of sorts where they sold liquor to travelers.

The process of encroachment began in February 1755, when Japheth Rickard, his wife, and their three-year-old daughter, Susannah, apparently not among the "worthy poor" of the colony, were warned out of Plympton. At that time Rickard probably first attempted to establish a residence for his family on or near the sheep pasture, for in August 1755 the couple's second child, Martha, was born "at a place called Parting Ways."[34] The birth of this child of impoverished and homeless squatters on the town's common land marks a crucial moment in the transformation of the sheep pasture from common land used for grazing to common land appropriated by poor and marginalized people for their own use. Still, the Rickard family was not secure in its residence. When Martha was only three months old the family, now described in the town records as "former residents of Plympton," was warned out of Kingston. Rickard continued shifting his residence back and forth between Middleboro and Kingston during the 1750s, working as a cordwainer, not always paid regularly by those who hired him.[35] At some point after 1758 Rickard probably returned to his earlier residence on or near the sheep pasture, now called The Parting Ways in local records. He found new neighbors when he arrived—the Seth Fuller family.[36]

Seth Fuller, like Japheth Rickard, had lived a marginal existence before he settled at The Parting Ways. No recorded occupation can be found for Fuller before 1776. He and his family had been warned out of Kingston in October, 1755, the month before the town had evicted the Rickard family. The Fullers then had attempted to establish a residence in Plymouth, but were warned out of that town, too, in December, 1755.[37] The family faced limited options at this point, for warnings out of town reflected a level of social undesirability and economic marginality so extreme as to effectively isolate and banish people. Three roads led away from Plymouth. The road north, toward Boston, led through a thickly settled area and offered few opportunities for a family facing the Fullers' plight. The road south, toward Sandwich and on around Cape Cod, would have appealed to a person with skills in the maritime trades, who might find work fishing or as a sailor. Nothing indicates that Seth Fuller, now in mid-life with at least one grown son settled in Middleboro, was a mariner. The family probably left Plymouth on the road leading west, toward Middleboro and Taunton. Following this route, the Fuller family would have passed through The Parting Ways.

Although Fuller's activities over the next eight years are undocumented, by the mid-1760s he and his wife had established a permanent residence at The Parting Ways. Because of its location, the sheep pasture was an ideal resting place for people traveling between Plymouth and the villages of Plympton and Carver, and both Japheth Rickard and Seth

Fuller attempted to capitalize on this advantage. In 1763 Rickard was charged with "selling strong drink without submitt[ing] the matter to the Court," but the charge against him was dismissed when Rickard paid court fees. Later that year, Fuller, perhaps somewhat wiser in his approach to the matter, applied for and received a license to sell "spirituous liquors," a request that was renewed annually through 1765.[38] Fuller apparently established a relatively permanent home on the old sheep pasture and sustained himself there informally as tavernkeeper during the 1760s. A perambulation of the boundaries between the towns of Plymouth and Kingston laid out in 1767 used as one marker "the house now possessed by Seth Fuller." That same year Fuller and his wife Deborah mortgaged her interest in the improved lands, their dwelling house, "and the small building set up adjoyning"—probably the Fullers' tavern—to Samuel Bartlett of Plymouth for nine pounds, eighteen shillings.[39] The birth of Martha Rickard at The Parting Ways in 1755 had marked the onset of relatively permanent residence on the public lands. By 1767 at least a portion of the original tract had passed, de facto, from public lands to private property.

The process of transformation continued as Fuller and Rickard translated the conventions surrounding squatters' rights into more formalized transactions signifying private ownership of the land. By October 1770 Fuller was apparently overextended and not able to repay Bartlett. He and Deborah left their home and inn at Parting Ways and moved to Kingston, where they lived with their old neighbor, Japheth Rickard.[40] The Fullers were elderly and without visible means of support, and as a result, they were warned out of Kingston in September, 1771. In 1773 their son, Archippus Fuller, intervened in their lives, paid the nine-pound debt his father had incurred with Samuel Bartlett (thereby clearing the elder Fuller's claim on the improvements, fencing, and buildings at The Parting Ways), and sold the tract to Elijah Leach, a yeoman of Bridgewater.[41] The following year, 1774, Japheth Rickard sold his "dwelling house and land lying at a place called The Parting Ways . . . said land being by Estimation about ten acres" to his kinsman Eleazar Rickard for one pound, fifteen shillings.[42]

Leach lived on the Fuller tract at The Parting Ways from 1773 to 1779, bringing to his tenure there a personal history of tragedy, economic failure, and petty criminal conduct. Like the other white squatters who had preceded him, Leach had lived neither a happy nor successful life.[43] The Rickard tract, either abutting or overlapping the sheep pasture, remained within the family and probably was used as grazing pasturage or for minimal grain cultivation. Eleazar Rickard subdivided the small parcel during the 1780s and sold one portion to his son and the other to his son-in-law. The Fuller tract, however, passed from Elijah Leach to Job Cushman, a man with a local reputation as "a thrifty farmer [and] public spirited citizen." Cushman may have acquired the Fuller tract in an effort to consolidate or expand his land holdings. The Cushman family had been well established in Plymouth County since the early years of the eighteenth century and had owned land abutting the sheep pasture since 1707. Cushman, a yeoman, probably used the Fuller tract for supplemental grazing or cultivation, at least for a brief period. In July, 1779, however, Cushman faced criminal charges related to an incident at The Parting Ways that threatened to tarnish his good name in the local community. He was accused of "stealing five bushells of Indian corn from Quash, a free Negro Man."[44] Although the court took no prosecutorial action, Cushman paid a fourteen-pound fine, and sold his property to Plato, "A Negro man of said Plimouth, mariner" all on the same day.[45]

Quash, or Quashey Quandey (ca.1726-1806), was an African who had been kidnapped into slavery as a teenager, around 1740, and brought to Boston where he had been sold to Dr. Lazarus LeBaron of Plymouth.[46] LeBaron, who already owned several slaves, attempted to rename the boy Julius Caesar, but Quashey held fast to his African name, even resisting the bribe LeBaron offered him of a fancy feathered hat. Quashey probably lived in the LeBaron household throughout his youth and young adulthood. In 1756, Quashey, now a thirty-year-old man, married Phillis, a slave owned by Colonel Theophilus Cotton of Plymouth, and the couple had a son in 1759 whom they named Quomony Quash, following the African tradition of assigning an Akan day-name to the child coupled with the name of his father.

Quomony Quash was born on the leading edge of an African-American baby boom in southeastern Massachusetts, an increase in births (and baptisms) that reflected a dramatically increased degree of self-determination and control over the details of daily life among African-American adults in the region. There, as elsewhere, the transition out of bondage began several decades before the 1783 *Walker* decision, and the increase in births during the 1750s was an early demographic indicator of the relaxed regulation of slaves, if not their outright manumission. After 1740 African-American men began marrying at a much younger age than they had in earlier decades, and between 1740 and 1774, the average age at marriage for men and women had equalized to, on the average, about twenty-nine years. Quash had been thirty when he married, about average for his cohort, and although is it not possible to date Phillis's age, there is no reason to think that she would vary significantly from the general pattern for women in her cohort. Still, Phillis and Quash did not enjoy full freedom. Their son, Quomony, had been born three years after his parents married. During the same period, while many were still enslaved, an average of 2.8 years elapsed between marriage and the birth of the first child for African-American couples. This, and the fact that no additional children appear to have been born to Phillis and Quash, suggests that the couple probably did not live together during the early years of their marriage, but subordinated their conjugal visits to the demands of their servitude in the LeBaron and Cotton households. For Quash and Phillis, as for practically all African-American slave couples, opportunities to maintain a normal family life remained irregular throughout the pre-Revolutionary decades.[47] There is no record of manumission for Quashey Quandey, but Lazarus LeBaron died in 1773, when Quash was in his late forties, and Quash probably moved onto The Parting Ways land around the time of LeBaron's death. He would live there for more than thirty years, until his own death in 1806.[48]

Quash had been about fifty-five in 1779, the year Job Cushman stole his corn. His son, Quomony, still owned by Theophilus Cotton, was away at the war, fighting for the Patriot cause and, simultaneously, earning his own freedom. Whether alone or with his wife Phillis, Quash had most likely simply squatted on a portion of the sheep pasture lands at about the same time Elijah Leach purchased the Fuller improvements, fencings, and buildings. He had been living at The Parting Ways five or six years when Cushman sold his interest in the Fuller tract to Plato Turner. To be sure, Cushman's Parting Ways transaction with Plato was concluded, at least at the level of an economic exchange, in Cushman's favor. Plato paid sixty pounds for his house and Cushman's right in the improved land, a price well above market value for property in the area of the sheep pasture. At the same time, Plato Turner, a mariner by trade, had taken a vital first step toward personal stability, attaining a secure home that might insulate him against a time of economic uncertainty.

By 1779, then, the sheep pasture at The Parting Ways had become a settlement for two African Americans, Quash and Plato, men who had chosen "liberty with poverty and discomfort to the mildest slavery that ever existed."[49] Despite the poverty and discomfort of life on the sheep pasture, however, the African Americans who settled at The Parting Ways enjoyed a measure of security and stability that eluded many others in rural New England. After 1780 towns throughout southeastern Massachusetts increasingly warned entire African-American families out of town and, in a more insidious pattern, began to bind out (or indenture) African-American children of impoverished families to domestic and industrial work in order to avoid expenses associated with feeding and clothing them. At the statehouse in Boston, legislators entertained a bill clearly directed at newly emancipated slaves. The law would have denied legal inhabitancy to African Americans unless that inhabitancy had been established prior to April 1767 and would relieve towns of responsibility for the support and assistance of indigent and infirm African Americans.[50] Apparently at least some citizens of the state of Massachusetts had hoped to avoid the social consequences of a substantial population of free but still dependent African Americans. While the proposed legislation was not permitted a third reading and thus never voted upon, like the local warnings out of town it reflected a building reaction in New England against the ending of slavery and an effort to implement more subtle forms of race discrimination. By the 1780s the settlement at The Parting Ways offered a thin blanket of protection against the perils of freedom.

A GRADUAL EMANCIPATION

In the remembered past of the 1858 Commemorative Festival, the Revolutionary War became a metaphor for the disappointment, betrayal, and contradictions Africans and their descendants had suffered in the British North American colonies. Yet, in the collective consciousness of the 1850s, the metaphor had obscured a legacy of New World political agency that paralleled the betrayal. In the lived moment of the Revolutionary Era, African Americans consistently had resisted slavery in a variety of ways, capitalizing on opportunities afforded by a plastic and structurally dynamic society in transition to translate personal vision into lived realities. The avenues of their resistance trace the fault lines in a rapidly changing world, although the shadowy, remembered details of that resistance had formed the subtext of the political agenda at mid-century.

Slavery had been in gradual decay throughout the New England colonies for fully a generation before the onset of the Revolution, and the conditions of this enslavement differed markedly from those coming to characterize slavery in the plantation economy of the Southern colonies.[51] The institution had never been as fully integrated into the social and economic fabric of the region as it would be in the antebellum South. New England slaves were as often skilled artisans, clerks, and industrial workers as they were domestic and agricultural laborers. As a result, many slaves acquired both a trade and a degree of literacy during the course of their bondage. Legally and religiously sanctioned marriages among slaves, as well as between slaves and free African Americans, were common throughout the region. The relatively intact and enduring family units they formed provided a legitimized domestic terrain and a degree of personal autonomy and privacy to New England slaves that mediated and muted their bondage. Additionally, a tendency for masters to provide in their wills for the manumission of their slaves gradually had expanded the population of free African Americans in the region; and this free and freed population brought the reality of personal liberty into immediate and daily focus for the still-enslaved.[52]

Putting his heroic action on King Street aside for the moment, we can trace through the case of Crispus Attucks the path of slavery's collapse in New England during the Revolutionary Era and identify one of the strategies African Americans devised to capitalize on an already weakened structure. According to the tale told and preserved, Attucks had been a slave who had run away from his Framingham, Massachusetts, master around 1750 and had disappeared into the Boston mélange. There he had lived, obscure and undisturbed for two decades. At a time when slavery had declined in utility and popularity, few who walked away from bondage were pursued vigorously or seriously by the women and men who owned them.[53] On the night of March 5, 1770, the "fugitive" of twenty years apparently had been inside a victualling house, probably eating and drinking with white Bostonians. He had voluntarily and without popular resistance attacked a white man.[54] He had acted as a leader of white men. For Attucks, as for others in 1770 in New England who had claimed their freedom by no more formal means than walking away from enslavement, the lines separating slave from free were blurred and ambiguous. The abolition of slavery that would follow within the decade simply affirmed in official language an already well-advanced process that resulted in a tenuous, conditional, and incomplete freedom for African Americans living in Revolutionary New England.

While the official ending of slavery in Massachusetts generally is located in the 1783 Massachusetts Supreme Court *Walker* decision, the erosion of the legal apparatus supporting the institution in British North America in general, and in Massachusetts in particular, began to collapse during the 1760s. As women and men like Crispus Attucks were seizing their freedom in solitary moments of opportunity, the colonial courts anticipated the subsequent collapse of the legal foundations for slavery in Massachusetts Bay. On March 2, 1762, in Ipswich, Massachusetts, Jenny Slew sued her master, John Whipple, for her freedom. Slew charged that Whipple had held her in bondage illegally, basing her claim on the fact that her mother was white. Given the prevailing climate of opinion, Jenny Slew's claim simply suggested a reasonable solution to an entirely unreasonable dilemma. Although the case initially was decided in Whipple's favor, Slew appealed and in 1766 the Essex Superior Court of Judicature in Salem decided for Slew in a jury trial. She was freed and awarded four pounds in "damages."[55] In one respect, Slew's successful challenge simply reinforced New World conventions regarding the inheritability of slave status, which was transmitted through maternal rather than paternal lineage. Jenny Slew, the daughter of a free white woman and an enslaved African-American man, had a clear legal claim to her freedom. At the same time, the *Slew* case reflected a persistent flexibility of the boundaries between slavery and freedom in mid-eighteenth-century Massachusetts. There, as elsewhere in the British North American colonies, legal prohibitions against conjugal unions between European colonists and non-Europeans (laws initially intended to suppress marriages between European men and Native American women) had been codified since the mid-seventeenth century. Particularly within the servant class, however, neither formal marriages nor more casual unions between white and African-American colonists were uncommon.[56] Jenny Slew's parents had married and established a family life; and their daughter had claimed and won her freedom despite a climate of opinion that might have preferred otherwise.

The second suit, which challenged legal jurisdiction over slaves, began three years later in Boston. In October 1769 James Sommersett, a slave, was taken by his owner from Boston to London. Sommersett remained there, in his master's custody, until October 1771, when he ran away, was recovered, and then placed on a ship bound from London to Jamaica. As was often the case with resistant slaves, Sommersett was to have been sold into a harsher enslavement in the British West Indies. A writ of habeas corpus prevented the ship from sailing from London, and in the hearing that followed, Lord Mansfield declared that Sommersett must be discharged, there being no "positive law" in the British North American colonies for such situations.[57] While the Mansfield ruling did not directly challenge the legal foundations of American slavery, it foreshadowed nineteenth-century legal and popular jurisdiction battles surrounding fugitive slaves. For the moment, however, the ruling set the precedent for British treatment of fugitives from slavery and put the American colonists on notice: there would be no British support for this peculiarly American institution.

In the interim between the *Slew* and *Sommersett* cases in the 1760s and the 1783 *Walker* decision (which effectively ended slavery in Massachusetts), African-American New Englanders had claimed their freedom in a number of ways. They bought themselves, submitted petitions and other appeals through a number of legal and quasi-legal channels, shouldered arms in the Revolution and traded military service for freedom, and simply walked away from their masters. Many joined other native-born New Englanders and European immigrants in the migration of the poor, the landless, and the fortune-seekers to the territories of the Old Northwest. African Americans required no period of theoretical foment to forge their notion of freedom and the particular strategies and avenues people followed to obtain their freedom varied rather widely, shaped as much by personal circumstances and considerations as by socially and politically structured opportunities. Perhaps those who had established homes and families were less eager to vanish anonymously into colonial urban life than Crispus Attucks had been, or perhaps those who could preferred to negotiate their own purchase rather than wait for the death of a master or legislative deliverance from their bondage. Whatever the details of explanation, African Americans throughout rural New England simultaneously followed a number of different strategies to liberate themselves from an already collapsing institution.

Four months after Crispus Attucks died, on July 9, 1770, in Dartmouth, Massachusetts, a small fishing village on Buzzard's Bay some twenty miles east of Newport, a "Negro Man slave Named Venter" bought himself, paying twenty-one pounds, six shillings, and five pence to his owners, Elnathan Samson, a blacksmith, and John Chaffee, a spermacite manufacturer.[58] There is no record of Venter's life before November 1768, when Elnathan Samson bought him at public auction from the estate of Jeremiah Childs. Following a central tenet of American slavery, Venter's fortunes had followed those of his master. The sale had been demanded by Daniel Russell, to whom Childs was deeply in debt when he died. Venter, like any piece of chattel property, had a market value that could be used to reduce the debt. While the price Samson paid for Venter was not recorded, following his purchase Samson "did afterwards reconvey one half of said Negro" to John Chaffee. Within the decade, men like Venter would gain their freedom through soldiering, and men like Samson and Chaffee would grant that freedom for half the bounty money their slaves received when they enlisted. But Venter, in his late forties when he bought himself, would not wait for the Battle of Bunker Hill and the opportunities for freedom that followed.

The forces that informed Venter's vision of freedom, like those surrounding the death of Crispus Attucks, reveal much about the nature of slavery and freedom for African-American New Englanders during the era of the Revolution. There are striking similarities connecting Venter and Crispus Attucks. Like Attucks, with the exception of this single recorded event, Venter remains an anonymous and obscure figure. Both men had been in mid-life in 1770, Attucks forty-seven when he died, Venter forty-six when he freed himself. Both had been bought and sold like livestock; and both eventually gained their freedom. Attucks ran away, or simply walked away from his bondage, while Venter's plan for his future had required years of self-discipline and hard work—quintessential New England virtues.

It is unlikely that Venter formulated his plan for freedom in a cultural or political vacuum, devoid of either ideology or practical example. Questions of civil liberty permeated the consciousness of white New Englanders, and Venter must have been aware of the political dissent building throughout the 1760s and 1770s. Public speeches, broadsides, and a variety of circulating pamphlets increasingly challenged the "voluntary slavery" of colonial status. For Venter, as for all African-American slaves, the contradictions between public rhetoric and personal circumstances must have been acute.

The political climate and preoccupations of the British colonists, however, were only one source of influence in Venter's life. The area that stretched south from Boston to Newport and then ranged east across the Buzzard's Bay area and looped north over the neck of Cape Cod to Plymouth—the Plymouth sheep pasture is squarely centered in this area—contained a relatively dense African and African-American population. Some of Venter's nonwhite neighbors had been free-born, and a scattering owned land. In 1766, just four years before Venter bought himself, his neighbor Cuff Slocum, an African, had purchased both his own freedom and one hundred twenty acres of land from his owner at the price of six hundred fifty Spanish milled dollars.[59] Slocum's abrupt change in status, from slave to freeholder, must have inspired others, and particularly his son, Paul Cuffe, who would fashion another kind of dream into reality in his own adulthood.

Cuff Slocum and Venter both put enormous energy and planning into buying their freedom. That process also had consumed many years of grueling labor for African-born Venture Smith, who lived less than one hundred miles south and west of Dartmouth in the 1760s. In his early thirties Smith grew "ambitious of obtaining" his freedom and, by making a ten-pound down payment on his future, gained the right to hire his own time. He shunned "superfluous finery . . . and all kind of luxuries" in order to save the price his master had set. By his own report, during the first six months of his quasi-freedom Smith cut "four hundred cords of wood, besides threshing out seventy-five bushels of grain." For this labor he earned twenty pounds.

Venture Smith was a family man, and when he had gained his own freedom he set to work to earn the freedom of his wife and children. Between 1769 and 1773 he bought his two teenage sons, Solomon and Cuff. Young and capable of hard work, Solomon and Cuff added tremendously to Smith's earning power and were able to ease the economic burden Smith had shouldered when he embarked on the task of buying his family's freedom. Working together, father and sons reunited their family. The sea offered a likely setting for a poor man to make money in the eighteenth century, and Smith hired Solomon out on a whaling voyage. When Solomon died of scurvy, Smith reported that "besides the loss of life, I lost equal to seventy-five pounds." Still, Smith was determined to free his family. With his surviving son, Cuff, he began hauling and trading wood in a rented sloop "of about thirty tons burthen, and hired men to assist me in navigating her." From the profits he bought his wife Meg, paying forty pounds for her freedom. The choice had been a practical one. There had been no time to waste. Meg was pregnant, and Smith rushed to complete her purchase before she gave birth "and thereby prevented having another child to buy." The reconstitution of his family nearly completed, for a time Smith combined fishing "with setnets and pots for eels and lobsters" with his coasting trade in commodities until he was able to buy his eldest child, Hannah, for forty-four pounds.[60]

Given the gradual erosion of slavery in Massachusetts, Quork Walker's 1783 freedom suit was anticlimactic. Walker claimed his freedom on the basis of his master's verbal promise of manumission. In his charge to the jury hearing the case, Massachusetts Supreme Court Chief Justice William Cushing observed that "slavery is inconsistent with our own conduct and Constitution."[61] Cushing's admonition reflected increasingly widespread public sentiments against the institution and the jury had little choice but to uphold Walker's assertion of his freedom. While individual cases of slavery persisted for another decade after the decision, the Walker case removed the final legal prop for the persistence of slavery in Massachusetts. Still, the Cushing court did not render a landmark decision, for a number of Massachusetts towns already had moved to effectively abolish slavery by simply voting to have no slaves in their midst. To be sure, community motives were probably as much practical as they were moral. With the failure of proposed state legislation in 1780 aimed at relieving towns of financial responsibility for newly emancipated slaves, the collapse of slavery and its attendant human obligation for masters to provide for their aged and infirm bondspeople would obligate towns to support emancipated, aged, infirm, and impoverished African-American residents.[62] Nevertheless, for still-enslaved African Americans in Massachusetts, the *Walker* decision marked the ending of one period and the beginning of another in the lived experience of the Revolutionary Era.

SOLDIERS, BUT NOT HEROES

By the time Cushing had delivered the 1783 *Walker* decision, Cato Howe, Quomony Quash, and Plato Turner had made their way home to Plymouth as free men. Quomony Quash probably joined his parents, Quashey and Phillis Quandey, who already were living at Parting Ways. Plato Turner and his wife, Rachel, also settled on the sheep pasture in the house he had purchased from Job Cushman in 1779, with their infant son, Plato Turner, Junior; and in 1785 Cato and Alathea Howe also established a household at The Parting Ways. The sketchy and fragmented details of The Parting Ways residents' lives depict a difficult and isolated existence.[63] With the exception of Turner, whose occupation consistently is listed as a mariner, the men worked as laborers and the families struggled with poverty and debt, getting by with their meager wages, assistance from the town of Plymouth, and occasional small loans from Howe's former master, Ephriam Spooner, during the 1780s and 1790s. Despite the difficulties of life on the old sheep pasture, however, African tastes and African customs survived. The families stored tamarind fruit, probably brought back from Plato Turner's working voyages to the West Indies in crockery jars "almost identical to West African pottery and unlike anything in the New England tradition."[64] At The Parting Ways, as elsewhere in the New World, ancestral memory informed and permeated the microroutines of daily life, even among

African Americans who were claiming and living whatever prerogatives of citizenship were available to them.

There were signs of difficulty in the little community as the veterans at The Parting Ways aged. Indebtedness, a chronic problem for poor people, always had formed a subtext of the relationship between The Parting Ways and white Plymouth residents, but in 1800, when Plato Turner was fifty-seven, James Thacher and Nathan Hayward charged him with nonpayment of a debt of $4.74. Thacher and Hayward failed to appear in court, however, and defaulted in their suit. Turner apparently disputed the debt, for he then successfully countersued Thacher and Hayward for $7.63. There were also signs of disharmony among The Parting Ways residents. In 1814 Cato Howe, also in his late fifties, was charged with assault against another African American, Prince Goodwin. Howe pled not guilty and was acquitted in a jury trial. Goodwin, a Plymouth resident and also a Revolutionary War veteran, probably lived at some time at The Parting Ways, but there is no evidence that his residence there was as stable or permanent as that of the Howe, Turner, and Quash families.

Quashey Quandey, the African who had held fast to his own African name and had named his son in the African manner, died of old age in 1806. He had lived eighty-one years, sixty-seven of them in the New World. During his final sickness Lazarus LeBaron's daughter, Priscilla, had delivered gingerbread and calves-foot jelly to the old man. Quashey's wife, Phillis Quash, survived her husband by thirteen years and died in the Plymouth Alms House on April 3, 1819.

Quomony Quash married Ellen Stephens in 1812 at the age of fifty-three. Their first son, Charles H. W. Quam, was born that year and died of consumption in 1856. Their second son, Winslow S. Quash, was born around 1817 and died in 1823. With their deaths Quashey Quandey's African lineage in the New World ended.

In 1818 Quomony Quash, Cato Howe, and Plato Turner were formally placed under the guardianship of Nathan Hayward by the Plymouth Probate Court. They had been "free" thirty years. Declaring the men incapable of caring for themselves "by reason of imbecility of body and mind," Hayward assumed responsibility for the management of their lives. One of his first official acts was to file applications for their military pensions. They each received eight dollars a month, from which Hayward deducted a one-dollar fee from each pensioner for administrative services. Hayward also recorded expenses for ploughing, food and related provisions, clothing, and medicine and physicians' fees as being deducted from the pensioners funds.

Plato Turner died on July 11, 1819, at the age of seventy-six, and his widow, Rachel, died on July 28, 1824. Their eldest son, Plato Turner, Junior, married Sarah Hayward and bought land in Bridgewater. James Turner, the first African-American child to have been born at The Parting Ways, married Nancy Hollis, a white woman. The couple bore no children. The Turner daughters, Sarah and Rachel, married and lived during their adult years in Boston.

Cato Howe's wife, Alathea, died at the age of seventy in 1820 and Howe remarried the following year to Lucy Prettison. There is no evidence that he fathered children from either marriage. Howe died in June 1824 at the age of eighty-nine. Nathan Hayward served as administrator of his estate. The inventory listed the typical belongings of a poor but stable and established household: a fire shovel, two tables, three chests, four chairs, a bedstead and bedding, a spinning wheel, a pair of handirons, iron kettles and pots, a spider, skillet, flat iron, two lamps, assorted tin ware, woodenware, six junk bottles, a coffee mill, a mortar, knives, forks, and spoons, family pictures, an axe, crockery and glassware in a cupboard, a wash tub, one rooster, four hens, one cow, a dwelling house, and a barn, valued altogether at $61.82. Hayward sold the cow to pay Howe's debts, and Howe's widow, Lucy Prettison Howe, abandoned the Parting Ways homestead, moved to Boston, and subsequently married John Rogers. At a town meeting in May, 1824, the Plymouth Selectmen appointed a committee authorized "to sell the property conditionally granted by the town to Cato Howe."[65] Quomony Quash died in 1833, at the age of seventy-four, the cause of his death given as rheumatic fever. His widow, Ellen, remarried in 1847.

Whether or not the families living at The Parting Ways participated in the life of the larger Plymouth community, attended religious services or town meetings, or joined in community parades and Fourth of July celebrations can only be surmised. The scant evidence about their lives in the decades after the Revolutionary War suggests that they maintained cordial if distant relationships with former masters and other upper-class white Plymouthers. Still, with no African Church, African Meeting House, African Society, or Free African School in Plymouth, the men and women who lived at The Parting Ways in such great poverty would have had to travel to Boston, Newport, or Providence to join in the rituals and festivals that fused African ancestry with American nativity for other

African Americans. There is no evidence to suggest that they made such trips. Yet their small community situated on the old sheep pasture seemed bounded by a certain cultural integrity: the African-style crockery they used for food storage, and the naming pattern Quash and then his son Quomony followed, locate the persisting sites of ancestral memory embedded in the routines of the community.

In a limited way, the community at The Parting Ways underscores a resonant and recurring theme in post-Revolutionary African-American cultural life—the search for a stable home in a stable place, the search for a homeland. For the Howe, Quash, and Turner families, Plymouth, Massachusetts provided that stable place. For others, the search would lead in quite different directions. For all African Americans who confronted their freedom in the new republic, the challenge lay in realizing cultural and spiritual freedoms that paralleled physical freedom.

CHAPTER TWO

"Sons and Daughters of Distress": A Theology of Liberation

*Be you assured that Jesus Christ the King of heaven and
of earth who is the God of justice and armies, will surely
go before you. And those enemies who have for hundreds
of years stolen our rights and kept us ignorant of Him and
His divine worship, He will remove.*

—David Walker, 1829[1]

DURING THE EARLY YEARS of the republic, for Americans of European
descent, loyalties to state and nation supplanted attachments to European
homelands, and an emerging national identity provided the foundation
for a unifying American historical memory. Drawing from this national-
ized consciousness, white citizens of the young nation gradually fashioned
a collective identity that minimized ethnic differences, and collectively
remembered events that had marked the nation's progress toward political
and cultural autonomy and unity became the sites of that constructed
national memory. However, for Americans of African descent, whether
they lived in rural areas, villages, or cities, cultural identity and historical
memory were problematic. Original differences in tribal heritage and
identity had been muted by the African Diaspora, and, as the distance
between real time—the lived moment—and an African homeland lengthened, ancestral memory had retreated into the collective unconsciousness.
With the loss of direct contact with the African milieu, the intersection
of personal and collective identity weakened.

That intersection might have been strengthened or replaced by the
abolition of slavery and by the full and unconditional inclusion of African
Americans into the life of the nation. To be sure, by 1780 freedom of

one sort or another had either materialized or had become inevitable throughout the Northern states, and in some places African Americans voted and entered more or less freely into local civic life and the political process.[2] Vermont had directly and explicitly abolished slavery in its 1777 state constitution, and while neighboring New Hampshire would not enact similar legislation until 1857, over the eight decades spanning these two legislative abolitions of slavery, all the Northern states implemented various strategies for bringing an end to human bondage. Responding largely to the fears of white citizens that an abrupt general emancipation would result in widespread social unrest, many states crafted legislation that ended slavery through gradual emancipation programs. Rhode Island, for example, provided in 1778 for unconditional manumission of slaves who enlisted in the militia, the following year prohibited interstate traffic in slaves, and automatically emancipated all African-American children born after March 1, 1784. Over the next twenty years, Pennsylvania (1780), Connecticut (1784 and 1797), New York (1799 and 1817), and New Jersey (1804) would provide for various forms of gradual, or phased emancipation, generally setting an arbitrary date after which no more children could be born into slavery and enslaved adults would be emancipated at the age of majority.

Even as the gradual emancipation movement proceeded, however, African Americans faced a critical dilemma of memory and consciousness. The lengthening distance between the lived moment and an African homeland had blurred African environments of memory, and the mythologized representations of a lost world had replaced or supplemented personal and autobiographical memories of that homeland. At the same time, while freed from perpetual bondage, African Americans as a group still did not gain automatic and full access to the prerogatives of citizenship enjoyed by white Americans. Taxed, but deprived of access to the formal machinery of politics, circumscribed and restricted socially and economically, they remained a powerless and marginalized group. Neither respectability, education, propriety, nor public virtue proved effective shields against race discrimination. In Boston and Philadelphia, the twin souls of white anti-slavery in the United States, as surely as on the rice plantations of the Carolina low country, African ancestry fixed the boundaries of personal opportunity. The prevailing conventions of class and the distinctions of status that applied to others had been suspended for Americans of African ancestry.

In response, throughout the urban North, African Americans countered their half-freedom by crafting a metaphoric homeland within the nation of their birth and constructing a civic culture that buttressed the daily realities of social, economic, and political oppression. They grounded that culture in a community-based infrastructure of mutual-aid and self-help organizations that aimed not to accommodate white racism through institutionalized subordination but, rather, to promote and foster race unity and race autonomy. Within a crucible of racial oppression, African Americans invented a new nation and a new nationalism that challenged the myth of assimilation and demanded both cultural integrity and civic equality for peoples of African descent living in the United States.[3] This civic culture supported the apparatus through which African Americans educated their children, worshipped without inhibition or restraint by white co-religionists, claimed and proclaimed their common African heritage, and promoted and crafted a definition of citizenship designed to counter an increasingly elaborate system of social and political restriction.

The protected terrain of the segregated world provided opportunities to forge a shared framework of cultural memories that informed a New World racial identity vastly different from that being developed among white Americans. The substance of that shared framework of meaning and memory bears the indelible stamp of middle-class morality and values, for in a world where race directly limited education, income, and the accumulation of wealth and real property, the African-American urban elite in the young republic defined its social position through behavioral, moral, and value differences and claimed its status through symbolic rather than material criteria.[4] Given the prevailing restrictions and limitations, it could not have been otherwise. In exercising its leadership, the elite promoted a behavioral and aspirational culture of middle-class respectability. At the same time, an organizational infrastructure grounded the African-American moral community, and a value system bounded by Christian virtue, mutual aid, and racial uplift formed the crucial cornerstone of the relationship between the elite and popular classes.

An address Prince Hall delivered in Boston to African Lodge No. 459 (the first African-American Masonic Lodge to be established in the United States) in 1797 anticipated the contours and the agenda of this moral community. Hall wove race unity, mutual aid, uplift, and the abolition of New World slavery into a single tapestry of African-American culture:

> Among those numerous sons and daughters of distress, I shall begin with our friends and brethren; and first, let us see them dragg'd from their native

country, by the iron hand of tyranny and oppression . . . to a strange land
and strange people, whose tender mercies are cruel; and there to bear the
iron yoke of slavery and cruelty till death as a friend shall relieve them.[5]

In Massachusetts, slavery had been abolished for more than a decade
when Hall delivered the address; yet for Prince Hall, as for millions of
other African Americans—those living in the nominally "free" Northern
states as well as those still enslaved—the memory and the reality of slavery
remained a galvanizing *lieu de memoire* in historical memory and political
culture. For Prince Hall and those who gathered in the fraternal lodges,
as for those who would come to Faneuil Hall in 1858, symbolic kinship
between enslaved and free African Americans hinged on two equally
compelling facts of daily life: a bond of a common ancestry that a
darkened skin signified, and a shared, racially defined oppression that
differed only in degree. Hall's point was clear and his argument direct:
until slavery had been abolished everywhere and the lingering residual
effects of the institution eradicated, no descendant of Africa in the United
States could be truly free. For the next two centuries that single
understanding would drive freedom movements that demanded an end
to the physical, spiritual, intellectual, and moral bondage imposed on
African Americans. From the outset a compelling call for cultural
unification was embedded in those demands.

MY DEAR AFRICAN BRETHREN

Cultural unification proceeds not from the acquisition of a common
physical space, but from an intellectual, moral, and ideological anchorage. During the 1780s and 1790s the resonant inner voice of the
emerging moral community turned to public discourse and pamphlets,
the most popular print medium of the day, to analyze and debate the
issues African Americans faced in their daily lives and to frame the
circumstances of lives delimited by race discrimination within politically
meaningful contexts. A new political consciousness informed the discourse of the urban elite, a consciousness not greatly different from the
political culture of the white elite, but one disrupted and thwarted by
the limitations of race. Educated, literate, and affluent African Americans—those most profoundly affected by the recurring cycle of rising
expectations followed by crashing disillusionment; those most likely to
realize great gains in status and stature through the eradication of racial
boundaries—began to speak and write to African-American audiences.

In this discourse the supplicative tone of earlier petitions against slavery was transformed into one of civil and moral protest.

Like citizen petitions, pamphlets were a common and popular medium in the young nation and had been used to circulate and gain mass support for various ideas and philosophies during the final decades of the eighteenth century. Aimed at a mass audience, but requiring less capital to produce than a newspaper, pamphlets were the principal vehicle for disseminating theological, political, philosophical, and moral arguments of the day. They were a logical medium for developing intellectual coalitions that derived from immediate social issues. They were easily transported, and the authors were relatively free from editorial control and constraint. For African Americans like Jupiter Hammon, Prince Hall, Absalom Jones, and Richard Allen, pamphlets offered an ideal medium for disseminating their ideas. These early pamphleteers helped to forge a resonant moral community among their audiences. Their writings were concerned with matters related to race—domestic slavery and its abolition, the African slave trade, contemporary race relations in the young republic—and emphasized moral and social responsibility, elaborating on the obligations of the more fortunate to the enslaved and profoundly impoverished.

Jupiter Hammon (1712-1800) was a member of an upper-class Patriot household, privileged in material well-being, literate, yet a slave writing primarily to a slave audience. Hammon lived in a complex and contradictory milieu. To be sure, he was a slave (who disclaimed a desire to be free), but slavery was a variegated state during the Revolutionary Era. Hammon was owned by John Lloyd of Long Island and Hartford; his bondage was mild and relaxed compared to the conditions under which other African Americans lived at the time, and this placed him in a unique intellectual and social position. Like Phillis Wheatley, Hammon was a poet and essayist, living in relative privilege within the secure terrain of an upper-class household. His writings were printed as the result of the support and encouragement he received from "my superiors, gentlemen whose judgment I depend on," and while he does not say so, without whose approval and endorsement the works would likely have been suppressed.[6] Hammon had been first a poet, his *Evening Thought. Salvation by Christ, with Penitential Cries* printed in broadside in 1760. Several other poems appeared during the following two decades; but he turned to the essay in the 1780s. His first essay, *Winter Piece,* printed in 1782, apparently met with some degree of success, at least among his superiors, for the following year Hammon wrote *An Evening's Improvement*, introducing the work by noting "it hath been requested that I would write something more . . . by my superiors."[7] At the same time, writing in old age, he explained that he spoke to other slaves "with the tenderness of a father and friend," believing those who received his words would be "more likely to listen to what is said when it comes from a negro, one of your own nation and colour."

A slave writing to other slaves, Hammon also wrote in a time of enormous social and political uncertainty. His essays reflect that turbulent climate and suggest the intellectual strategies African Americans employed to reconcile the contradictions and ambiguities in their circumstances. Addressing always his African brethren in his essays, and grounded in the Protestant piety that had fueled the moral justification of the Revolution, Hammon's remarks are particularly instructive in understanding the tenuous beginnings from which African Americans crafted and manipulated moral and theological symbolism for uniquely racial political purposes.

The war for national independence had been won by the time Hammon's first essay appeared in print. The new nation was struggling through a difficult period of postwar financial chaos, and the revolutionary spirit that had driven the war had also transformed the political ideas of ordinary people. Samuel Adams's call for a "Christian Sparta" reflected the overpowering millennialist thought that had intensified the prevailing popular connection between religion and politics. Jupiter Hammon lived very close to the center of this political and intellectual world, and his writings reflect the fervor of the period. His master, John Lloyd, was an enthusiastic Patriot who had fled from New York to Hartford in September 1776, taking Hammon with him. There master and slave had waited out the end of the war in relative physical safety but certainly not in isolation from the prevailing popular ideological intersections of religion and politics that fueled the Revolution. Hammon's essays, written between 1782 and 1787, are weighted heavily with the language of Christian salvation and focus on the connection between secular behavior, temporal freedom, and spiritual salvation. Considered together, these essays underscore Hammon's keen awareness and understanding of evangelical Protestantism, especially its connection with the politics of the Revolution and its applications to the uncertain future of Africans and their descendants in the United States. These same connections formed the spiritual and religious contours of the emerging African-American moral community.

At the same time, Hammon's writings also trace the tension many African Americans felt between civil and sacred authority. In the Northern states, the decay of slavery in the postwar period posed hopeful possibilities to African Americans for full inclusion in the civic life of the nation; and although the Articles of Confederation had remained silent on the question of citizenship for Africans and their descendants, when representatives to the Constitutional Convention gathered in Philadelphia in May 1787 to begin their deliberations on the issue, African Americans anticipated a providential ruling and waited hopefully for the outcome. Jupiter Hammon's *Address to the Negroes of New-York* (1787), written during those deliberations, reflects both his full awareness of the citizenship debate and his thorough understanding of the issues surrounding it. Foreshadowing the extent to which African-American military valor in the Revolutionary War would come to define and anchor subsequent African-American demands for full and unconditional citizenship, Hammon asked, "how much money has been spent and how many lives have been lost to defend *their* liberty?" Hammon and his audience could not have been unaware that some of those lost lives had been African-American, and must have seen the paradox of their military service. African-American slaves had fought primarily for the political liberty of their white masters and neighbors. Still, his consciousness fixed within the psychosocial boundaries of dependency, Jupiter Hammon declined in the end to challenge the secular authority embodied in the representatives to the Constitutional Convention: While Hammon had "hoped that God would open their eyes, when they were so much engaged, to think of the fate of the poor blacks, and to pity us," he conceded that the freedom of the soul and spiritual salvation must remain the central concern of all Christians.[8]

The implicit claim embedded in Hammon's text of the equality of all souls before God serves as a bridge from the tradition of spiritual autobiography to the civil religion of the African-American moral community.[9] For Hammon, as for others, this crucial assertion of autonomous and subjectively derived moral consciousness of necessity preceded and grounded collective demands African Americans advanced for civic equality. While Hammon emphasized the inevitability of a separation of civil and sacred authority and counseled prayer for divine intervention in secular affairs rather than violent resistance to white oppression, the subtext of his essays foreshadows the theology of social action and the politicization of spiritual salvation that have become the defining characteristics of African-American Christianity from the bourgeois Protestantism of Absalom Jones and Richard Allen to the sectarianism of Father Divine's Peace Mission and the liberation theology of the Reverend Martin Luther King, Jr.[10]

In the more immediate context, Hammon's concern in his final essay, *An Address to the Negroes of New-York* (1787), for the bonds of reciprocity and responsibility that united free and enslaved African Americans anticipated the core themes that would ground the moral community: mutual aid and racial uplift.[11] Jupiter Hammon, like all late-eighteenth-century exhorters, aimed to foster a greater understanding of the path to spiritual salvation, "to encourage my dear fellow servants and brethren, Africans, in the knowledge of the Christian religion." The advice and counsel he offered in this essay followed closely that established and conventional path: submission to the will of God, repentance, and grace are the only routes to spiritual salvation. In *A Winter Piece* he forthrightly invoked the Calvinist admonition to "avoid bad company" in secular affairs. In his *Address to the Negroes of New-York* Hammon broadened this theme, cautioning his audience to "let not the example of others," even wealthy masters and other white gentlemen who hold authority over slaves in a secular society, "lead you into sin."[12]

While Hammon aimed to advance religious understanding, he also addressed the most immediate and central concern of African-American New Yorkers, his message veiled in the language of conventional evangelical Christianity: "Many of us are seeking a temporal freedom," he acknowledged, "and I wish you may obtain it." For reasons that can only be surmised, Hammon set himself entirely apart from the emancipation debate:

> I now solemnly declare that I have never said nor done anything, neither directly nor indirectly, to promote or to prevent freedom. I am a stranger here, and I do not care to be concerned or to meddle with public affairs.[13]

Writing at a relatively advanced age, perhaps Hammon could not transcend the psychosocial dependencies slavery had created, or perhaps shrewd practicality of intellect, the understanding that he must sacrifice the possibility of personal liberty in order to secure freedom of thought and expression, had shaped his public ambivalence regarding his own freedom. Or, Hammon's motive may simply have reflected a straightforward and honest loyalty to and affection for John Lloyd, a man who was obviously a more important figure in his life than the conventional master-slave relationship would suggest. Whatever the details of motive may have been, having distanced himself from the emancipation issue,

Hammon's tone remained cautious and conditional, offering barely a hint of the radical intersection of spiritual and secular liberation that within the decade would drive the ministries of Absalom Jones and Richard Allen. Following a Biblical tradition that ranges from Jeremiah to Paul, Hammon partitioned sacred and secular authority and then fused that tradition with Calvinist inventions regarding predestination: "If we are slaves it is by the permission of God, [and] if we are free it must be by the power of the most high God."

Hammon's application offered a measured interpretation of American slavery, a slim and subtle message of hope, urging those who desired temporal freedom to pray "that God would grant your desire, and that he may give you grace to seek that freedom which tendeth to eternal life." Prayer and faith, the most elusive tools in the Christian arsenal, were the only resources Hammon the exorter could provide to slaves longing for their freedom: "Cannot the same power that divided the waters from the waters for the children of Israel to pass through make way for your freedom?" At the same time, Hammon counseled integrity in the performance of secular duty, urging his brethren to "be not discouraged, but cheerfully perform the duties of the day, sensible that the same power that created the heavens and the earth and cause the greater light to rule the day and the lesser to rule the night can cause a universal freedom."[14]

Hammon's tone and text changed noticeably in his third and final essay, *An Address to the Negroes in the State of New-York.* First printed under the aegis of the African Society of New York City in 1787, the essay addressed both enslaved and free African Americans. (Apparently well received and widely read, the pamphlet was reprinted the same year by the Pennsylvania Society for Promoting the Abolition of Slavery and appeared a third time, printed posthumously by three unnamed citizens of Oyster Bay, New York, in 1806.) Although still enslaved, Hammon wrote now with remarkable candor when he discussed the concerns of his African brethren. The circumstances resulting in his release from Lloyd's editorial control are not clear, although the evidence of his literary and intellectual autonomy from John Lloyd is unmistakable. Perhaps the inevitability of the gradual emancipation legislation, or the increasing latitude enslaved African Americans claimed as freedom neared were factors influencing his apparent detachment from Lloyd. Whatever the details may have been, writing at the age of sixty-seven, Hammon counseled honesty and admonished slaves to neither steal from their masters nor malinger in the completion of their labor. Begging the question of the morality of slavery, Hammon simply urged the enslaved among his audience not to debate "whether it is right, and lawful, in the sight of God, for them to make slaves of us," but to have faith that freedom, if not obtained during this lifetime, would be forthcoming in the next.[15]

In this essay Hammon also spoke directly to the practical matter of living in a world circumscribed by "the poor, despised, and miserable state" of slavery and other forms of race prejudice. Writing more with resignation than with condemnation, he reminded slaves to be mindful that "we depend upon our masters for what we eat and drink and wear." Given this reality, Hammon counseled obedience, honesty, and faithfulness to duty, and outlined an ethic for living set against a backdrop of spiritual salvation. Writing at a time when African Americans in New York State were preoccupied with freedom and emancipation, Hammon addressed those issues directly. "Now I acknowledge that liberty is a great thing, and worth seeking for, if we can get it honestly, and by our own good conduct prevail on our masters to set us free." Seeming to endorse the state's gradual emancipation plan, he believed "many of us, who are grown up slaves and have always had masters to take care of us, should hardly know how to take care of ourselves; and it may be more for our own comfort to remain as we are." Nevertheless, he would "be glad if others, especially the young negroes, were to be free." Certainly, Hammon agreed, freedom is a desirable state, as "we may know from our own feelings, and we may likewise judge so from the conduct of the white-people, in the late war."

Hammon concluded this address with remarks directed especially toward those who were already free, and in this section of the essay his remarks foreshadow the texture of the relationship between the African-American (moral and intellectual) elite and popular classes in the coming decades. Anticipating the call for race unity that would ground the African-American spiritual and moral community throughout the nineteenth century, Hammon forged an enduring ethical bond between enslaved and free African Americans: "The most of what I have said to those who are slaves may be of use" to those who are free, he began, "but you have more advantages . . . than they. You have more time to read God's holy word, and to take care of the salvation of your souls. . . . If you do not use your freedom to promote the salvation of your souls, it will not be of any lasting good to you." Anticipating the emphasis subsequent African-American leaders would place on middle-class behavioral values, Hammon concluded his address by fusing the public image of respectability with the principle of moral responsibility and mutual aid:

Besides all this, if you are idle, and taken to bad courses, you will hurt those of your brethren who are slaves, and do all in your power to prevent their being free. . . . Let me beg of you, then, for the sake of your own good and happiness, in time, and for eternity, and for the sake of your poor brethren who are still in bondage, to LEAD QUIET AND PEACE-ABLE LIVES IN ALL GODLINESS AND HONESTY [16]

This slave, speaking primarily to other slaves, had been required to mask his views on secular concerns and political issues behind a theme of spiritual salvation. Yet Hammon's material advantage, combined with his clearly powerful intellect, doubtless shaped his thoughts, for his advice and counsel trace the contours of the middle-class respectability that dominated the oratory of the free African-American elite during the early decades of the nineteenth century and formed the core of the moral community this elite would create. To suggest that Hammon identified with and modeled the values of the ruling class would be an oversimplification of the situation and of Hammon's life. Like Hammon, future members of the African-American elite sought to set themselves apart from the less fortunate in the moral community, and all understood the central and causal position slavery held in the institutionalized racism that circumscribed their world. Their view of that social world placed them in an organic and interdependent relationship with other African Americans, bound together by the disadvantages of race and vested by virtue of their material and intellectual advantage with certain responsibilities for fostering uplift of the less privileged and promoting race unity within the community. For Jupiter Hammon, as for other African Americans of privilege, the moral community revolved around and depended upon the development and maintenance of race unity.

CONSTRUCTING A MORAL COMMUNITY

While Jupiter Hammon was exhorting African Americans in New York to attend to their spiritual salvation as they waited for secular freedom, those who were already free began constructing the institutional apparatus and the civil religion within which a tenuous secular freedom would be lived. Working within organizations born from the needs and concerns of local communities and often created as responses to local racism, privileged African Americans reached out to their less advantaged neighbors and to each other, crafting spheres of influence and a network of alliances grounded in the integrative principle of race unity. During the final years of the eighteenth century, in Newport, Boston, New York, and Philadelphia—urban areas where African Americans lived in great numbers—mutual-aid and religious societies began providing various forms of economic and social support that buttressed the otherwise capricious and difficult circumstances African Americans faced.

Led by a bourgeois nucleus, African Americans living in these concentrated settings formed into a critical mass; rejected and marginalized, they turned their energies toward the construction of a racially segregated world in which they might exercise their tentative and conditional liberty. In Philadelphia, New York, and Boston—the urban commercial and cultural centers of the young republic—and in the area around Newport, Rhode Island, where the maritime trades dominated the economy, African Americans laid the cornerstones of a segregated world—schools, churches, mutual aid, and fraternal societies—where they mingled without restraint and relatively uninhibited by the social conventions of a white-dominated world. The women and men who organized and sustained the infrastructure of the moral community—and who also guided the freedom movements—faced an enormous challenge of identity that had been building for fully a generation.

While immediate local issues and self-interests generally shaped the contours of community infrastructures, the larger paradox of African-American slavery drove the freedom movements that developed within those infrastructures. To be sure, the plight of slave brethren formed a critical and persistent subtext in African-American historical consciousness, but the freedom movements broadened beyond the physical to include spiritual, intellectual, and civic domains. The concrete and horribly irrefutable fact of physical bondage became the metaphor for the spiritual, moral, and mental enslavement of all African Americans. The nationalism of the freedom movements implicitly demanded sweeping structural change and the moral redemption of American society.

From the outset, the consciousness of the moral community, the contours of African-American nationalism, and the agenda of the freedom movements were shaped by an interaction of spiritual and secular agendas. In Boston, Prince Hall (1748-1807) figured prominently in this process, grounding his civic and political activities in a Christian vision. A product of the rich racial and cultural mélange of the eighteenth-century New World, Hall had been born in Bridgetown, Barbados to an English father and an African-French mother. Apprenticed to his father's trade in leather work as a youth, Hall had resisted the craft, seeking instead to emigrate to America. In 1765, acting in direct opposition to his parents' wishes, Hall had struck a bargain with the captain of a ship bound for Boston. The eager and ambitious teenager worked aboard ship for his passage to a new life that would be filled, he hoped, with broader opportunities than those Bridgetown offered. Once he arrived in colonial Boston, Hall followed a rigorous personal program of hard work, frugality, and education by private tutors hired at his own expense. By the age of twenty-five Hall had acquired property and become a taxpayer and a voter. Measured by the prevailing standards of colonial America, Prince Hall was a wealthy man.

In the 1770s, when Hall was in his late twenties, politics and religion combined to become a driving force in his life. Like Jupiter Hammon, Hall had been profoundly affected by the evangelical movement that swept pre-Revolutionary New England. He had joined the Methodist church and then the ministry, and there he had found both spiritual and political kinship. Crispus Attucks, Samuel Gray, Jonas Caldwell, and Samuel Maverick—all killed in the Boston Massacre on March 5, 1770—had been founding members of Hall's congregation at his Cambridge church, and they had been his friends. Drawn to the Patriot cause, Hall began to take an active role in Revolutionary politics. At the same time, however, Hall's deep religious commitment profoundly shaped the course of his life. Acting on that commitment, he had sought membership in a Boston Masonic lodge, but his application was denied on racial grounds. Still, Hall regarded Freemasonry as an opportunity to extend and strengthen his religious commitment, and he sought other avenues to Masonic membership. While firmly remaining a Patriot, in 1775 he had slipped into a British encampment with other African Americans to obtain admission to Masonry from British Lodge No. 58.[17] Hall could not have foreseen the extent to which his actions that night would create the medium through which he and many other African Americans would define and act upon their political beliefs, for by the 1820s Freemasonry would provide a unifying operational framework for the African-American elite in urban areas throughout the North. For the moment, however, when the British encampment withdrew from the city, Prince Hall and the others began meeting as an independent lodge in a rented room at the Golden Fleece Tavern. The group petitioned the Provincial Grand Master of Modern Masons of Massachusetts for a charter, but their application was rejected, once again on racial grounds.

Driven by race-consciousness, in 1775-6 Hall led a delegation of free African Americans who appealed to General George Washington for admission to the Continental Army. Their request was provisionally granted, and Prince Hall enlisted in the army. Believing the Revolution would bring an end to slavery, and acting on the advantage Washington's provisional decision afforded him, Hall also petitioned the Boston Committee of Public Safety to enlist local African-American slaves in the defense of the city as a way of preparing for the freedom he believed would follow the war. While the committee denied the petition, Hall's proposal stands as a bold, even visionary action. Within months Washington willingly would accept African-American soldiers into the thin ranks of the Continental Army. In 1777, perhaps impatient for that inevitable ending to slavery he had accurately anticipated, Hall headed a petition to the Massachusetts General Court, turning to the vocabulary and the ideology of the natural-rights philosophers to frame a petition demanding an end to slavery in that state and a restoration of "the Naturel Right of all men." Hall and the other petitioners presented a simple and straightforward claim: Africans and their descendants, "Sons and Daughters of Distress," had been "detained in a State of slavery in the Bowels of a free and Christian Country." Yet, like all people, they had "a Natural and Unaliable Right to that Freedom which the Grat Parent of the Unavers hath Bestowed equalley."[18]

In 1784 Prince Hall applied to the Grand Lodge of England for a warrant to establish an independent Masonic lodge for African Americans. He received the warrant in 1787, smuggled back across the same military barriers that he and his companions had crossed to obtain admission to the Masonic order, and established African Lodge No. 459 in Boston. Within a decade lodges also had been established in Philadelphia and Providence, and by 1812 there were African lodges in all the major Northern cities. Largely as a result of Hall's energetic leadership, black Freemasonry grew rapidly into a powerful and influential national organization. Between 1797 and 1818, for example, the Philadelphia lodge maintained a membership roster of more than one hundred men, including Richard Allen, James Forten, and Absalom Jones. Throughout the antebellum period black Masons promoted education, protested against illegal kidnappings, and agitated for an ending to slavery. Some lodges served as stations on the Underground Railroad.

Hall had been a familiar figure in Boston politics since the 1770s. A small, light-skinned man, he probably could have passed as white in Boston, but chose, instead, to claim his African heritage and to press demands for racial equality in every social arena of Revolutionary Boston. Ten years later, when slavery in Massachusetts was a horror of the recent past rather than a suffering of the present, Prince Hall again invoked the vocabulary and the spirit of natural rights to seek immediate civic freedoms and access to public facilities for Boston's African-American citizens. Prince Hall understood well the crucial importance of education for African-American children, and in 1787 he initiated a petition to the city for separate schools for African-American children, claiming that education is one "out of many . . . privileges of free men."[19] Among African Americans, Prince Hall spoke with enormous authority, but the 1787 school petition was no more successful in instigating structural change than Hall's earlier efforts had been. The city of Boston provided no formal support for the education of its African-American children. Nevertheless, Boston's African school, supported by subscription, began meeting in the home of Primus Hall, a member of African Lodge No. 459. The children Prince Hall had described as "our rising offspring" would not be allowed to "grow up in ignorance in a land of gospel light." They received instruction from the most educated men in Boston's African-American community: Thomas Paul, Jr., the son of Boston's first African-American minister, and John Russwurm, a graduate of Bowdoin College who in 1827 would collaborate with New Yorker Samuel Cornish to establish *Freedom's Journal,* the nation's first African-American newspaper.[20]

Prince Hall publicly challenged the moral contradictions embedded in secular authority, and when that challenge was ignored, Hall mobilized the collective resources in Boston's African-American community for the sole purpose of providing black children one of the basic and fundamental "privileges of free men." However, black Bostonians were not alone in their concern for the education of the children. In 1787, as Prince Hall submitted his petition in Boston, the New York (City) Manumission Society organized a Free African School. Originally intended to assist that city's African Americans in their transition from slavery to freedom, from the outset the school provided instruction in reading, writing, mathematics, and geography as well as vocational training to children and youth during the day and to adults in the evening, a pattern of ethnically grounded education that Jewish immigrants to the United States would repeat in the late nineteenth and early twentieth centuries. Peter Williams, Jr., chaired the home visitation committee, a group of African Americans charged with the responsibility of meeting with parents whose children were not attending school, and Samuel Cornish guided the fund raising committee.[21] The New York African Free School would grow at an astonishing rate during the coming decades, listing seven separate facilities in the City Directory by 1834, when the schools were incorporated into the New York City public school system. During the first decades of the nineteenth century, the community-supported African Free Schools, which followed the monitorial system, the most progressive educational model of the times, counted among their graduates: Ira Aldridge, an internationally recognized Shakespearean actor; Patrick Reason, a commercial artist and engraver; Charles Reason, a teacher and writer; Reverend Alexander Crummell; Reverend Isaiah DeGrasse; and Samuel Ringgold Ward.[22]

While Jupiter Hammon had alluded to a theology of liberation and Prince Hall had crafted a Christianized political agenda, Philadelphians Richard Allen (1760-1831) and Absalom Jones (1746-1818) brought the principles of an African-American civil religion into clear and vivid focus. Their ministries, so completely fused to the social as well as the spiritual needs of black Philadelphians, and so utterly linked to the politics of their era, translated the abstractions of the natural-rights philosophers and of evangelical Christianity into daily reality for their parishioners. Their clerical model, emphasizing immediate social application of the Gospel, set the agenda for African-American Christianity well into the twentieth century.

Both Allen and Jones were born into slavery, Allen in Philadelphia and Jones in Sussex, Delaware. The Allen family, owned by a Philadelphia lawyer, was sold to a Delaware farmer when Richard was a child. In 1777, the seventeen-year-old youth experienced a religious conversion so obviously powerful and compelling that he subsequently conducted religious services in his master's home. Self-educated, Allen obtained his freedom around 1781, then worked for a time as a woodcutter, and in 1784, at the age of twenty-four, was received into the Methodist ministry and licensed to preach. The Reverend Bishop Asbury guided Allen's early career as a traveling preacher. Gaining no financial support from the Methodists, Allen worked at odd jobs to support himself during this period. He recalled that he had "got myself pretty well clad through my own industry—thank God—and preached occasionally" to both whites and African Americans throughout Delaware, New Jersey, Pennsylvania, and Maryland. He described a grueling schedule: "I frequently preached twice a day, at 5 o'clock in the morning and in the evening, and it was not uncommon for me to preach from four to five times a day." During this clerical apprenticeship Allen was awakened to the spiritual neglect of "my African brethren, who had been a long forgotten people and few of them attended public worship." Richard Allen had found his calling. In 1786 he accepted the invitation of the elders at St. George's Methodist Episcopal Church, Philadelphia, to minister to increasing numbers of African Americans among the predominantly white congregation, and returned to the city of his birth, where he would live until the end of his life.[23]

Conversely, Absalom Jones had passed his childhood and youth in rural Delaware and was brought to Philadelphia in 1772, at the age of twenty-six. There he was employed as handyman and clerk in his master's store, attended Anthony Benezet's school, and married a slave. After fourteen years of marriage, Jones and his wife, with the assistance of local Quakers, bought their freedom in 1784.[24] Absalom Jones was thirty-eight years old. Two years later Jones joined St. George's and there met Richard Allen, the twenty-six-year-old charismatic preacher newly arrived in the city, and joined Allen in his efforts to minister to the Philadelphia African-American community.

Richard Allen took his ministerial charge at St. George's seriously. Seeing a need "to erect a place of worship for the colored people" attending St. George's, he established a segregated prayer meeting and subsequently was regarded as a "nuisance" by the elders who initially had invited him to join St. George's. Allen recalled, "here I met with opposition" by a white elder of the church, "who used very degrading and insulting language to us." Feeling "ourselves much cramped," in 1787 Allen, Absalom Jones, William White, and Dorcus Ginnings formed the interdenominational Free African Society and laid plans to establish an independent African Church. Despite vigorous opposition from the white elders, the four led the Quaker-type prayer meetings the Free African Society held in rented rooms.[25]

During the early formative months the African Americans who met together for prayer in the Free African Society meeting room continued to attend regular worship services at St. George's. However, the simmering racial tensions at St. George's erupted on April 12, 1787, when Allen, Jones, and other African-American congregants suffered an interruption of their prayers. The men had taken seats in a new gallery at the church they mistakenly believed had been reserved for African-American congregants. When ordered to move, Absalom Jones requested that they not be interrupted during their prayers. In response, church trustees dragged the men from the gallery on their knees.

In the days following the incident Allen and Jones led a withdrawal of African Americans from St. George's. Allen later recalled that "we went out of the church in a body, and they were no more plagued with us."

Despite subsequent apologies by the white elders and efforts to draw the African-American congregants back into the church, those who had led the withdrawal "were filled with fresh vigor to get a house erected to worship God in." Still, the white members of St. George's did not easily release the people they had disdained and humiliated, and a struggle followed the withdrawal. The white Methodists threatened to have the African Americans "read publicly out of meeting," but the group persisted, "hired a store-room, and held worship by ourselves."[26]

Both Allen and Jones would later establish and head African-American congregations, Jones as an Episcopal pastor and Allen as the founder of the African Methodist Episcopal denomination, whose organizers vowed they would "admit none to be enrolled as members but descendants of the African race."[27] During the 1780s, however, the two clergy directed their considerable energies to the development of the Free African Society. Guided by a vision of racial unity and cultural autonomy, the organization established and supported a variety of mutual-aid and self-help programs for its members.

Proclaiming themselves "men of the African race" in the society's Preamble, the Philadelphians echoed Jupiter Hammon's admonitions to the free African Americans in New York. The organization required and expected of its members lives circumscribed by sobriety, mutual aid, and the protection of the nuclear family and provided within the structure of the society for the discipline to enforce those expectations.[28] Members who drank, gambled, or disregarded their marriage vows were warned, then fined, and if their behavior persisted, expelled from the society. Still, membership in the Free African Society, as in mutual-aid societies elsewhere throughout the urban North, provided a crucial safety net for people whose material resources were profoundly limited. From its monthly dues the Free African Society provided burial expenses, relief to the sick, and limited financial support for widows and fatherless children. Despite sometimes vigorous white opposition and occasional open hostility to their efforts, the members of the Free African Society continued to meet for worship, envisioning the erection of a church and then a schoolhouse as the crucial first elements of community infrastructure. In both values and programs, the Philadelphia Society mirrored the Free African Union Society that had been established in Newport in 1780; and the African Society of Boston, established in 1796, and the New York African Society for Mutual Relief, established in 1809, would parallel the Newport and Philadelphia organizations. In these and other mutual-aid and self-help societies being organized throughout the urban

North, African Americans claimed an authenticity of identity through a theology of liberation.

"STRANGERS IN A STRANGE LAND"[29]

Guided by a theology of moral uplift and social action, the social programs that the mutual-aid societies organized—primarily centering on education and financial assistance to members during times of crisis—constituted only one dimension of these complex organizations. Grounded in the official discourse of mutual aid, racial uplift, and race unity, the African Societies provided a slim margin of reserve to people whose lives were circumscribed by profound economic limitations, but the disadvantages African Americans suffered in the secular world were not limited to the material. Honor, prestige, esteem, respectability—all were withheld from the "strangers in a strange land," as the members of the Newport Free African Union described themselves. The Proceedings of the Free African Union reflect the Newporters' keen awareness of this symbolic disadvantage and the members of the society took specific steps to avoid the perils that the judgment of whites could bring to them. Struggling during the 1780s and 1790s to protect themselves against the vagaries of race prejudice and discrimination, the Newporters set forth in the Proceedings of the Free African Union elaborate procedures to be followed at the death of a member. These procedures reveal a great deal about how these African Americans managed their bifurcated identity and about the role that middle-class respectability played in their image management.

The death of a member of the Free African Union Society demanded immediate notification to "each Member by the Sexton, or some other Person appointed for that Purpose." All members of the society who were "well in Body & of perfect mind and Memory" were expected to participate in all the rites and rituals surrounding the funeral. The detailed and unambiguous instructions for those rituals were written into the society's official record: Society members would unite in a formal and public procession to the deceased's home and there join the public procession to the burial ground, the members taking their place in the procession in an order that reflected the hierarchy of the society— "President & next officers shall immediately follow [the next of kin]," the other members forming into pairs behind the officers.

Like Jupiter Hammon, the architects of the Free African Union Society were particularly sensitive to the deportment and public image projected by those among the membership who were free, and image management formed an important subtext of the society's guidelines for attending and participating in funerals. The proceedings record that the officers "particularly recommend to all and every Member that shall find freedom," but particularly to those who were already free, to "dress themselves and appear decent on all occasions, that so they may be useful to all and every such burying as above, and within described, *that all the Spectators may not have it in their Power to cast such Game contempt, as in times past.*"[30] Those spectators were, of course, the white people who gathered along the roadside to watch—and sometimes jeer at—the black people dressed in their funereal finery.

Despite persistent white contempt and the periodic eruptions of violence directed against African Americans, normalized relations with the surrounding white community remained a desired goal. While public rituals offered structured moments when African Americans could present a face of respectability, less predictable opportunities also were presented from time to time. In Philadelphia a public health crisis proved such a precipitating moment. In August, 1793, a "malignant fever" began to spread rapidly through Philadelphia. By early September the epidemic nature of the disease, identified as yellow fever, had become frighteningly apparent. Many of the sick were going unattended and many of the dead unburied because of the fear of contagion. During the early weeks of the epidemic, few African Americans seemed to have contracted the disease. With little scientific understanding of contagious disease, many in Philadelphia believed rumors attributed to Carolina planters that their slaves were immune from the yellow fever epidemic there. Mathew Carey voiced this popular belief when he reported as fact "the black people . . . were exempted in a peculiar manner from the contagion."[31] As a result, a public call went out soliciting "people of color to come forward and assist the distressed, perishing, and neglected sick" of the city. Richard Allen, Absalom Jones, and William Grey organized the members of the Free African Society, which worked under the guidance and instruction of Dr. Benjamin Rush. The fever ran its course and by the winter months of 1793-4 had subsided, but in the aftermath Carey publicly accused African Americans of taking advantage of the crisis by charging excessive amounts for their nursing services and of behaving in unprincipled ways; specifically, neglecting the sick they had been hired to care for and stealing from the dead.[32]

The rhetorical exchange between Carey, Allen, and Jones offered little in the way of empirical proof to clarify the specific situation.

Whether or not African Americans, as Carey had charged, took advantage of the sick and dying in Philadelphia during a public health crisis is less important than his accusations and the strategy African-American leaders employed to counter them. Carey clearly was condescending as he crafted his charges. "As the value of labour is generally estimated by the trouble it costs," he reasoned, "the blacks would naturally . . . take advantage of the time, to get as much for their labour as they could."[33] Allen and Jones countered Carey's accusations in *A Narrative of the Proceedings of the Black People, During the Late Awful Calamity in Philadelphia, in the Year 1793, and A Refutation of some Censures Thrown upon them in some late Publications,* which provided an accounting of the expenses Philadelphia's African-American community had incurred in the course of providing nursing and burial services during the city's yellow fever epidemic. Addressing the issue of financial gain, they explained that according to their records, expenses exceeded all payments received. They also described the conditions at Bush Hill, the temporary hospital that had been opened to care for the sick and dying throughout the fall and winter months of 1793-4. The facility had been sorely lacking in sanitation; and they cited case after case of African-American women exhausted from nursing around the clock without relief, falling ill with the fever themselves, and being turned out of private homes or the Bush Hill facility, refused the same nursing care they had been providing to others. "We sought not fee nor reward," Allen, Jones, and Grey explained, "until the increase of the disorder rendered our labour so arduous that we were not adequate to the service we assumed."[34]

Carey had turned to a racist innuendo to explain his charges of profiteering. "It should be considered," he wrote, "that their education has been such as to keep them in ignorance of the finer feelings of nature . . . that the time afforded tempting opportunities."[35] Allen and Jones had assumed a rationality that probably did not exist, or at least did not apply to race and class prejudice. Reasoned discourse had been no more effective a weapon against prejudice than had piety, sobriety, and bourgeois respectability. Still, doubtless aware that their pamphlet would receive wide notice among white as well as African-American Philadelphians, Jones and Allen used their narrative of the epidemic months to comment on slavery and race prejudice. They appended three additional essays to the body of the yellow fever epidemic narrative—one addressed to slaveholders, one to slaves, and one to whites described as "the Friends of Him Who Hath no Helper."[36] Read together, the essays formed a complex commentary on slavery.

In the essay to slaveholders, Allen and Jones obviously aimed to counter and refute the stereotyped beliefs Mathew Carey had expressed about the relationship between race and the "finer feelings" of human nature. They wrote: "a black man, although reduced to the most abject state human nature is capable of, short of real madness, can think, reflect, and feel" as fully as white people. Citing the downfall of kings and princes "that God hath destroyed for their oppression of the poor slaves," Allen and Jones echoed Jupiter Hammon, urging slaveowners to acknowledge the fundamental humanity of their slaves and thereby repent, condemn their former conduct, "and become zealous advocates for the cause of those whom you will not suffer to plead for themselves."[37]

In 1790 the members of the Free African Union Society considered how they might organize a return to their homeland. As the members explained in a letter to "the Affricans in Providence," they sought, quite simply, to return to their "own country" where they believed they would "be more happy" than they were in the United States. Corresponding with African Americans in Boston, Providence, and Philadelphia, and planning to send a "surcular Letter to our free Blacks [in] all the States," the society proposed sending "a number of Men from among Ourselves" to the African west coast to negotiate "by gifts or purchase of some Kings, or chief people, Lands proper & sufficient to settle upon."[38]

Through William Thornton, an English Quaker physician already involved in the Sierra Leone Company, the members of the Newport Society had been invited to join the Sierra Leone colony then being organized on the African west coast. Thornton described his vision of a new life in the British colony to members of the Newport African Union Society when he invited them to join the venture: "The ground ought to be divided in equal lots," he wrote, "one to each Settler, on his becoming Subject to the Laws and Regulations of the Community." Continuing to describe a society fused from two cultural legacies, Thornton elaborated the relationship between private property and public responsibility: each settler would be "Bound with Life and property taxed according to the exigencies of the community, but by the voice of the Representatives of the People who would be elected by their free and uncorrupted Suffrage."[39]

Thornton's meticulous attention to matters of civil rights may have been intended to reassure the anxious Newporters, for he carefully explained that the new African community would protest and embrace religious toleration, equality of civil liberties, and the right to bear arms.

The African Union Society apparently circulated Thornton's correspondence among various other mutual-aid societies with whom they were in contact, for Samuel Stevens wrote from Boston that "we do not approve of Mr. Thornton's going to settle a place for us: we think it would be better if we could charter a Vessel, and [send] some of our own Blacks" to locate a suitable settlement site. Anthony Taylor replied to Stevens on behalf of the Free African Union Society, whose membership concurred with the Bostonian's sentiments: "We have much the same Opinion of Mr. Thornton," Taylor wrote. "We think he ought to be treated with respect, and to be encouraged in his honest Zeal to promote the welfare of the Affricans, while we behave with caution." Maintaining distance from Thornton and the English abolitionists who were organizing the Sierra Leone colony, the Newporters and other African Americans in the urban Northeast continued their correspondence with each other on the matter of African emigration. In 1794 the African Society in Providence petitioned the Rhode Island General Assembly for assistance in the emigration venture and proposed to the Newport Society sending "three black men on this Important Business" of locating a settlement site on the African west coast. Three delegates were needed, they opined, "on Account of Accidents."[40]

In 1797, after seven years of deliberation and correspondence—but twenty years before Paul Cuffe would sail for Freetown with thirty-one emigrants aboard *Traveller,* and fully a generation before the American Colonization Society would initiate the U.S. colonization of the African west coast—the Newporters agreed that James McKinzie of Providence could represent those desiring to emigrate in preliminary negotiations with authorities in Sierra Leone. Once he arrived in the colony, McKinzie encountered some difficulties in his negotiations with British authorities and, in the end, arranged only a limited emigration: British authorities agreed to accept twelve families sent by the Providence Society. Those families would receive ten-acre land grants, town lots, and full admission to British citizenship, with the stipulation that the emigrants would provide testimonies of their good moral character.[41] The women and men who waited in Providence and Newport for McKinzie's return must have felt enormous disappointment when they received his news, for thereafter local interest in an African emigration subsided and most people simply returned to the business of living their daily lives as best they could.[42]

While the 1790s emigration initiative may have been premature, the brief and aborted attempt by the Providence and Newport Societies to sponsor a return to Africa anticipated a movement that would become refined and elaborated in subsequent decades. The emigration question reflected a fundamental and pivotal problem African Americans confronted in living genuinely free lives, and the centrality of that problem persisted long after African emigration had been rejected by the African-American majority. (Even then, a number of African Americans—Paul Cuffe, James Forten, John Russwurm, and Martin Delany being the most prominent—would continue to promote African emigration as a viable alternative to life in the United States.)

Those who turned away from emigration to Africa did not necessarily embrace the United States. Faced with bitter personal and collective disappointments, many became resigned to the knowledge that full citizenship would not be forthcoming and proposed Canada, Haiti, and even the far western United States as viable resettlement sites. What began in the 1780s as a movement toward a beloved homeland gradually would be transformed into a search for a concrete territory where African Americans could realize the freedom they had been promised but had never received. Between 1820 and 1860, 20 percent of the free African-American population quit the United states to establish new lives in Liberia, Haiti, the British West Indies, and Canada.[43] These streams of migration were the focus of recurrent and passionate debate within the African-American community throughout the first half of the nineteenth century. Carried on in convention halls during the 1830s, in public meetings, and in the pages of the abolitionist press during the 1840s and 1850s, the emigration debates infused African-American cultural memory with an irrevocable transnational impulse that aimed to reconcile the paradox of African ancestry and American nationality.

As the African Union Society's committee of correspondence went about its work, putting down on paper a common set of ideas, concerns, problems, and proposed solutions, then circulating those formalized statements to similar organizations in other cities, the machinery of coalition-building had been put into motion. Not always in agreement, the groups in Boston, Providence, and Philadelphia with whom the Newport Group corresponded and who, in turn, circulated their own memoranda became each others' critical audiences. Members of these local organizations gained a new awareness of each other and of the concerns and circumstances they shared. The bonds among the groups that developed during this process created the nuclei of an emerging translocal moral community.

MEMORY, IDENTITY, AND THE MORAL COMMUNITY

By the onset of the new century, in the Southern states slavery had hardened and there was little promise of legislative relief for 90 percent of the African-American population who were held in bondage. Throughout the rural areas of the Northern states, scattered and isolated African-American families struggled quietly in places like The Parting Ways to survive the harsh realities of their hard-won freedom, but in places where free African Americans lived in more concentrated numbers the members of mutual-aid societies sought avenues for fostering collective support and encouraging those who were already free to lend a helping hand to those who were not. For most, vision was limited to immediate spheres. Few had the luxury to look beyond the boundaries of physical community. Paul Cuffe was an exception. Within a decade the son of Cuff Slocum, the slave who had bought himself in 1766, would envision a different world and then translate his private hopes and imaginings into a profoundly politicized global program that aimed to permanently disrupt the enslavement of Africans by attacking the system at its root. Cuffe envisioned a world in which the descendants of Africa would return to their homeland and establish a moral and economic fortress against slavery, a colony informed by "Christian benevolence," set in the midst of the west African coastal slave trading centers. In 1815 Captain Cuffe transported thirty-one African-Americans to the Sierra Leone colony in his favorite ship, *Traveller*.[44]

Despite such efforts as Cuffe's, however, African-American visions of liberty and equality went largely unrealized, for isolated and localized efforts—such as the settlement at The Parting Ways in rural Massachusetts—to claim the human rights promised by both divine and civil authority were limited in scope and effect. In the urban North, however, the signs of collective unrest and of an emerging moral community that could mediate that unrest were unmistakable. Within this milieu, calls for race unity and race autonomy sought explicitly to mobilize a moral fortress against racial oppression and African Americans resisted accommodation to white supremacy. While this resistance was largely localized and only loosely organized, it anticipated the subsequent development of more specifically focused freedom movements. From the outset these movements were fueled by divine authority and guided by divine inspiration, and while they assumed many forms, all signaled a growing restlessness and a heightened dissatisfaction with the biracial world that had resulted from a Constitutional paradox that simultaneously protected (white) liberty and made slavery possible in the United States. David Walker's *Appeal, in Four Articles,* would be written in the tradition inspired by these movements. Reverberating with passionate energy, setting aside the civility previously used to address white audiences, no longer needing to mask their frustration and anger with a veneer of rhetorical reserve, within the freedom movements African Americans spoke to each other in a vocabulary of race unity and cultural autonomy; and from those movements an ethnic identity grounded in a common mythic African heritage welded from a blend of autobiographical and generational memory emerged and crystallized. For African Americans, that identity anchored a cultural world separate and apart from the nation that oppressed them. This was the legacy of David Walker's *Appeal.*

David Walker reflected the diversity of experiences and intellectual perspective the African-American elite of the early nineteenth century brought to the freedom movements they guided. Born to a free African-American woman in North Carolina in 1785, the forty-four-year-old Boston used-clothing dealer challenged the core of the invented American myth of assimilation when he published the *Appeal.* Walker had been born the year after the United States signed the Treaty of Paris with Great Britain, in the first year of the republic, and he had no direct knowledge of the Revolution. Yet memories of the Revolution inspired Walker's vision of civil liberty as surely as they informed other African-American freedom movements throughout the new republic during the early decades of the nineteenth century. Walker justified his call for a violent revolt against racial oppression by diminishing the nation's collective sufferings under the tyranny of Great Britain, calling them merely "one hundredth part as cruel" as the conditions white Americans had imposed upon people of color. Walker's *Appeal, in Four Articles* (Boston, 1829) simultaneously claimed cultural integrity and demanded civil equality for peoples of African descent in the United States. A riveting manifesto of African-American nationalism, the *Appeal* combined an unequivocal condemnation of slavery and American racism with an incisive analysis of the corruption of Christianity to the political agenda of white Americans. In the pamphlet, which circulated widely among African-American communities in both the Northern and Southern states, Walker declared that "the greatest riches in all America have arisen from our blood and tears" and demanded that the citizens of the United States "make a national acknowledgment to us for the wrongs they have inflicted on us."[45] Walker's *Appeal* went through three printings in less than a year, electrified African-American readers, and evoked intense alarm among white Americans. Not surprisingly, David Walker died under mysterious circumstances within months after the publication of the *Appeal*. In Walker's case, as in many others, white Americans retaliated decisively, immediately, and with violence against a person of color who voiced and acted upon his dissatisfaction with the American racial matrix.

Environments of Memory, 1800-1835

INTRODUCTION

For African Americans living in the nominally "free" states of the North during the early decades of the nineteenth century, consciousness and identity revolved around two events: 1807-8 federal legislation prohibiting ships sailing under the United States flag from participating in the African slave trade; and, the Haytian Revolution. Both provided fertile psychosocial environments in which memories of the past intersected with realities and opportunities of the moment. From the outset, romanticized images of Africa as a lost homeland figured prominently in shaping African-American perceptions, understandings, and interpretations of the two events. To many, the 1807-8 legislation seemed to promise an end to the sufferings and degradations people of African descent had endured in the United States. The discourse that memorialized and celebrated that legislation invented a shared ancestry—tribal distinctions blurred by the African Diaspora—and anticipated for African Americans a reunification with a lost cultural legacy. Parallel to that legislation, the Haytian Revolution provided African Americans with a model of political agency and racial achievement denied in the United States. In African-American constructions of Toussaint's Hayti, images of a lost past combined with the material reality of a New World democracy created and ruled by people of African descent, and the representations of liberty embodied in African-American descriptions of Hayti contrasted sharply with the incomplete and limited freedoms they endured in their native country. Confronting the paradox of nationalism resulting from these representations, many must have asked themselves, as W. E. B. DuBois would a century later: *"Am I an American or am I a Negro? Can I be both?"*[1] The dilemma posed by African ancestry combined with American nativity would present a continuing challenge to identity for African Americans, and it never would be entirely resolved.

A generation of Revolutionary War veterans had responded to this confusion of identity by directing ancestral memory inward, establishing and sustaining institutions that formed the racially grounded infrastructure of their communities. They organized local churches and schools, mutual-aid and fraternal societies in urban areas throughout the North, and they claimed and proclaimed their common, mythologized ancestry in the names of those organizations. In African churches, Free African schools, and African Benevolent societies, nebulous African environments of memory anchored both personal and collective identity, and schoolmasters and clergy kept alive the spirit of individual liberty in segregated classrooms and from segregated pulpits. Within this segregated world a few of the free African Americans living in the Northern states responded to the images and imaginings of freedom beyond their immediate sphere by leaving the country to establish permanent homes elsewhere. Some migrated to Africa and others dreamed of an emigration to Hayti.[2] For the majority, however, many generations removed from a lost and mythologized homeland, the invented and celebrated ancestral past formed the core of psychosocial identity and proved the fulcrum of a community unity vested in the principles of mutual aid and racial uplift.

In 1815, when Paul Cuffe sailed at the helm of *Traveller* carrying thirty-one emigrants bound for new lives in Sierra Leone, the debates surrounding emigration were less intense than they would be in later decades, as African Americans increasingly resisted American Colonization Society efforts to remove free blacks from the United States to Liberian settlements. For Cuffe, and for those who followed, motives for emigration were complex, and idealized visions of a lost Africa were freshened by the persistent and enduring alienation from U.S. environments. For many the Liberian settlements represented both cultural reunification and personal opportunities to realize the sorts of freedoms that eluded them in the United States. Probably few understood that the Africa to which they returned was, ironically, a product of the same global forces that had produced slavery.

In 1829 a riot and race crisis in Cincinnati tested the power of the mutual-aid and racial-uplift ethic, an organizing principle of community life for African Americans in the United States. Initial concern for the plight of the black Cincinnatians intersected with already well established and continuing opposition to the work of the American Colonization Society.³ In September 1830, eleven months after the riot, as the fate of slightly more than two thousand African Americans remained suspended in the unbalanced equation of civil rights, racist legal codes, and white fear, Baltimore ice dealer Hezekiah Grice suggested to Richard Allen that he convene a meeting of concerned African-American leaders to consider what action might be taken to support the Cincinnatians and, in a broader sense, to advance "the condition of the free people of colour throughout the United States."⁴ Acting on the suggestion, Allen convened a clandestine meeting of forty self-selected delegates at Bethel Church, Philadelphia, that same month. The National Convention Movement, the first civil rights movement in the United States, was born from that tragic eruption of New World racism.

By the time the 1830 Philadelphia meeting had adjourned, those present—who vowed to convene annually—had forged a political agenda that brought concerns for civil rights, the goal of eradication of the moral, economic, intellectual, and political bondage associated with African ancestry in the United States, and a statement of unity with African Americans living in Canadian refugee settlements under a single, unifying rubric. While it had a relatively brief life—the first national convention met in 1830 and the last in 1835—the National Convention Movement would shape the African-American political agenda for the next thirty years. The architects of the movement transformed race identity for free African Americans into a political resource upon which two major twentieth-century liberation movements would draw to fuel their agendas. Within the National Convention Movement, African-American concerns about emigration in general, and about the Canadian refugee settlements and opportunities for resettlement in Hayti in particular, anticipated the impulse for cultural unification of people of color that would also drive twentieth-century Pan-Africanism. At the same time, and complementing the focus on citizenship and the improvement of the status of free African Americans, the movement aimed to eradicate structural and legal sources of racial oppression. In this way it foreshadowed the political and economic agendas both of post–Civil War Reconstruction in the Southern states and of the 1960s Civil Rights Movement.

CHAPTER THREE

From Laws and Revolutions, Freedom Lieux

Let the history of the sufferings of our brethren, and of their deliverance, descend . . . to our children, to the remotest generations.

—Absalom Jones, 1808[1]

FOR AFRICAN AMERICANS living in the Northern United States at the onset of the nineteenth century, the gradual abolition of slavery, the Haytian Revolution, and 1807-8 federal legislation that forbad American ships' masters from trading in African slaves all held forth the elusive promise of full and unconditional inclusion in the nation's civic culture and thus seemed to signal the onset of a new national era. In very different ways, these three events challenged the basic cultural assumptions surrounding the legacy of suffering to which Absalom Jones[2]—rector of St. Thomas African Episcopal Church, Philadelphia—had referred in his 1807-8 sermon. All roused resonant hopes for deliverance from the disadvantages associated with African ancestry in New World environments. All seemed to promise an ending to the personal sufferings and collective degradation that shadowed life for Africans and their descendants living in British North America. All evoked widespread anticipation of a radically transformed future; and although the implicit promises embedded in these events proved, in the end, illusory, all were commemorated, memorialized, celebrated, and mythologized as they were drawn through the lens of collective African-American memory.

FREEDOM CLAIMS

In 1807-8, the United States government forbad American ships' captains from importing Africans into the country. That legislation further reinforced widespread expectations for personal freedom and seemed to foreshadow a broader moral, social, and political commitment to a general emancipation. Driven by a complex and shifting equation of practical politics—both domestic and international—and moral pressure, on March 2, 1807 the United States Congress ratified legislation prohibiting the participation of ships sailing under the United States flag in the African slave trade. While Thomas Jefferson wrote passionately about ending "those violations of human rights which have been so long continued on the unoffending inhabitants of Africa," the president remained silent on the continuing violations of human rights within the borders of the new republic.[3] Jefferson probably could not have anticipated the deeper meaning African Americans found in the legislation, a meaning vested not in the moral redemption of the United States but, rather, in the spiritual reunification of a people torn from their ancestral homeland. While the legislation, like the nation's commitment to universal freedom and equality, lacked both moral strength and enforceability, for African Americans the law seemed to anticipate the reconciliation of a lost past and a promised future.

Disillusionment inevitably followed each moment of heightened hopes and expectations. Freedom won through military service or granted in the years following the Revolution had proved conditional and incomplete. The anticipated general emancipation did not follow the 1807-8 legislation. The African slave trade continued, and domestic slavery dominated the social and economic fabric of the nation. In the Southern states slavery prevailed, and throughout the nominally free states of the North, seamstresses, used-clothing dealers, ministers, and washerwomen alike, whether born free or enslaved, comfortably middle-class or impoverished, lived in the margins of the republic. In this milieu Africans and their descendants forged a racial identity born of paradox and anchored in a fundamental reinterpretation of contemporary events. The freedom festivals commemorating the 1807-8 legislation, which most believed—at least for a time—had abolished the African slave trade, trace the contours of an emerging historical consciousness that simultaneously constructed a common ancestry and claimed a common future.

ANCESTRAL INVENTION

On New Year's Day, 1808, the day the law took effect, African Americans gathered to worship together and to celebrate at St. Thomas Church in Philadelphia and The African Church in New York City. Those who had come together that day sat from morning to afternoon, singing, praying, and engaging in "delightful reflection . . . that [the] sinful traffic which has wrested so many of our brethren from their parent country, and doomed them to painful and incessant servitude, has been recently extirpated."[4] They declared their "pious gratitude" for a promised and envisioned moment of deliverance. Most soon realized that the legislation contained no real relief from either domestic slavery or the transatlantic traffic in human cargo. Still, the promise of a universal and unconditional abolition of slavery, that moment when "the sun of liberty shall beam resplendent on the whole African race," was not easily relinquished.[5] At the onset of the nineteenth century, few African Americans living in the Northern states could personally recall an increasingly remote African homeland, for at that time, less than 15 percent of the adult black population living in the North had been born in Africa.[6] As a result, the psychosocial distance between real time and an African homeland had lengthened. Despite the increasing gulf between ancestral memory and real time, when Peter Williams, Jr.[7]— rector at St. Phillips African Church, New York City—joined the deliverance of Africans from the destruction of the slave trade with the emancipation of the descendants of Africans living in the United States under a single rubric, he probably reflected a contemporary longing for the lost homeland that transcended autobiographical memory. His words describe a resonant impulse among African Americans born in New World environments to reunite with their ancestral past:

> Rejoice, Oh! Africans! No longer shall tyranny, war, and injustice, with irresistible sway, desolate your native country: no longer shall torrents of human blood deluge its delightful plains . . . no longer shall its shores resound with the awful howlings of infatuated warriors, the death-like groans of vanquished innocents, nor the clanking fetters of wo-doomed captives. Rejoice, Oh ye descendants of Africans! No longer shall the United States of America, nor the extensive colonies of Great-Britain, admit the degrading commerce of the human species.[8]

African Americans celebrated the 1807-8 legislation from its implementation on January 1, 1808, into the 1820s. The early First of January celebrations and commemorations of the legislation anticipated both a reunification of Africans and their descendants in the New World and a general emancipation of slaves in the United States. As the years passed, and both the slave trade and American slavery continued, commemorative sermons and orations delivered in African churches and the halls of African fraternal and mutual-aid societies reinterpreted and transformed the meaning of that legislative moment. Anticipating an American future in which the promises of a democratic society would be fulfilled, oratory and ritual constructed a culturally significant African-American memory of an invented common past. Commemorations of the 1807-8 legislation abolishing the slave trade became a vehicle for forging a politicized consciousness that reconciled the discontinuities between past and present. Anchored in thoroughly conventional early nineteenth-century Christian theology, images of a lost African homeland joined with more immediate, New World environments of memory and aimed to claim the future by reinventing the past.

Peter Williams, Jr., who would support Captain Paul Cuffe's[9] 1815 Sierra Leone venture and then Haytian emigration in the 1820s, had delivered the New Year's Day, 1808, oration at St. Phillip's African Church in New York City. He spoke as both a descendant of Africans and as an American, describing the lost homeland as an Africa of "simplicity, innocence, and contentment," a land corrupted by the "enterprising spirit of European genius." The result of that corruption had been an unhappiness "beyond measure and without control." Williams detailed that unhappiness by describing the sweeping and destructive impact of the slave trade economy: "Its baneful footsteps are marked with blood; its infectious breath spreads war and desolation; and its train is composed of the complicated miseries of cruel and unceasing bondage."[10]

Turning from the two-hundred-year history of the slave trade to the more immediate, New World past, Williams recalled for the congregation at the African Church that moment "when the spirit of patriotism erected a temple sacred to liberty." Giving the 1807-8 legislation contemporary meaning, Williams assured his audience that at long last the nation created as an "instrument of divine goodness" had acted "in the vindication of our rights, and the improvement of our state." Williams counseled caution, however, warning that "the waves of oppression are ever ready to overwhelm the defenseless." Echoing the sentiments Jupiter Hammon had expressed in the 1780s and the concerns about the judgments of white people that had fueled the cautious public deportment guidelines the Free African Union Society in Newport had written into their Proceedings in the 1790s, Williams advised the congregation to guard their rights as citizens "against fatal encroachments . . . by a steady and upright deportment, and by a strict obedience and respect to the laws of the land" even as they anticipated that moment when "Ethiopia shall stretch forth her hands; when the sun of liberty shall beam resplendent on the whole African race."[11]

In Philadelphia, Absalom Jones also preached a sermon of thanksgiving on January 1, 1808. He began with the exodus from Egypt and, like Williams, turned quickly to the African slave trade, painting with words the horror of the reality. In a lesson on geography and economics Jones traced the ecology of the slave trade from the African west coast to the Caribbean islands and then to ports in the United States. Biblical text faded. Jones chronicled the legal events leading to the abolition of the slave trade first by Great Britain and then by the United States, and then he focused on national and regional domestic matters. African Americans, he said, had many reasons for offering up prayers of thanksgiving, especially "for disposing the hearts of the rulers of many of the states to pass laws for the abolition of [domestic] slavery; for the number and zeal of the friends He has raised up to plead our cause; and for the privileges we enjoy, of worshipping . . . in churches of our own."[12]

Like Peter Williams, Absalom Jones included a morality lesson in his sermon that echoed Jupiter Hammon. He urged those present (and presumably those who would read the text printed in pamphlet form) to "conduct ourselves in such a manner as to furnish no cause of regret to the deliverers of our nation." He explained that personal conduct circumscribed by sobriety, temperance, humility, peaceability, frugality, industriousness, honesty, and personal honor was informed by a common heritage that bound African Americans together and provided a source of symbolic strength. Williams forged the bonds of race within the metaphor of kinship. "An African slave, ready to perish, was our father or our grandfather." Given the perils and anguish those ancestral slaves had survived, Jones reasoned, every African American was fortunate to have come into existence at all, and personal conduct, "regulated by the precepts of the gospel," would reflect that good fortune. Reflecting contemporary efforts to create a separate and independent African-American community infrastructure, Jones urged education of the children, especially in "a knowledge of useful trades . . . and the principles of the gospel of Jesus Christ."

Although the promise of universal and unconditional abolition, that time when "the sun of liberty shall beam resplendent on the whole African race," would be long delayed, in 1807-8 African Americans had reason to remain hopeful.

Calling for annual public recognition of the 1807-8 legislation and for an interpretation of that legislation within a context defined by the unique and tragic circumstances that had brought Africans and their descendants to the New World, Absalom Jones anticipated the revisionist history of the 1960s:

> Let the first of January, the day of the abolition of the slave trade in our country, be set apart in every year, as a day of publick thanksgiving for that mercy. Let the history of the sufferings of our brethren, and of their deliverance, descend by this means to our children, to the remotest generations.[13]

Many who gathered that day in Philadelphia and New York City believed that with the abolition of the African traffic, the ending of African slavery in America surely would be forthcoming. In declaring that the violation of Africa must be indelibly imprinted on the historical record, Jones extended those expectations to reunification with a lost homeland and a lost people. In the annual celebrations that followed the implementation of the 1807-8 legislation, the freedom-festival oratory fused two distinct cultural traditions and located the connection between cultural memory and political agency at the intersection of two competing sources of African-American identity: autobiographical and cultural memories of a lost African homeland, and the shifting struggle to define and claim freedom in United States environments.[14]

Although the piety of the original First of January celebrations continued for a time, after 1810 the oratory that anchored the events shifted noticeably in emphasis from sacred to secular contexts, and from African environments of memory to New World political environments.[15] Inevitably, as New World events displaced African milieux, race discrimination dominated the celebrations. Early on, issues surrounding the problematic nature of citizenship were linked to the First of January freedom celebrations. On the first anniversary of the ineffectual 1807-8 legislation, New Yorker Joseph Sidney addressed this bitter truth directly, and his comments anticipated the protracted and difficult African-American struggle for full and unconditional U.S. citizenship that would continue into the twentieth century. Declaring the New England experiment in gradual emancipation successful, Sidney urged African Americans in the Northern states to turn their attention to "these duties which have devolved on us, in consequence of our having recently obtained our freedom." While reflecting the successful legislative effort that year by the Federalist party in New York state to suppress the African-American vote, Sidney's admonitions also foreshadowed the core issues that would drive civil rights movements throughout the nineteenth and well into the twentieth century. The right of suffrage was primary, Sidney declared, and carried with it "the indispensable duty of bestowing our votes on those, and on those only, whose talents, and whose political, moral, and religious principles, will most effectually promote the best interests of America."[16]

Those who delivered the sermons and commemorative addresses at the annual First of January freedom celebrations after 1810 continued to reformulate and expand the earlier visions of freedom and deliverance to which Absalom Jones and Peter Williams initially had subscribed. As the circumstances of public life changed for African Americans living in the Northern states, the freedoms deriving from civic and political inclusion were equal in importance to freedom from bondage. The Reverend William Miller[17] began his 1810 commemorative sermon at the New York City African Church with a straightforward claim intended to directly challenge white charges of inherent racial inferiority. Miller bluntly asserted the historical superiority of Africans over Europeans: "The inhabitants of Africa are descended from the ancient inhabitants of Egypt . . . the first learned nation was a nation of blacks."[18]

Joseph Sidney, speaking in 1814 at the African Asbury Church in New York City, also challenged the ideology of inherent racial inferiority, refocusing both the politics and the geography of historical events. He made Africans in the United States who were "worthy of the greatest esteem and respect" the centerpiece of his address, weaving an impressive list of contemporary African-American writers, visual and performing artists, and artisans into the tapestry of his oration: the poets—Wheatley, Hamilton, Varick, Latham; the orators—Williams, Sipkins, Teasman, Carmer, Hamilton, Derry; the self-taught printers "composing devices of almost every description"; and the composers of sacred music.[19] The artistic and literary achievements of these "self-taught and venerable" women and men, Sidney declared, could not have been the product of an inferior race.

By 1816 African environments of memory no longer dominated the oratory of the First of January celebrations. More immediate issues focused the attention of the African-American orators. That year, in his remarks before several African Benevolent Societies gathered in Philadelphia to commemorate the 1807-8 legislation, Russell Parrott invoked explicitly New World memories to advance the principal aim of his address: "to defend our degraded race from the foul aspersions which the united efforts of malevolence and interest have cast upon us." Setting aside the vocabulary of the Enlightenment and relocating the milieux of memory that increasingly would ground freedom celebrations and freedom movements in New World environments and expectations, foreshadowing William Cooper Nell's retrojective use of African-American military service, Parrott argued that African-American military valor during the Revolutionary War provided "in abundance all the rich materials for the formation of the good, useful citizen." During that time, "when the country engaged in the perils of war, with disasters accumulating on her head, the negro shrunk not from what he felt to be the performance of his duty . . . [and] in the glorious and eventful struggle on the waters of Champlain and of Erie . . . there too did he assist" in achieving both military victory and national autonomy.[20] The following year Parrott similarly would cite military service in the War of 1812 to buttress his protest against white initiatives for African colonization.[21] Foreshadowing African-American claims to citizenship that would be advanced in unequivocal language by the 1850s, this crucial relocation of African-American environments of memory increasingly located freedom celebrations and freedom movements in an American-centered popular historical consciousness. Still, for a time, the 1807-8 legislation had served as a powerful site of cultural memory, a moment lifted from the movement of history and recrafted from event to moral and spiritual vehicle for the reconstruction of a lost past. In its recrafting, the legislation had extended a particularly powerful promise to a colonized people, welding images of a lost ancestral legacy and a New World redemption of that loss into a shared framework of meaning that gave form to both consciousness and identity.

FREEDOM IN THE NEW WORLD

In the years following the Revolution, freedom—whether won through military service or granted through other means—had proved conditional and incomplete. Yet, in a milieu circumscribed by racism, the promise of full and unconditional inclusion in national civic life shaped a shared framework of meaning that gave form to collective consciousness and identity grounded in New World experiences. At the same time, the Haytian Revolution and the proclamation of a black republic in the New World in 1804—a process that began as a slave revolt in 1791 and continued over thirteen years of bloody warfare against the Haytian planter class and French, British, and Spanish military forces—extended African-American consciousness beyond the borders of the United States. Black and white Americans were keenly aware of events in Hayti, and official policy toward the nation—as well as more privately held attitudes about the nation's leaders, particularly Toussaint—hinged on a combination of trade arrangements and dependencies between the United States and Hayti and on U.S. policy toward France after 1780.[22] Whether Toussaint[23] was a model of racial moderation, "an important symbol of stability and reason in an otherwise chaotic world ruled by passion and violence," as many whites believed, or an African Spartacus, leading a people in their struggle against oppression, as many African Americans believed, he represented without question the triumph and superiority of New World forces over European and colonial dominance to both blacks and whites in antebellum America.[24]

African Americans probably learned firsthand about the Haytian Revolution through the refugee *affranchis,* or *gens du couleur* who fled Hayti with the surviving Creoles during the final, cataclysmic stages of the revolution in 1803-4. After Toussaint's capture in 1802 and his deportation to France, Jean Jacques Dessalines and Henri Christophe led the final fight against the French forces.[25] Dessalines, in particular, lacked Toussaint's moderation and shrewd sense of diplomacy, and with the defeat of Donatien Rochambeau and the withdrawal of French troops from the island, Dessalines launched a massacre designed to drive out or annihilate all whites and their freed black supporters.

The freed men and women who fled Hayti and settled in U.S. urban centers, primarily New Orleans and Philadelphia, during the first decade of the nineteenth century, had much in common with free African Americans whose communities they joined. Although many had been relatively wealthy, in Hayti they also had been subject to a wide range of restrictive legislation based on race rather than on economic or legal status. As a group, the Haytians were politically sophisticated, relatively well-educated, and probably predisposed to embrace racial ties that transcended political boundaries. Many prospered and most merged easily into local African-American communities.[26]

Apart from the revolutionary dispossession the Haytian refugees represented, Hayti offered material New World evidence that directly challenged the ideology of Anglo-European world supremacy.[27] Foreshadowing the anticolonialism, cultural unification, and self-determination of twentieth-century Pan-Africanism, the Haytian Revolution and the republic created and ruled by peoples of African descent offered a resonant *lieu de memoire* for African Americans during the antebellum period. While the African-American mandate for racial unity hinged on the mythic common ancestry forged from African environments of memory, the Haytian *lieu* inspired African-American visions of a civic culture and a democratic future.

Some African Americans embraced Hayti while Toussaint still struggled to unify St. Domingue and throw off the French colonial regime. In 1800, in Henrico County, Virginia, Solomon, Martin, Gabriel, and Nancy, property of tavern-keeper Thomas Prosser, dreamed of freedom and mobilized slaves to seize their liberty by force. Inspired by Toussaint, crafting their revolutionary demands for secular freedom from scriptural precedent, calling up African lore and magic to assure their victory, they marched on Richmond beneath a banner proclaiming "Death or Liberty," the motto of the quintessential black freedom movement in the New World, the Haytian Revolution. Then, thwarted by a torrential rainstorm, they failed and died, as other slaves would in the coming decades.[28] Rumors circulated of a similar revolt in the area around Charleston, South Carolina, also inspired by the St. Domingue insurrection.[29] White voices, pro-slavery and anti-slavery alike, pointed to the bloody carnage of Toussaint's revolution as evidence of the barbarity surrounding chattel slavery, the former arguing for the necessity of the institution to civilize and control Africans, the latter pointing to the evil embedded in a system "God and the slaves themselves would destroy."[30]

For some African Americans, Toussaint's revolution held more direct and personal meaning. Even as the Haytian Revolution proceeded, Prince Hall, like Gabriel and his comrades in rural Virginia, found in Toussaint's Hayti the hope for an abrupt ending of slavery in the United States. In a charge to his Masonic brethren in Cambridge, Massachusetts in 1797, Hall asked those who sat before him in discouragement at the persistence of slavery in the United States to

> remember what a dark day it was with our African brethren, six years ago, in the French West Indies. Nothing but the snap of the whip was heard, from morning to evening. Hanging, breaking on the wheel, burning, and all manner of tortures, were inflicted on those unhappy people.

Toussaint, with divine guidance, had transformed St. Domingue from an island of hopeless slaves to a nation created and ruled by black people whom African Americans should and must "receive as their friends and treat as their brothers." Anticipating antebellum freedom movements led by African Americans in the Northern states and foreshadowing twentieth-century Pan-Africanism, Hall predicted: "Thus doth Ethiopia stretch forth her hand from slavery, to freedom and equality."[31]

Haytian images served both moderate and radical African American political agendas throughout the antebellum period. On the occasion of his graduation from Bowdoin College in 1826, John Russwurm chose *The Conditions and Prospects of Hayti* as the topic of his valedictory address and three years later, in 1829, David Walker punctuated his *Appeal, in Four Articles,* a militant call for revolt against Southern slavery, with the term *citizen* and invoked the history of Hayti as a model for the United States revolution he hoped to inspire. The African-American migration to Hayti already had begun when Samuel Cornish and John Russwurm[32] explained the purpose of the new newspaper in their first editorial in *Freedom's Journal:* "We wish to plead our own cause," they wrote. "Too long have others spoken for us." *Freedom's Journal* aimed to provide a channel for public discourse for five hundred thousand free African Americans in the United States, to enlighten, to educate, and to inform them on issues of common interest and mutual concern. Hayti, "where despotism has given place to free governments, and where many of our brethren now fill important civil and military stations," could serve as a new model of the possibilities for African Americans in the United States.[33]

In 1834, with the migration to Hayti in its second decade, Haytians attending the National Convention for the Improvement of the Free People of Colour signaled the strength of ongoing ties between peoples of African descent in the United States and Hayti. Hayti's universal appeal, bridging the chasm between advocates of violent resistance and advocates of constitutional procedure to end slavery in the United States, persisted into the 1850s. Henry Highland Garnet linked Toussaint to his call for a slave revolt, and at the 1858 Boston festival John S. Rock, the first African American admitted to practice law before the United States Supreme Court, addressed the charge of African-American cowardice commonly issued by white apologists of slavery by observing that the Haytian revolution stood as ample evidence that "the black man is not a coward . . . [and] will be a lasting refutation of the malicious aspersions of our enemies."[34]

The oratory that celebrated, commemorated, and interpreted the 1807-8 federal legislation prohibiting U.S. ships from participating in the slave

trade foreshadowed a much broader African-American intellectual journey from individually lived and autobiographically remembered pasts to
a collectively crafted historical memory. During the course of a journey
that spanned the eight decades between the American Revolution and
the Civil War, African Americans fused two disparate elements of
identity: an increasingly remote African ancestry and cultural heritage,
and a popular historical consciousness shaped directly by a corpus of New
World experiences. To be sure, that consciousness traced and chronicled
enslavement and despair. At the same time, it embodied intersecting
moments of resistance to and triumph over racial oppression, and it
consistently anticipated promised but elusive deliverance from the
sufferings of loss and degradation. The Haytian Revolution was the first
of those moments, a catalyst for a race consciousness and a racial identity
formed in New World environments of memory.

CHAPTER FOUR

Africa Envisioned, Africa Found

Tell my brethren to come: not to fear. The land is good.
It only wants men to possess it.

—Daniel Coker, 1821[1]
From Goree, on the African West Coast

IN NINETEENTH-CENTURY NEW ENGLAND, African-American men often
made a living working in the maritime trades. The work was physically
grueling, and it was dangerous. For those willing and able to endure the
physical demands, however, the sea might provide a decent living for an
entire family. For Captain Paul Cuffe, as for his friend James Forten, the
sea offered great wealth. For Paul Cuffe, the sea also offered an avenue
for political action. Cuffe envisioned a settlement of African Americans
on the African west coast, a plan described by the New Bedford *Mercury*
as fundamentally "an offspring of Christian benevolence." To be sure,
Cuffe's personal motives were philanthropic. He intended that the colony
would "ultimately prove beneficial to his brethren of the African race
within their native climate" and, at the same time, provide opportunities
for free people of color in the United States to engage in commerce and
missionary work along the African west coast.[2]

A prosperous maritime merchant and a devout Quaker, Cuffe had
conducted business within an international mercantile community for
more than twenty-five years when he initiated the Sierra Leone venture.
As a result, his vision blended philanthropy, politics, and mercantile
capitalism. He enjoyed warm and intimate friendship with the English
evangelicals—William Wilberforce, Thomas Clarkson, William Allen,
and others who had guided the British abolitionist movement and
supported African colonization that aimed to force an end to the African
slave trade. Cuffe ardently shared their goal and their vision and, like

the English evangelical philanthropists who had been instrumental in establishing the Sierra Leone colony twenty-five years earlier, he believed that slaving would be driven from the international trade economy only when it had been replaced by a more profitable trade medium. As a result, he viewed his emigration venture, at least in part, as a contribution to that new world economy. Yet Cuffe's vision was more expansive than the English one and was explicitly grounded in African-American New World experiences. He believed the emigrants from the United States would take with them to the African west coast a moral commitment and a religious obligation that derived as much from the bond of race as from the Christian missionary imperative. Cuffe intended that agricultural products would displace human cargo in the transatlantic trade and that Christianity would bring spiritual salvation, temperance, and industry to the American emigrants' African brethren. Cuffe originally had attempted to interest the United States government in the venture, hoping that federal support could ease the financial burden he and the emigrants must bear. Pleading the exigencies of war, the federal government demurred, and in the end Captain Cuffe financed the venture himself.

Cuffe had promoted this vision as he recruited emigrants for the voyage among African Americans in Baltimore, Philadelphia, New York, and Boston. His description of life's possibilities in Sierra Leone must have struck a harmonious chord among some. On August 13, 1815, Stephen Womsbey of Providence, Rhode Island wrote to Captain Cuffe: "I am a black man," Womsbey explained, "and want to know . . . when the [*Traveller*] is to sail" for Sierra Leone. Womsbey asked Cuffe to "write me back as quick as possible and let me know so that I many get reddy." Twelve men in Charlestown, Massachusetts, also wrote, offering character references and making application for the voyage. Reporting themselves ready to sail, they assured Cuffe that they and their families would "make wholesome colonists." From Little Compton, Rhode Island, a coastal village a few miles from Cuffe's home, another man wrote, explaining that he was trying to arrange his affairs in order to be ready for the sailing. Prince Saunders, who later would direct his energies to a Haytian emigration project, recommended several Boston families to Cuffe for the Sierra Leone venture. Two Philadelphians, Anthony Severance and Samuel Watson, volunteered for the voyage, as did Perry Locke. Cuffe, his crew, and thirty-one passengers sailed for Sierra Leone in December 1815 with a full cargo of provisions, farm implements, American values, and African-American dreams.[3]

Those aboard *Traveller* shared an American experience of racial oppression, and the bonds of race that tied them to Africa were uniquely American in origin. For most, particularly those who had personal memories of the American Revolution, that bond derived from a continuing struggle to claim the promises of democracy for which they and their generation had fought. Perhaps for others, certainly for passenger Anthony Severance—one of the free people of color who had sought asylum in the United States following Toussaint's remarkable overthrow of French rule in Saint Domingue—claims to an African ancestry, either direct or symbolic, had been born in the dispossession rather than the promise of revolution. Political oppression had driven Severance and other free men and women, generally privileged mulattos, from Hayti. Those refugees had brought to African-American communities in the United States an expanded vision of racial bonds, as connections that transcended political boundaries.[4] As a result, the promises of democracy that Paul Cuffe and his generation embraced had been born of fresh and personal memories rooted in two New World revolutions.

AFRICA FOUND

The Sierra Leone to which Paul Cuffe and his passengers sailed in 1815 was a relatively young colony, clinging precariously to the African west coast less than ten degrees north of the equator, set squarely in the center of the slave trade. Less than a generation had passed since the formation of the Sierra Leone Company, and those aboard *Traveller* found Freetown to be a remarkably cosmopolitan city of five thousand inhabitants, a cultural mélange of Europeans, Nova Scotians, Jamaicans, and members of various African tribes. Resettlement of the region had begun during the late eighteenth century at the instigation of English philanthropists and merchants. Men like Granville Sharpe, who enjoyed personal as well as public images as "men of benevolent character," had been moved most immediately by the miserable circumstances of the African slave-Loyalists who had removed to London after the American Revolution and there fallen into "the most distressed situation." In 1787, believing that the long-range economic benefits of African resettlement would outweigh the direct costs of transportation and relocation, the philanthropist-colonizers sought and obtained support from the British government for a program of African resettlement on the western coast.[5]

English merchants had enjoyed a century of prosperous commerce on the African west coast when they issued their appeal for assistance; and they anticipated the dire economic consequences that would follow from the abolition of the slave trade if adjustment in the current trade economy were not initiated. Most feared that banning the slave trade would not end it but would, rather, drive the African traders into partnership with the French and Portuguese and serve only to bankrupt British commercial interests on the African continent. At the same time, most also regarded the region as potentially "equal in salubrity and superior in production [of rice and cotton] to any of the West India islands."[6] Proposals to resettle emancipated Africans in the area around the Sierra Leone River promised an opportunity to capitalize on established elements of a trade economy that never had been based exclusively on slaves and thereby salvage English financial interests in Africa.

Accordingly, from the outset the program envisioned, initiated, and administered by the Sierra Leone Company was intended to be a profitable venture, serving as an economic and moral fortress against the ongoing slave trade. Declaring that they would "not deal in slaves themselves, nor allow of any slave trade on their ground," the directors of the Sierra Leone Company intended to develop the colony into a slave-free trading center with interests extending down the western coast and penetrating inland along the rivers.[7]

Still, a transition from a trade economy centered on slaves to one driven by cotton and rice and supplemented by livestock, camwood, ivory, and cloth required a labor force willing to produce and supply those goods. The company directors understood that established African merchants would not be likely to willingly shift away from an established, lucrative, and proven trade economy—which included slaves—to a more speculative one, and they also believed that Europeans were unable to labor in the African sun. The Africans they recruited, first among the London Loyalists and then from the Loyalist slaves who had been removed to Nova Scotia during the American Revolution, were to provide the work force they needed to realize their vision.[8] Paul Cuffe fully understood and embraced this agenda when he formulated his own Sierra Leone colonization plan. Cuffe, with close personal and business ties to English evangelicals and abolitionists, including Sharpe, had followed the development of the Sierra Leone Company from a much closer vantage point than had most Americans.

Whatever personal expectations for autonomy and equality those initial emigrants to Sierra Leone had held at the moment of their passage from London and then Nova Scotia to the African west coast were thwarted by two sets of circumstances that were well beyond their control: First, stringent economic restrictions on the colony had been imposed by the company directors. Second, overt—if anticipated—hostility from Africans severely hampered the well-being of the settlers almost from the beginning. Perceived by the English (and later, the American) whites as the colonized, but regarded by the Africans as the colonizers, the emigrants held an intermediate and contradictory position in the social structure of the Sierra Leone colony, as would African Americans in subsequent decades in Liberia. As a result, community-building on the African west coast proved a consistently difficult task for returning Africans and their descendants through the late eighteenth and early nineteenth centuries. The first wave of settlers, four hundred sixty men, women, and children "in the most distressed situation," sailed from London for Sierra Leone in May 1787. The Company Directors added to the group sixty additional whites, "chiefly women of the lowest sort, in ill health and of bad character." Eighty-four of the colonists died during the passage and one hundred or more died during their first months in Sierra Leone, victims of the "African Fever" that plagued all new arrivals to the African continent, black and white alike. The colonists quickly discovered that the Africans were as hostile as the tropical climate. Although the directors believed they had negotiated treaties and arranged land transactions in advance of the colonists' arrival, the fragile settlement was attacked soon after the group had landed by Africans already living in the area. This, even though many among the settlers, according to King Naimbanna, were well aware of "the horrid depredations committed by all countries that come to trade" and had kinspeople "now in the West Indies, carried away" by Danish, Portuguese, and English slavers. Naimbanna himself remained relatively loyal to the Europeans despite the hostility of his tribespeople, a loyalty probably bought by both the French and English through the education they had provided Naimbanna's sons and other less obvious benefits accorded the king directly.[9]

As the Londoners sailed for Sierra Leone, some African Americans also were looking to Africa for a homeland where they might emigrate and settle. In Boston Prince Hall and seventy-five other petitioners, perhaps inspired by the English program, appealed to the Massachusetts General Court for assistance in emigrating to Africa, and in Newport the African Union Society initiated a search for African lands where some seventy among their membership could settle free of white European economic and political control.[10] Although neither of these efforts resulted in an organized emigration, African Americans clearly were aware of the British initiative and embraced images of a remembered African homeland waiting to be reclaimed, despite differences in tribal origins and, for many, a separation of generations from that homeland.

Still, the English resettlement program proceeded for a time without African-American participation. In 1792, three years after the London Africans had established a precarious foothold in Sierra Leone, the company directors recruited 1,131 Nova Scotian Africans, also British Loyalists, who had removed to the colony from the United States at the end of the Revolution. When presented with the company offer to emigrate, although few among them were African-born, the Nova Scotians were eagerly receptive. They had known little except poverty and discouragement during their time in Nova Scotia. One applicant for the Sierra Leone venture, describing the circumstances of his friends and neighbors as well as his own, recalled for Thomas Clarkson his original hopes to receive an allotment of land and three years' provisions from the British government as his reward for his loyalty to the Crown during the American Revolution. "On the contrary," he explained to Clarkson, "instead of receiving our promised and proper allotments upon our arrival in the province, the greatest part of us have received small allotments of soil so run over with rocks and swamps that vegetation, without utmost care, is barely sufficient to keep us in existence."[11] Most had regarded their residence in Nova Scotia as a "second servitude." Promised individual land grants in Sierra Leone of twenty acres per household, with additional allotments of ten acres for a wife and five acres for each child in the family, most of the Nova Scotians perceived emigration as a much longed-for end to servitude.

The company directors, seeking laborers for their economic venture, required only "satisfactory testimonials of [the emigrants'] character." They were initially pleased with the group they had recruited and believed that "this rising generation of well-educated blacks [would lead] the gradual improvement of the colony."[12] Like other displaced descendants of Africa who would follow them to the African west coast throughout the nineteenth century, the Nova Scotians suffered terribly during their period of adjustment to the climate. Only 80 percent of those who began the emigration survived the voyage and their first year in Sierra Leone. (Sixty-five emigrants died during the transatlantic passage and ninety-eight died during the first rainy season.) Yet for some, the difficulties of passage and of beginning a new life in the swampy tropical wilderness must have been offset by the anticipation of their return. For at least one Nova Scotian, that anticipation translated into dramatic reality. The man, who had been kidnapped fifteen years earlier from a beach site in Sierra Leone, recognized the place of his landing as the site of his capture. He and a number of the other emigrants were

> standing together, not long after their arrival, when a body of natives, led by curiosity, came down to see the settlement. An elderly woman of the party was observed by some of the settlers to have her attention arrested and very peculiar emotions excited whenever she could observe the face of this Nova Scotian . . . at length, fully recognizing his countenance, she ran up to him and embraced him; she proved to be his mother.[13]

The initial exhilaration many among the Nova Scotians must have felt when they witnessed that reunion between mother and son quickly dissipated during their first year of settlement. Almost immediately upon landing the emigrants began to confront a series of broken promises and disappointments that consistently characterized white hegemony in economic and political transactions with peoples of African descent. Promised land allotments were not forthcoming. The directors had laid out the town of Freetown in advance of the emigrants' arrival, intending to settle the company's imported labor force on four-acre town lots rather than the larger tracts that had been promised. The directors believed this adjustment necessary because "the labour of cutting paths, and measuring so large a tract, would have been too great for one season."[14] In short, the directors accurately judged that the Nova Scotians could not simultaneously lay out and begin cultivation on their own farms and provide the labor necessary to the company's projects. Clearly, the Nova Scotians were intended to be laborers for the company first, independent farmers second. Discontent mounted throughout that first year of settlement, exacerbated by the limited supply of provisions and a critical lack of public services. Wages remained miserably low and the settlers were heavily taxed on wilderness land as soon as it became productive.

Led to expect far more than they received, the Nova Scotians voiced objection through a self-created, ad hoc governance system. When the company's local representative announced a land tax, the Nova Scotians "assembled to consider whether it were best to accept . . . and pay the impost." Conflict between the settlers and the company escalated when company soldiers disrupted their meeting. The Nova Scotians took up an armed defense and then "combined, by leaving their work, to raise the price of labour" in the colony. Unable to settle the labor dispute in negotiations with local managers, the Nova

Scotians sent a delegation to London "to lay their complaints before the Court of Directors." In a strongly worded petition they complained of "the high price of the Company's goods; the low wages for labour; the nonfulfillment of promises stated to have been made them by Clarkson, and many trifling instances of supposed misconduct in the succeeding governor." The directors received and judged their complaints as "founded on mistake and misinformation" and urged the Nova Scotians, should complaints arise in the future, to speak directly with the company's Sierra Leone governor.[15]

Despite the power struggle between the settlers and the company, economic development and the details of building Freetown and the colony proceeded. First houses, single rooms no more than 12 feet by 18 feet, "merely temporary, wattled, plastered with clay, and thatched with long grass," were replaced by two-room structures of larger dimensions, raised up off the ground, with wooden floors and siding and shingled roofs. Crops of rice, yams, eddoes, cabbages, Indian corn, and cotton all grew well, and the worst crimes reported among the emigrants were petty theft and adultery. On the whole, the Nova Scotians were regarded as a temperate and pious group. Nevertheless, they persisted in challenging the authority of the English officers sent by the London-based Sierra Leone Company to manage their affairs.

Although the Nova Scotians sat on all juries in the colony, a company officer routinely acted as judge in both civil and criminal cases; and while the Nova Scotians formed and maintained their own militia company, British law prevailed. The colonists consistently and chronically complained that the company gained "unreasonable profits at their expense"; and they were said to have been publicly rude to company officers, exhibiting what their English overseers described as "symptoms of ambition."[16] The pious and temperate Nova Scotians aspired to self-government.

The "unreasonable profits" to which the Nova Scotians objected derived from an "agricultural incentive" program the company had developed. From the outset, the directors had intended the colony to be a fully operational trade center when the slave trade was finally ended. Economic success depended on establishing an economic foundation for a new trade economy that would be in place as the slave trade waned. Believing when that moment arrived, Africans "habituated to European articles shall find that nothing will be taken in return but the product of their land and labour," the company directors had sent a group of "managers," or planters, out from London to the

Freetown settlement specifically charged with organizing a cotton-based plantation system. The Nova Scotians were at first encouraged through the dispensation of "premiums" to cultivate rice, yams, plantains, eddoes, cabbage, and Indian corn as secondary crops on their own lands. Clearly, they had judged the "premiums" the company offered inadequate and unfairly low.[17]

Unrest between the Nova Scotians and the English officers in Sierra Leone continued for five years, and during the final years of the eighteenth century the company imported some five hundred Jamaican maroons to serve as a military force to subdue the rebellious Nova Scotians.[18] Brought to Sierra Leone following a bloody revolt on the island, the Jamaicans generally were regarded as ruthless and fearless. Immediately upon landing, they were armed and charged with specific military objectives, which they "obeyed with alacrity." The group contrasted sharply with the pious, Christianized Nova Scotians. They were hard-drinking warrior-outlaws, "ignorant and careless of agriculture," who clung fiercely to their maroon identity. It was reported that many practiced polygany with "simplicity and gusto." The Nova Scotians, who had entered into the Sierra Leone venture with trust in the English and high hopes for their own futures, were said to be "completely disheartened" by the situation. Many deserted their farms and some eventually quit the colony in the face of the violence that followed the Jamaicans' arrival in Sierra Leone.[19] Paul Cuffe had not been ignorant of these events when he sailed for Sierra Leone in 1815. He had made his first trip to Freetown in 1794 and his second in 1810.

Yet the socially fractured colony of several thousand, with Europeans, Nova Scotians, Jamaicans, and African tribes competing for political and cultural hegemony, also had grown at a remarkable rate in the time between Cuffe's first trading visit there and the 1815 voyage of *Traveller*. The colonial population, beginning with less than five hundred people in 1787, had increased to some two thousand during the first decade of the nineteenth century and had risen to five thousand by 1811. Cuffe the businessman would not have ignored such a demonstrated growth record, and Cuffe the philanthropist, intent on realizing a vision, might have seen in that mélange the beginnings of a Pan-African world.[20]

"MY SOUL CLEAVES TO AFRICA"

Paul Cuffe's efforts failed to stimulate a widespread interest in African emigration among African Americans in the United States. The reasons were several: The cost of passage and resettlement was prohibitive for most. In 1821, for example, Lott Cary[21] paid $1800, his entire life savings, for his family's passage aboard the American Colonization Society ship *Nautilus* from Norfolk, Virginia to the society's settlement at Cape Mesurado. Few free African Americans could have produced such a large sum of money to finance their relocation. Cuffe's failed attempt to win government support for his venture probably doomed it from the outset. Additionally, the population from which Cuffe had recruited was relatively small and many remained hopeful that conditions in the United States would improve. Finally, despite a widely promoted idealized vision of Africa, African Americans understood the hazards and risks they would face in a world where the economy remained vested in slaving. Still, these factors, while limiting, were not insurmountable, for many had received Cuffe's ideas enthusiastically, and prominent African-American community leaders throughout the urban North had actively supported Cuffe and the venture. Had circumstances been otherwise, Paul Cuffe's 1815 colonization plan might have marked the onset of a relatively large African-American emigration fueled by the same longing for cultural reunification with a lost homeland that had informed community-building efforts in the United States.

Many who might have been drawn to the African emigration movement as a result of Cuffe's efforts were repelled by the ideology of the American Colonization Society. American evangelicals, with roots in the eighteenth-century revivalist fervor that swept through New England, were deeply concerned with all varieties of social ills and the circumstances of the disadvantaged; they first advocated the resettlement in western Africa of emancipated blacks who would be trained as missionaries to carry the Christian message to the uncivilized continent during the final years of the eighteenth century. William Thornton had promoted this plan to the members of the Free African Union Society in Newport during the 1790s. White Newporter Samuel Hopkins had attempted to craft an alliance with Granville Sharpe and the directors of the Sierra Leone Company at about the same time that Paul Cuffe began organizing his Sierra Leone venture. Sharpe had encouraged Hopkins, as he had Cuffe, indicating that African Americans would be welcomed into the colony. Neither Hopkins nor Cuffe had been able to interest the U.S. government in supporting American colonization on the African west coast, but as the number of free blacks in the Northern states increased, so too did popular and quasi-official interest in the African colonization scheme. In 1816 the Reverend Robert Finley of New Jersey, "an Evangelical of energy and resource," took up the cause of African colonization and organized fund-raising among white missionary and Bible societies to support the transportation of free African Americans to west Africa. In November 1816, Finley and his associates launched the American Colonization Society (ACS).[22]

African Americans uniformly met the American Colonization Society agenda with outraged protests: From Richmond, African Americans sent a memorial to Congress requesting a land grant in one of the territories along the Missouri River where they might settle and live apart from white Americans, in peace and safety.[23] From Philadelphia, African Americans issued a declaration that "our ancestors (not of choice) were the first successful cultivators of the wilds of America [and] we, their descendants, feel . . . entitled to participate in the blessings of her luxuriant soil." From Baltimore, African Americans issued a simple declaration: "when we desire to remove, we will apprise the public." From New York and Boston, similar sentiments echoed the resounding rejection of the ACS deportation plan. Men who had supported Paul Cuffe's plan—James Forten and Peter Williams, Jr.—and men who would support Haytian emigration—Richard Allen, Russell Parrott, Samuel Cornish—led a solid opposition to the American Colonization Society proposal for the resettlement of all free African Americans in an independent colony on the African west coast.[24] All understood the implicit deportation sentiments embedded in the quasi-governmental plan. Yet, despite mass protests in major cities throughout the Northern states, the ACS recruitment efforts met with a degree of success; Cuffe's efforts had provided a concrete legacy for those who emigrated to western Africa in the years after 1820.

The Friendly Society, established at Cuffe's suggestion, stood as an American cultural outpost in Freetown, receiving and welcoming the African Americans who came seeking new options for their lives in west Africa after 1820. Yet the Friendly Society and other efforts to foster cultural reunification and mediate the destructive impact of the slave trade had only limited influence in the area. Just beyond Freetown, in the areas of Cape Mesurado, Grand Bossa, and the River Shebar, locations destined to come under the control of American Colonization Society settlements, ship's captain Samuel Swan reported lively and profitable trading in ivory and camwood, although others reported that local tribes in the region "were so engaged in war and slave dealing that the ground was left uncultivated."[25] Despite intense resistance among African Americans in the United States and equally fierce opposition to the program among African tribes in the area, during 1818-9 the American Colonization Society recruited eighty-nine people, thirty free African-American families, and three whites—Reverend Samuel Bacon, an Episcopal rector and representative of the U.S. government, and two ACS agents, Dr. Samuel A. Crozer, a physician, and John P. Bankson— to sail from Baltimore on its first ship, *Elizabeth,* in 1820.

Departure from New York City was scheduled for January 31, 1820, although the ship became ice-locked and was not able to sail until February 6. Despite the delay, the sailing took place amid the pomp and fanfare that would be expected of a great and monumental beginning. African Americans "assembled at the African Church to the number of several thousand, to witness the solemnities expected on the occasion, and to join a procession to the vessels." Foreshadowing the racial divisions of authority that would follow African Americans to the ACS settlements on the African west coast, white ACS agents feared the black crowd and intervened in the public and collective joy of the gathering. "Foreseeing that some disaster might be the consequence of such a multitude assembling at the water," Reverend Bacon "mounted on a piazza" and distracted those who had gathered to bid their friends farewell. As he delivered a spontaneous address, the emigrants "were conveyed to the ship" in relative secrecy by other ACS agents. With this beginning, *Elizabeth* sailed from her anchorage on the North River, through New York Harbor, and out into the Atlantic Ocean. Daniel Coker[26] and Elijah Johnson[27] were among the passengers aboard *Elizabeth.* Both would later play crucial roles in the stabilization and early development of the colony at Cape Mesurado, later Monrovia, Liberia. Even during the voyage, Coker recorded an eruption of simmering tensions between the ship's crew and the emigrants, predicting that the "mutinous spirit" of those initial disruptions "would be likely to break out, and give trouble, as soon as a favourable opportunity should offer." The opportunity came when the ship's captain threatened to shoot emigrant Peter Small's dog. The animal had got into a fight with the ship's dog, and "the captain called for his pistols." Coker intervened, the dogs were separated, "the colored people were all got below," and outright violence was averted, but the tension and unrest persisted. On the twenty-fifth day at sea, the "mutinous spirit" once again exploded when the white ACS agents were offended "by reason of some improper expressions made use of by some emigrants." Coker convened all the men in the party and urged them to sign a statement of "full confidence in the judgment and sincere friendship of the agents." All but two of the men complied with Coker's request.[28]

On March 3 *Elizabeth* passengers sighted the Cape Verde Islands. Coker recorded the moment in his journal: "May these children ever cherish a grateful remembrance of this [moment] . . . and tell it to their children and their children to their children." *Elizabeth* made initial African anchorage at Freetown on March 9, 1820. At the moment of his symbolic homecoming Coker experienced profound emotions. "Streams of tears ran down my cheeks" he wrote in his journal, and then wrote in a letter to his friend Jeremiah Watts in Baltimore that, "my soul cleaves to Africa in such a manner as to reconcile me to the idea of being separated from my dear friends and the comforts of a Christian land."[29] Following courtesy calls to the ship by local tribespeople and British officials, during that first evening, "at the time of prayer," the *Elizabeth's* passengers began to meet other African Americans who had preceded them to Freetown. Among them was Perry Locke, who had come out to Africa with Cuffe. "He was so happy at seeing us he could not contain himself," Coker recorded in his diary. Despite the enormous distance separating them, Locke had not lost touch with his family in the United States. Coker delivered "a letter to him from his brother in Baltimore," correspondence written "in answer to one brought to America by Mr. Burgess," a (white) representative of the American Colonization Society.[30]

Visiting between the *Elizabeth's* passengers and the African Americans already settled in Sierra Leone continued throughout the ship's anchorage in Freetown and then again at the Liverpool trading post on the Mano River. In the course of those encounters the *Elizabeth's* passengers gained a deeper understanding of the world in which they would settle. Religious ritual and spiritual life bridged the wide distance between the United States and the African west coast. African Americans already established in the colony joined the emigrants on board the *Elizabeth* for Sunday worship and Coker, an ordained clergyman, "was invited to dine with the Interceding preacher" in Freetown. Conversation must have turned to secular matters and the details of daily life when an elderly man from Nova Scotia described to Coker and his companions recent attacks on the colony by both the French and the African natives.[31] Through such moments as this, the newly arrived emigrants gained a heightened awareness of the hostilities and dangers they would likely encounter in the coming months.

While *Elizabeth* lay at anchor in Freetown, ACS agents and the party of settlers met a member of Cuffe's Friendly Society named John Kizell, a west African native who had been kidnapped as a child and sold into American slavery. He had joined the British during the Revolution, was evacuated to Nova Scotia, and returned to Sierra Leone in 1792. Kizell knew the local languages and cultures and had served as a negotiator between the British governor of Sierra Leone and African tribespeople. He had recommended Sherbro Island to Cuffe as a settlement site and had bought land there himself. He recommended the location to the ACS agents and traveled to the Sherbro Sound area to facilitate their negotiations for land where they might establish a colony. A decided Pan-Africanist, Kizell believed the tribal lands for which he negotiated "belong to Africans abroad, as well as those now in this country; and if they are disposed to return, land they must and shall have. They have not forfeited a right to the inheritance of their fathers, by being carried by force from their country."[32]

When the negotiations had been completed, *Elizabeth* left Freetown and continued on down the coast toward Sherbro Sound, pausing at the Liverpool trading post on the Mano River to obtain fresh supplies. The stop at Liverpool probably relieved many of the anxieties the emigrants were feeling regarding their decision to go out to Africa. There Coker and his companions met another member of the 1815 Cuffe party, the trading post superintendent, who lived surrounded by his children and grandchildren in their family's compound, which must have seemed idyllic to those among the emigrants who had endured enslavement in the United States. The man was delighted with the arrival of *Elizabeth*, confiding to Coker he had been "anxious to see [my] brethren in American return to this country." Another member of the Cuffe party who was living at Liverpool, formerly a ship's carpenter from Boston, echoed the trading post superintendent's enthusiasm for life on the African west coast. He assured Coker and the others "it was best for the people of colour, who are now in America, to come to this country." Both men advised Coker that skilled artisans and mechanics would find ready work in the African settlements.[33]

While *Elizabeth* still lay at anchor in Freetown harbor, a number among the passengers and the (white) ACS agents began to present symptoms of the "African Fever," but *Elizabeth* weighed anchor for the short sail to Sherbro Sound despite the onset of the sickness. Within the first two months after the ship's arrival at Sherbro sound, however, the fever took a terrible toll and as the colonization society physician/ agent lay dying, he charged thirty-five-year-old Daniel Coker, the son of an English indentured servant and an African slave, a "colored preacher of the Methodist Episcopal denomination [with] the whole burden and responsibility of providing for the welfare of the colony."[34] Coker faced a formidable task, and for twelve months he and another of the *Elizabeth* passengers, Elijah Johnson, struggled against what at times must have seemed insurmountable difficulties to keep the small group of emigrants together. When many grew discouraged and wanted to return to the United States, Elijah Johnson rallied failing spirits when he declared, "two years long I have wanted a home. Here I have found one. Here I remain." Still, the "spirit of insubordination" that had surfaced during the *Elizabeth's* voyage persisted. The settlers "knew no authority, and would not be controlled, stealing, and pilfering wherever an opportunity offered, and threatening the active agent, if he attempted to restrain them."[35] Johnson was a few years younger than Coker, a veteran of the War of 1812, and a native New Yorker; he organized and assumed command of a militia force and Coker administered the other affairs of the group.[36] The society sent the colonists a shipment of fresh supplies and the captain who delivered them reported that Coker had fallen into "a state of the greatest despondency." Still, Coker guided the settlement, established a Sunday school, and was teaching spelling and reading when he wrote to the society on September 12, 1820, saying "Tell my brethren to come: not to fear. The land is good. It only wants men to possess it."[37]

In an attempt to impose some order on the colonists, Coker and Johnson moved them from Sherbro Island to a plantation on Fourah Bay near Freetown. Twenty-three of *Elizabeth's* passengers had died that year. When additional colonists arrived and joined the group in 1821, the white ACS agents negotiated a settlement site at Cape Mesurado and made plans to move the Americans once again. In conference with "some of the American blacks who went out with Paul Cuffe," ACS agents assessed the state of the colony as they found it a year after its founding and concluded that Coker and Johnson "had managed the business of the expedition . . . in as judicious a manner as the circumstances of the case would admit."[38]

The ACS eventually obtained a permanent site for the colony at Cape Mesurado, but Daniel Coker and six others chose to remain at the Fourah Bay site. Self-government and self-determination, central elements in Paul Cuffe's vision and principles conditionally endorsed and anticipated by American Colonization Society agents during their earliest planning for the Liberian settlements, had become a temporary reality. At Cape Mesurado Elijah Johnson and Lott Cary assumed the leadership roles Coker and Johnson had held by default at Sherbro Island many months earlier. Johnson served as Commissary of Stores and Cary held several ad hoc positions of responsibility and leadership.

Lott Cary had been born a slave near Richmond in 1780, had been a tobacco worker and a Baptist preacher in the United States, and brought to the settlement both a missionary zeal and a powerful sense of nationalism. In the United States he had dreamed of an African home "where I shall be estimated by my merit—not my complexion." He and ministerial colleague Collin Teague began as early as 1813 to plan their emigration. The Cary and Teague families sailed aboard the ACS ship *Nautilus*, which had sailed from Norfolk, Virginia in 1821 carrying twenty-eight women, men, and children. From the outset, Cary's intellectual powers and Baptist piety placed him "in a conspicuous station and gave him wide and commanding influence" among the colonists at Cape Mesurado. When the colony's white physician died, Cary "applied his powerful mind to the subject" and became a medical practitioner.[39]

The Cape Mesurado settlement faced the same internal and external problems that had plagued the early Sierra Leone colonists. Provisions were in short supply and neighboring Africans remained hostile and threatening. During one particularly fierce attack, brought about apparently because the colonists at Cape Mesurado "had put a stop to the slave trade" in the area, Lott Cary led a raid on the colony's storehouse "and by force took from the public stores" the food and ammunition necessary for the colony's immediate survival that were being withheld by white ACS agents.[40] When other settlers became discouraged and wanted to abandon the Cape Mesurado site, Cary urged them to "hold fast." He and Elijah Johnson organized the settlers' defense during the attack, rejecting British assistance offered by the captain of a gunboat who requested in return for his military support a small grant of land on which he might hoist the Union Jack. Johnson was said to have responded: "We want no flag staff put up here that will cost more to get it down again than it will to whip the natives."[41]

The settlement survived those early attacks and by 1822, two years after *Elizabeth* first dropped anchor in the Freetown harbor, ACS ships made Monrovia, not Freetown, their first anchorage. Lott Cary, now serving as physician, educator, and missionary in the settlement, reported in correspondence to friends in the United States "a promising little crop of rice and cassava and . . . about a hundred and eighty coffee trees" under cultivation at the Cape. Although tribal chiefs in the area continued to trade with Spanish, French, and Dutch slavers, the ACS settlements maintained an irregular commodity trade with the United States. Yet, the colonists were often "without Provision, Powder, lead, or any kind of ammunition" and tribal hostility toward the colonists at Cape Mesurado remained high. Liberated Africans, emancipated slaves, and free-born African Americans came to a place dominated by "low, swampy jungles" along the coast in a climate many found "at times almost suffocating." During the dry season the site was polluted by "the miasma rising from the marshes . . . exhaling a naucious odor from the decomposed vegetation."[42] And still, emigrants continued to arrive, and the colony grew. The *Strong* delivered thirty-seven emigrants in 1822, many recently kidnapped Africans who had been rescued from slavery and returned to Africa, although not necessarily to their homes. Instead, they were "settled in a community by themselves" and there, on the African west coast, the processes of acculturation to an Americanized life style began. They were placed "under a judicious superintendent who was directed to regulate their hours, lead their family devotion, and instruct them in reading, writing, and arithmetic, and the principles of the Christian religion." Prevented from returning to their tribal homes (suggested by the depositions they gave to the Baltimore agent of the ACS while they were detained prior to the sailing of *Strong* as no more than a two- or three-day walk from the coastal settlement site), the group served as forced laborers for a perimeter defense system for the settlers. Predictably, they began deserting the settlement within weeks after their arrival.[43]

The society reported a population of about one hundred thirty people at Cape Mesurado when *Oswego* delivered sixty additional settlers in 1823. *Cyrus* brought an additional one hundred hopeful African Americans to their ancestral homeland in 1824. The majority were free-born and literate adults from Maryland, Pennsylvania, and Virginia. Monrovia, like Freetown, grew rapidly from a frontier settlement into a bustling city, although provisions, clothing, and ammunition remained in short supply. Tensions between society officials and the settlers persisted, generally revolving around Society efforts to control and ration provisions.[44]

Lott Cary attempted to mediate the disputes but on June 19, 1824, a number of the settlers threatened a general strike in protest against reduced rations, vowing "to aid in no survey of the lots or in any public improvements; to leave uncleared and uncultivated the land which had been assigned to them" until changes were made in the rationing system.

The ACS agent initially responded by threatening to withhold all provisions from those who refused to submit to his authority. When rations were stopped the colonists "proceeded to the store-house, where the commissary was, at that moment, issuing rations for the week; and seizing, each, a portion of the provisions, hastened to their respective homes."[45] Inevitably, the dispute was resolved, for the ongoing hostilities with neighboring tribes presented greater threats to survival than power struggles within the colony.

During the 1820s, each new ship's arrival brought fresh personnel and supplies to the fragile settlement. Following the *Oswego* in 1828 and the *Cyrus* in 1824, two ships arrived in 1826: *Vine* brought thirty-four emigrants, the majority—including Newport Gardner—from Newport, Rhode Island, and a printing press and books. Perhaps reflecting the protracted longing for an African return among that state's lacks, the Rhode Islanders had organized themselves as a church congregation prior to their sailing in preparation for their return and resettlement. *Indian Chief* brought 154 settlers from Virginia and North Carolina. Lott Cary routinely attended the sick. Others made cartridges and fought off slave traders and hostile tribes. On November 8, 1828, loose powder on the floor of the munitions supply house caught fire, exploding the cartridges and mortally wounding Reverend Lott Cary.[46]

COMPETING LOYALTIES

Lott Cary had played an heroic role in establishing the colonial environment from which Liberia would emerge in 1847. He had negotiated a major land purchase, "all that tract of land on the north side of the St. Paul River, beginning at King James' line below the establishment called Millsburg settlement," from several tribal kings while serving as agent of the colony. He had recruited settlers for the colony, writing to local colonization societies, appealing to free African Americans to quit the United States and come out to Liberia, a land where "the people are industrious, and the children attend the schools . . . [and] everything depends on the sobriety and industry of the Colonists."[47] Cary had helped create a homeland where, he believed, people were, indeed, estimated by their merit, not their complexion.

But Cary had been largely forgotten in the United States, where the American Colonization Society met firm and unrelenting resistance among the majority of free African Americans throughout the 1820s. During that decade the society transported less than one thousand

African Americans to the Liberian settlements, which Samuel Cornish and John Russwurm described as "an unhealthy region . . . [with] a horrible climate." For most, nationalism overpowered Pan-Africanism. Thomas Jinnings of New York explained:

> Our claims are on America, it is the land that gave us our birth; it is the land of our nativity, we know no other country, it is a land in which our fathers have suffered and toiled; they have watered it with their tears, and fanned it with sighs.
> Our relation with Africa is the same as the white man's is with Europe.
> . . . We have passed through several generations in this country, and consequently we have become naturalized, our habits, our manners, our passions, our dispositions have become the same. . . . I might as well tell the white man about England . . . and call him a European, as for him to call us Africans. [48]

Nevertheless, within the ACS settlements, houses were built, gardens planted, and substantial acreage cleared. In Monrovia a school designed "along the Lancasterian plan," which also informed public education in Boston and New York and which Prince Saunders introduced into the Haytian republic, began the task of educating the children in the colony. The library boasted two hundred volumes. A college had been established at Fourah Bay. The agriculturists among the colonists cleared in excess of five hundred acres and brought twenty-seven plantations into production during those early years of settlement. The artisans constructed public works for the growing town. [49]

By mid-1829 Cornish and Russwurm softened their editorial opposition to the Liberian settlements that had been so overt the previous year. Straightforward reportage replaced anti-colonization rhetoric in the pages of *Freedom's Journal*. American readers learned that cows had been introduced into the colony and a butchery had been established in Monrovia. Colonists had initiated a ship-building industry and the Monrovia shipyard had turned out four schooners. Public works had progressed, opening a path from the city into the colony's interior. Francis Devaney, the high sheriff of the colony, had imported a horse and several other colonists had horses on order. The bulk of the earliest settlers were involved in the coasting trade (the trade Paul Cuffe had predicted would be sufficiently prosperous to drive an economic wedge into the slave trade) and many colonists were "beginning to add both to their comfort and their independency by agriculture." Those who had arrived more recently were in more pressed circumstances, their houses not yet complete, their circumstances limited because of few financial or material resources. The most recent arrivals were still living in public houses, primarily because they had not yet adjusted to the tropical climate and were unable to work. On the whole, by mid-1829 *Freedom's Journal* described a dynamic, potentially prosperous colony of African Americans building personal and collective lives on a reclaimed homeland.[50]

In 1830 John Russwurm, having concluded that for African-Americans talk of enjoying citizenship in the United States was "a mere waste of words," emigrated to Monrovia and put the printing press that had arrived in Monrovia aboard *Vine* in 1826 to good use. Under his editorship the *Liberia Herald* came to be regarded as a first-class newspaper.[51] In many respects, by 1830 those who had taken the risk and gone out to Africa on one of the ACS expeditions were realizing Paul Cuffe's vision, combining a Christian mission, a fortress against the hideous traffic in human cargo, and economic and political autonomy. That year, the year of Nat Turner's Rebellion in Southampton County, Virginia, the year the First National Negro Convention met in Philadelphia, the citizens of Monrovia prepared an address to the "Free People of Colour in the United States" in which they made clear their motives for emigration:

> The first consideration which caused our voluntary removal to this country . . . is liberty—liberty in the sober, simple, but complete sense of the word. . . . We did not enjoy that freedom in our native country; and from causes which, as respects ourselves, we shall soon forget forever, we were certain it was not there attainable for ourselves or our children. . . .
>
> In Africa we are the proprietors of the soil we live on and . . . our laws are altogether our own.[52]

That same year forty African Americans responded to Richard Allen's call and gathered in a clandestine meeting at Bethel Church in Philadelphia. Allen had invited the group to consider what actions might be taken to advance "the condition of the free people of colour throughout the United States."[53] The delegates to the Bethel Church meeting seemed to be turning away from ties to an African ancestry that had informed the thoughts and actions of an earlier generation. Images of an idealized and mythologized African homeland had been persistent and powerful in the lives of African Americans. Even among those who did not or could not join the post-Revolutionary return-to-Africa ventures, a memory—auto-biographical for some, culturally reconstructed for others—had fueled a racial identity permeated by African themes. The oratory of Jupiter Hammon and Prince Hall had been addressed to "beloved African brethren." Those who had founded the Free African Societies, the African churches, and the African schools throughout the urban Northeast during the final decades of the eighteenth century had publicly claimed and proclaimed both their freedom and their African ancestry. The popular support Paul Cuffe had enjoyed for his Sierra Leone venture, and the willing volunteers who filled the ACS ships bound for the Liberian coast, reflected a persistent power of that identity in the popular historical consciousness of African Americans.

Now, parallel to this impulse to reclaim a lost legacy and homeland, a new cultural memory and racial identity had been forged by a consciousness of nativity and explicitly American milieux of memory, for the actions at Bethel Church involved considerably more than a triumph of one political strategy over another. Abandoning African environments of memory, the men who gathered at Bethel Church embraced that New World collective consciousness when they formed the American Society of Free Persons of Colour, for Improving their Condition in the United States, for Purchasing Lands, and for Establishing a Settlement in Upper Canada.

CHAPTER FIVE

Moral Community, Ethnic Identity, and Political Action

We claim to be American citizens, and we will not waste our time by holding converse with those who deny us this privilege, unless they first prove that a man is not a citizen of that country in which he was born and reared. Those that desire to discuss with us the propriety of remaining in this country . . . must first admit us as a cardinal point, their equal by nature, possessing like themselves, from God, all those inalienable rights, that are universally admitted to be the property of his creatures.

—William Whipper, Alfred Niger,
and Augustus Price, 1835[1]

DURING THE WEEKEND OF AUGUST 22, 1829, Cincinnati, Ohio, a bustling river town of eighteen thousand, exploded in a moment of racial violence, although neither the frontier river town nor the savage white attack on African Americans that precipitated the violence was particularly exceptional in the cultural texture of early-nineteenth-century America. Despite the frontier venue, far removed from the urban concentrations of African Americans along the eastern seaboard, the circumstances and conditions surrounding the riotous burning of the tenements in Cincinnati's "Little Africa" epitomized the subtext of fear, violence, and intimidation that characterized race relations in the antebellum United States.[2] Racial tolerance in Cincinnati, as elsewhere, was tenuous and based on utilitarian considerations.

Despite the unremarkable nature of the Cincinnati riot, the events that unfolded in the weeks and months following that violent eruption foreshadowed a gradual but dramatic change in the texture of the American cultural landscape, for the Cincinnati Crisis of 1829 galvanized African-American public opinion throughout the Northern states. The first mass civil rights movement in the United States emerged in its aftermath, guided by African-American community leaders who mobilized collective energies and resources from within a moral community molded around the principle of race unity and increasingly focused on New World sites of cultural memory. Ironically, a racial identity that had informed the construction of segregated worlds during the early years of the nineteenth century became a springboard in the 1830s for organized social action and political demands that took as their centerpiece full and unconditional inclusion in the civic culture of the nation.

African Americans throughout the nominally free states initially responded to the threatened displacement of some thousand black Cincinnatians with disbelief and urgent concern. *The Rights of All,* published and edited by Samuel Cornish in New York City, had anticipated the outbreak of violence; in the months following the tragedy the paper initially had interpreted the riot in terms of local economic conditions and then cast the local event into the larger arena of the citizenship debate.[3] As a result, African Americans in the urban Northeast, whether or not they were connected to the biracial anti-slavery movement, were well aware of the building crisis in Cincinnati. Although Cincinnati was far removed from their daily lives, the interpretation of the events there provided in the pages of *The Rights of All* produced a shared understanding of the circumstances surrounding the riot and the threatened expulsion of the city's black population. The tragic byproduct of New World racism provided an unexpected new mooring for African-American environments of cultural memory that increasingly revolved around New World milieux.

CINCINNATI, 1829

Cincinnati, Ohio, in 1829, like Montgomery, Alabama, in 1959, afforded an ideal setting for an eruption of racial animosity. During the early years of the nineteenth century race relations in Cincinnati had remained relatively stable, but by the mid-1820s evidence of racial tension pervaded all spheres where the lives of black and white citizens intersected. The immediate sources of tension lay in a combination of historical precedents that fixed the status of African Americans in Ohio midway between enslaved and free and the labor competition embedded in the expanding local economy. Although in Cincinnati, as elsewhere, African Americans always had been consigned to the economic margins of the community, they had enjoyed a degree of economic stability in the prosperous river town. At the same time, while slavery was prohibited in the Northwest Territory and then in Ohio, legislation adopted at the organization of the State of Ohio in 1807 had incorporated so-called "Black Codes" from the Northwest Ordinance into the new state's Constitution, thereby affirming the established caste-like biracial social structure. The initial legislation required all African Americans to post a $500 bond guaranteeing good behavior and certifying their free status. Additional legislation prohibited African Americans from serving on juries or from offering testimony (against whites) in a court of law, denied them the opportunity to attend public schools, prohibited their service in the state militia, and refused them access to state institutions and services.[4] Compliance with the Black Codes at the local (or municipal) level varied enormously and in Cincinnati enforcement had been quite relaxed during the early years of the century.

By the 1820s, however, white public opinion had hardened on racial matters, at least in part a reaction to the rapid expansion of the African-American population during the preceding years. In 1825 the editor of *Liberty Hall*, a local newspaper, had described that population increase as "a great evil" for the city.[5] In addition to the jingoism of native white Cincinnatians, however, increasing numbers of German and Irish immigrants were competing fiercely, at times viciously, with African Americans for employment in the construction of roads and canals and as porters, vendors, shoeblacks, messengers and domestic workers. These jobs previously had provided steady employment for African-American women and men in the city's expanding commerce and manufacturing enterprises.[6] By the middle of the decade the American calculus of race and jobs had fostered intensified racial animosity between black and white working-class Cincinnatians. At the same time, during the warm months each year the Cincinnati population was swelled by wealthy white planters who came up from Mississippi, Alabama, and Louisiana to summer residences in and around the city. Their cultural perspective and social influence compounded already heightened racial tensions. Predictably, and probably in an effort to mask mounting tensions, white Cincinnati fortified the city's color line. African-American children were banned from the city's public schools, and black community efforts to organize a school for their disenfranchised children were undone by a combination of black poverty and white hostility. Tensions mounted.

African Americans began to avoid public places—theaters, hotels, and public conveyances—and found they were no longer welcome in white churches.[7]

In response and protest, local blacks began to exercise the few freedoms they did enjoy. They were led by John Malvin, a free-born African American who in 1827 had left Virginia and headed west in search of a more racially tolerant climate. Malvin had walked three hundred miles from his Virginia home to the Ohio River, and from there had taken a boat to Cincinnati, only to find the racial climate "little better than Virginia." Initially, the protests Malvin encouraged were covert. Under his guidance, his friends and neighbors opened their homes to the fugitives from Southern slavery who routinely crossed the Ohio River and passed through Cincinnati on their way to Indiana and Canada. As a result, the Underground Railroad gained many new waystations in the Cincinnati area. Eventually, Malvin urged more overt action, and with his guidance members of the local African Methodist Episcopal church organized a petition drive calling for a repeal of the Ohio Black Codes.[8] Outraged by this clear signal of black protest, local white community leaders had responded by summarily giving the entire African-American population—slightly more than 2,200 people—thirty days to post the $500 surety bond required by law or leave town.[9]

Within the African-American community initial disbelief quickly gave way to organized action. The required fee was beyond reach for the majority. Most had no choice but emigration, and while they might have gone out to Hayti, still popular, or Liberia—certainly the choice of many white Cincinnatians *for* them—African Americans dispatched Israel Lewis and Thomas Cresap, two trusted members of their community, to Upper Canada to identify a resettlement site and initiate negotiations with the governor of Upper Canada for the purchase of land (from which they believed they would never again be evicted by white capriciousness). At the same time, in an effort to obtain financial assistance for a move few could afford, black Cincinnatians sent other members of the community to New York, Philadelphia, Boston, and other Northeastern cities where they appealed to more stable African-American communities for financial help.[10]

Malvin negotiated a sixty-day extension of the deadline the town had imposed on its black citizens. As black Cincinnatians waited for word from their agents, Lewis and Cresap, concerning the Canadian land and from those who were soliciting money to finance the migration, much of the African-American residential area in Cincinnati was burned in a fierce riot. Some two hundred left for Canada immediately.[11] At that point, members of the town council, realizing that a mass emigration would siphon off the town's cooks, waiters, and washerwomen, intervened with black community leaders. In the face of promises for a cessation of the violence and suggestions of a restoration of racial collaboration if not harmony, many black Cincinnatians abandoned their emigration plans.

Little changed in the daily lives of those who chose to stay in Cincinnati. Ohio did not repeal the Black Codes, but instead reinforced the color line by enacting new racially restrictive legislation. Labor discrimination persisted. African Americans were barred from the skilled trades and from apprenticeships. Yet, there were also gradual improvements: a school that enrolled one hundred twenty-five young black scholars and provided evening classes for adults; a lyceum that sponsored twice-weekly lectures "on scientific and Literary subjects"; a circulating library of one hundred volumes. John Malvin moved to Cleveland, joined forces with white abolitionists, and extended his unrelenting attack against the Black Codes in particular and race discrimination in general to a statewide arena.[12]

The events in Cincinnati differed little from the racial violence and social conditions that punctuated and limited the lives of African Americans throughout the antebellum Northern states, where free black communities routinely battled the disadvantages of poverty and racism and relied on the delicate balance between private tolerance and public civility for their personal as well as collective safety. As black homes were burning in Cincinnati, whites disrupted and "rioted upon a black camp meeting" in Gloucester, New Jersey. In New Haven the African Improvement Society struggled with limited resources to "assist in the recovery of this numerous class from their present state of degradation by encouraging and promoting . . . useful trades . . . and keeping out of debt." In Boston and Philadelphia, cities where publicly supported primary education generally was available to white children, African-American children were educated in subscription schools open only to those whose parents could afford the tuition.[13]

Still, because black Cincinnatians had dispatched agents "to various parts of the United States to solicit aid from the people of color who were more favorably situated," their local crisis was transformed into a national issue. In Cincinnati in 1829 as in Montgomery, Alabama, and other Southern cities in the 1960s, African Americans compensated for their relative powerlessness against local white political and economic elite by inviting "third parties" into the local arena. In the Cincinnati case, in the absence of a viable national press and at a time when white public opinion, even in radical abolitionist circles, rarely supported the notion of full civic equality for African Americans, these third parties, groups outside the immediate environment, were mobilized through exclusively black media—the African-American press, black churches and fraternal organizations, and community-based mutual aid societies. Through these media the events in Cincinnati were transformed from a local crisis into a representation of the common plight of free black Americans throughout the United States.[14] As would be the case in the 1960s, economic marginality and race discrimination were transformed from a personal disadvantage into a mass-movement political resource.

In the aftermath of the crisis, Hezekiah Grice, a Baltimore ice dealer, suggested to Richard Allen, the presiding bishop of the African Methodist Episcopal Church, a convention that could serve as a forum for designing and coordinating unified (translocal) action to assist the Cincinnatians in their Canadian emigration.[15] Allen seized on the idea as an opportunity to forge a national African-American political alliance. The genius in Allen's leadership, in this situation as in others, lay in his ability to transform the profoundly negative into a positive. The heightened awareness and race consciousness that followed the Cincinnati crisis provided the catalyst for the first mass African-American civil rights movement. In a call for race unity the Convention Movement had been born.

RICHARD ALLEN'S PUBLIC

The public to whom Richard Allen appealed were beneficiaries of half a century of freedom in the North. While they were, to be sure, economically disadvantaged and politically marginalized, they were, at the same time, readers of newspapers and members of fraternal, mutual-aid, and social-reform societies. They had learned the art of debate and bourgeois deportment in literary societies and African churches; and through such organizations as the Free African Society; The Daughters of Abysinnia; The Society for the Relief of Worthy, Aged, and Indigent Colored Persons; The Female Society for Colored Orphans; The Female Dorcas Society; and The Mental and Moral Improvement Association, women and men in Boston, New York, Philadelphia, and many smaller cities and towns in the Northeast regularly put into practice the principles of mutual aid and racial uplift that had been preached in black churches and advocated in black fraternal organizations for fifty years. The generation that grew to maturity after 1820, trained within African-American community organizations, held high expectations for both their own lives and the future of the race. They noted and objected to the contradictions in day-to-day routines that their parents had masked behind self-constructed racial separatism. Yet free-born or former slave, comfortably middle class or struggling laborer, all lived, as had their parents and grandparents, in the racial margins of the United States.

By the 1820s, the potential public of free African Americans had expanded numerically and matured politically, and the discourse directed to that public reflected a sense of urgency and discontent. The new journalism that emerged during the decade blended political commentary, racially grounded interpretation of contemporary events, and biting social criticism. In 1827 John Russwurm and Samuel Cornish had claimed the right of African Americans to an autonomous political voice in their opening editorial of *Freedom's Journal*. Echoing the sentiments African Americans in Boston and Newport had expressed in the 1790s regarding arrangements for emigration to Sierra Leone, Russwurm and Cornish once again claimed the right of self-determination. "We must wish to plead our own cause," they had written in the paper's first issue. "Too long have others spoken for us." David Walker had made similar demands in less temperate language in 1829. His *Appeal in Four Articles* thrilled and challenged African Americans in both the Northern and Southern states.[16]

The audience for this writing had broadened considerably in the decades since Jupiter Hammon and Prince Hall's pamphlets had circulated in the eastern corridor from Boston to Philadelphia. *Freedom's Journal* was distributed in all major urban areas along the eastern seaboard, throughout upstate and western New York villages, in Hayti, and in the Canadian provinces, where a growing number of fugitive slaves were establishing new lives and communities. Providing an open forum for discussion of racial oppression, the paper marked a radical departure from the spiritual confessions, cautious rhetoric, and heavily moralized racial-uplift literature that had prevailed in earlier decades. *Freedom's Journal, The Rights of All*, and the newspapers that followed raised issues that were debated and argued in the African-American press for the next fifty years. The question of a homeland and the problem of national identity were intense concerns, divisive and never fully resolved. Debates over both would recur into the twentieth century.

While there was always unity on the abolition of slavery, opinions divided on strategies to achieve it, as they would in the 1960s on strategies to eradicate the Jim Crow traditions and conventions. In the early nineteenth century suffrage, education, temperance, and Canadian, Haytian, and African emigration all claimed the attentions of African-American journalists and their readers.

The press consistently carried contemporary accounts of Haytian and Canadian events, a reflection of the expanded psychosocial boundaries of Africans in the New World and an emerging transnational, Pan-African community grounded in New World milieux. Toussaint L'Ouverture was elevated to an heroic level. Readers charted Henri Christophe's ascent from slavery to royalty, and they came to know Jean Pierre Boyer as a "remarkable man." During the 1830s, William Jinnings, Boston agent for the *Colored American,* traveled to Hayti to provide firsthand accounts of agriculture and of government support for African Americans who entertained emigration.[17]

At the same time, the press praised Canadian soil and climate, optimistically suggesting that crop production in Canada would surpass that in Virginia and the Carolinas. Traveling reporters described life in the Canadian communities, often observing that while the refugees who lived there were in chronic need of material assistance, their communities nonetheless were soundly based and potentially prosperous. Most reporters observed that despite physical and material hardships, the communities offered the refugees sanctuary and security that were unavailable in the Northern United States.[18]

By the 1830s the press had nurtured a national popular consciousness that transcended local identity among a generation less psychologically receptive to a collective past built entirely on enslavement than their parents had been. For many, particularly for those who reached adulthood during the 1820s and 1830s, a personal memory of slavery had been replaced by events from a more immediate past: the Haytian Revolution and the emergence in the New World of a self-governing black republic (1801); the abolition of the slave trade (1808); the emancipation of slaves in the British West Indies (1834). As a result, this new generation confronted the future better informed of contemporary circumstances, better able to envision and debate alternatives to their disadvantaged condition, and better prepared to take collective action to achieve collective goals than any previous generation of African Americans. The 1829 crisis in Cincinnati had put that preparation to the test.[19]

PHILADELPHIA, 1830

For five days in September, 1830, forty self-selected delegates traveled from Brooklyn, Rochester, Wilmington, Baltimore, and Boston to meet in secret session behind shuttered windows at Mother Bethel Church in Philadelphia. The similarities between the proceedings at Bethel Church that September and the first sessions of the Continental Congress during another September more than half a century earlier in Philadelphia's Carpenter's Hall probably were not coincidental. Like the delegates to the Continental Congress, the men who met at Bethel Church struggled to define their common ground and to forge a collective political agenda, and they vied for hegemony over the proceedings. They also fully understood the revolutionary implications, personal dangers, and historical importance of their deliberations, for they decided that "come what may," they would make public the proceedings of their meeting. They summarized those proceedings in three deceptively simple resolutions: First, following prevailing public opinion, they rejected the American Colonization Society's African emigration scheme. Second, acting in concert, they affirmed the New World bonds of race that increasingly would compete with national identity and loyalties when they pledged financial assistance to the African Americans who had been forced to seek asylum in Canada. Third, in a bold claim to civic equality, and anticipating the issues Garrison and other abolitionists would debate in the coming decades, they affirmed the democratic principles in the Declaration of Independence as the appropriate vehicle for elevating the status of free African Americans and for attacking slavery.[20] In the end, the delegates to the Bethel Church meeting fashioned the foundations of contemporary race consciousness and racial unity around the crucial issue of civil rights.

In 1830 many Americans, if not the majority, both black and white, regarded the social and economic problems of black communities as the domain of African benevolent societies and churches. The men who met in Bethel Church offered a radical revision to the assumptions surrounding those problems, which they defined as artifacts of race discrimination and racial inequality rather than the result of moral flaws of individual character or inherent racial inferiority. By drawing on American cultural and political environments to refocus and redefine the nature and locus of African-American social problems, the delegates to the 1830 Bethel Church meeting claimed the democratic principles in the Declaration of Independence for their own pragmatic purpose. These principles, standing alone, supplied the guidelines for elevating the status of free African Americans. The delegates to the Bethel Church meeting had taken a crucial step toward relocating the sources of black poverty and ignorance. To be sure, the problematic status of slavery in a democratic society had been argued within liberal political circles for some time, but the question of racially structured disadvantage, whether formally legislated or informally crafted by custom and convention, had been accepted without question. The notion of the inherent inferiority of Africans and their descendants held iconographic status in the minds of white Americans. In Philadelphia that September, forty men invoked the principles of democracy to challenge that icon and, in much the same fashion as David Walker had challenged the American myth of assimilation the preceding year, the delegates to the Bethel Church meeting had politicized race in America.[21]

African emigration, like American slavery, had been at the forefront of African-American concerns for half a century when the delegates to the Bethel Church meeting deliberated on the matter. While several hundred African Americans already had gone out to Africa under the ACS program and many more would follow, the rejection and condemnation of the society's program by the delegates to Richard Allen's convention simply buttressed prevailing African-American popular consensus on the issue. African emigration had been in disfavor with many among the free African-American elite since 1817 (the date that simultaneously marked Paul Cuffe's death and the formal organization of the ACS). That year the society first had suggested that the solution to the troublesome dilemma posed by the ending of slavery and the immediate emancipation of several million slaves might lie in their return to an African "homeland." Many African Americans had recognized the ACS proposal immediately as a deportation plan. Still, the actions at Bethel Church involved considerably more than a triumph of one political strategy over another, for the delegates also were turning away from ties to an African ancestry that had informed the thoughts and actions of an earlier generation. Images of an idealized and mythologized African homeland had been persistent and powerful in the lives of African Americans. Still, there is some evidence to suggest that Richard Allen capitalized on the Cincinnati Crisis to upstage New York black leaders. Allen's action reflected a simple squabble over geography, not ideology. While the free black leadership generally opposed African colonization, Allen's call to convene at Bethel Church neutralized the New Yorkers' plan to hold the *first* national anti-colonization meeting in New York City and thereby control the proceedings.[22]

As a counterpoint to David Walker's *Appeal*, an electrifying condemnation of racial oppression in the United States as well as a call to action, the 1830 Bethel Church proceedings foreshadowed the contours of debates among the African-American elite over competing strategies to combat racism that would extend into the twentieth century. Faith in the democratic process and the Constitution on the one hand, and the imperative for direct and possibly violent action on the other, repeatedly would challenge race unity. The Bethel Church delegates did not detail the sources of American racial oppression in the language or the spirit of Walker's *Appeal*. In that document David Walker had clearly located oppression in American institutions and conditions: "our wretchedness in consequence of slavery . . . in consequence of ignorance . . . in consequence of the preachers of the religion of Jesus Christ—in consequences of the colonizing plan."[23]

Richard Allen and his colleagues had declared a political, social, and economic agenda intended to guide more moderated action against those sources of racial oppression David Walker had so vividly and explicitly named in *The Appeal*. In the most immediate sense, these competing strategies would divide and eventually fracture the Convention Movement, but the debate had broader implications as well. The Bethel Church meeting forged a legacy from which twentieth-century African Americans would draw both legal philosophy and practical strategies for successfully challenging structural barriers to racial equality in the United States. At the same time, those who advocated more direct and aggressive action against all sources of racial oppression, and who would within a decade support not only Canadian emigration but also resettlement in Hayti and Africa, constructed the foundation of the twentieth-century Pan-African call for cultural reunification. For the moment, however, the 1830 Bethel Church meeting had outlined a sweeping and revolutionary political agenda. The abolition of slavery and the acquisition of civil equality for free blacks had been fused under a common rubric, race consciousness and race identity. The concluding call for an annual convention to continue the work initiated during those five days in Bethel Church launched a national drive to unify a disinherited people.

IDENTITY AND SITES OF MEMORY, "UNDER THE TREES THAT WE HAVE PLANTED"

The repertoire of strategies that black leaders employed to initiate unification was uniquely American in form and origin. Throughout the winter of 1830-1 in cities and towns throughout the Northeast, African Americans held public meetings in which they discussed and debated the issues surrounding the Cincinnati crisis, came to terms with the acute and critical needs of the Canadian refugees, and adopted a series of resolutions reflecting a firmly fused racial and national identity. In New York City, Boston, Baltimore, Brooklyn, and Washington, DC, African Americans proclaimed their attachment to the land of their birth, their "only true and veritable home." New Yorkers who gathered at the Boyer Lodge Room in January, 1831, declared emphatically that "here we were born and here we will die." Memories and reconstructed images of Africa had been replaced by a resonant national identity; and yet, attachment to the United States transcended autobiographical memory, combining personal experience with generational memory and lore in much the same fashion that earlier generations had claimed their African ancestry. "Beneath [this] sod," the New Yorkers declared, "lie the bones of our fathers." Concrete claims to an American identity were linked, often in dramatic language, with resistance to African colonization. "We object," African Americans in Boston declared, "to the plan of dragging us to Africa." Although some had gone out to Africa during the early years of the century, first with Cuffe and then with the American Colonization Society's Liberian ventures, in the 1830s many African Americans envisioned their ancestral homeland as a "howling wilderness . . . a country unknown to us, except by geography." At the local meetings, as at Bethel Church, African environments of memory had been eclipsed by American events, the most striking of which was the Revolution.

To be sure, the Revolution served for all Americans as a resonant site of national identity and cultural memory. For African Americans, it had come to represent their ironic contribution to the building of a nation that had rejected them. Many recalled that "for it some of [our fathers] fought, bled, and died."[24] They must have felt enormous betrayal, yet in the 1830s, claims to national identity combined immediate personal experience with generational memory and lore. One reader of *Frederick Douglass' Paper* who signed his name only as "F" reacted to colonization schemes by proclaiming, "Here we were born—here we will live, by the help of the Almighty—and here we will die, and let our bones lie by our fathers." "D. Jenkins," whose letter to Douglass appeared in the same issue of the paper, responded to a series of lectures in Cincinnati intended to promote African-American emigration to Canada and Liberia. Jenkins issued a similar claim to his American identity, grounding his declaration not in cultural memory or political theory but, rather, in his autobiographical memory of his own labor: "I have not heard anything that has had a tendency to change my mind on remaining in the United States, under the trees that we have planted."[25] At mid-century, Douglass and his generation would validate their right to their American identity not in the vocabulary of ancestral memory but in terms of their own labors and their own accomplishments in their own real time.

By the spring months of 1831, as preparations were under way for the second annual meeting of the American Society of Free Persons of Colour, the African-American public had signaled clear support for the Bethel Church agenda. Representatives from eleven states (Connecticut, Delaware, Maine, Maryland, Massachusetts, New Jersey, New York, Ohio, Pennsylvania, Rhode Island and Virginia) and the District of Columbia joined under the banner of race unity. Following a routine that would become increasingly predictable at the national conventions, the delegates reviewed the material conditions of the People of Colour in the United States and the state of affairs in the Canadian settlement(s). As they would at each annual meeting, the delegates condemned the American Colonization Society and its African emigration plan, and they explored various strategies to foster moral uplift and economic improvement of the free black population in the United States. Still, in the course of the five-year period from 1830 to 1835 the national movement lost the focused sense of purpose that had informed the initial meeting at Bethel Church. By 1835, a movement initially forged by racial unity appeared to founder.

Richard Allen had died the month before the American Society of Free Persons of Colour 1831 convention held its first session, and many delegates to that meeting must have felt the vacuum left by the death of a man most had regarded as extraordinary and exceptional.[26] Nevertheless, the business of the convention proceeded, and the delegates probably received the report on the Canadian settlement established by the Cincinnatians with a certain satisfaction. The tragically destitute community of refugees from American racism and violence had prospered. The initial settlement of two hundred had become a community of two thousand. Newly erected log houses had replaced temporary shelters. The settlers had cleared and put under cultivation five hundred acres of Canadian wilderness. The delegates to the 1831 convention responded by urging that "the different Societies engaged in the Canadian Settlements be earnestly requested to persevere in their praiseworthy and philanthropic undertaking."[27] While those who had gone out to Africa seem to have been viewed, at least initially, as collaborators with the despised American Colonization Society, the African Americans who emigrated to Canada during the middle decades of the century had not broken the New World bond of race. They were, quite simply, refugees from American racism, and they deserved as much economic and spiritual support as African Americans in the United States could provide.

At the outset of the Convention Movement, race unity had transcended political boundaries; and although the national convention proceedings do not reflect the ongoing and steady emigration of African Americans to Hayti, during the three decades from 1820 to mid-century, an estimated thirteen thousand free black Americans left the United States for a home in a place they perceived as "a strong, powerful, enlightened, and progressive Negro nation."[28] Hezekiah Grice, who had urged Richard Allen to convene the Bethel Church meeting in 1830, went out to Hayti in 1832, the year after Allen died.

During the 1840s, Haytian emigration, sustained by combination of sentiments—the deconstruction of the African *milieux de memoire,* a spirit of racial unity inspired by Toussaint's glorious defeat of Napoleon's army, and a general disillusionment with life in the United States— would intersect with the Canadian refugee emigration, and the two diasporic movements of African-American peoples from the United States renewed and expanded the impulse for cultural unification among black Americans. In many respects, the recurring waves of New World migration also would become sites of resonant cultural memory. For the moment, however, material support for the Canadian settlements dominated the concerns of the American Society of Free Persons of Colour.

The Society also had aimed to "promote the elevation [of African Americans in the United States] to a proper rank and standing." Formal education constituted a crucial component in the program of improvement that emerged from the Convention Movement, and delegates to the 1831 annual meeting defined that program in terms of a national College for the Education of Young Men of Colour. Certainly, such an institution would meet a critical need, for while there were individual exceptions in 1830 that represented extraordinary human effort and achievement, there was no evidence that American colleges and universities willingly would open their doors on a routine basis to African-American youth. Perhaps the delegates drew on their initial success in mobilizing resources for the Canadian settlement as they devised an effective strategy to implement their new vision. At the same time, the ambitious plan for a national college probably derived from a combination of factors that transcended the historical moment: the delegates' understanding of the natural relationship between education and upward mobility that prevails in truly democratic societies; their own personal struggles to become literate and educated people; and their efforts at the local level to establish and maintain even elementary educational facilities for black children.

Whatever considerations may have informed their plan, the delegates to the 1831 convention unanimously endorsed a resolution to establish a national College for the Education of Young Men of Colour. Anticipating the movement to educate freed African Americans in the South after 1865, the school would be organized on the manual labor system, an educational model that welded scientific and liberal-arts education to training in mechanical and agricultural skills. Certainly, similar educational models had been incorporated into American public and private education for some time. Throughout the period of gradual emancipation in the Northern states, abolitionism consistently had been linked to education in "principles of virtue and religion . . . and useful mechanical arts." The New York Manumission Society had incorporated industrial training into the curriculum of the New York City African Free Schools during the final decade of the eighteenth century and had adopted the Lancastrian system during the 1820s.[29] The resulting emphasis both on individual academic achievement and on the acquisition of useful trades and skills probably guided the educational philosophy of the 1831 convention delegates.

At the same time, education proved the unintended vehicle by which the language of moral reform became superimposed onto the movement's political agenda, and this connection between politics and morality would create the wedge that by 1835 would bifurcate the leadership and fracture the national movement. The connection was in place at the inception of the plan for the national college. Delegates to the 1831 meeting believed that such an educational environment could best foster three crucial and interconnected virtues—education, temperance and economy—"among our brethren who have a desire to be useful." At the same time, however, broader cultural concerns also informed the planning. The convention delegates selected New Haven as the best site for the school, in part because of the "literary and scientific character" of the town but also in part because many believed that wealthy "coloured residents of the [West Indian] Islands would send their sons [to New Haven] to be educated" rather than to Europe, as was presently the custom. In this prelude to Pan-African cultural unification, the delegates hoped that such an arrangement would promote "fresh ties of friendship" and thereby enhance racial unity with people of color in the West Indies.[30]

At the time the plan was unanimously approved in convention session, an unnamed (but probably known, at least to those who designed the plan) "benevolent individual" already had subscribed one thousand dollars to underwrite the school. The delegates, calling for an additional nineteen thousand dollars in subscriptions, followed the fund-raising strategy they had effectively employed to generate support for schools at the local level and for the Canadian refugee settlements. They turned to local communities, where they intended to appeal to barbers, black-smiths, washerwomen, and cooks, as well as to preachers, teachers, and businesspeople for the support they needed. They elected Samuel Cornish to the position of "General Agent" for the fund-raising enter-prise and appointed Provisional Committees in fifteen Northeastern communities to guide local fund-raising activities and otherwise assist Cornish in his efforts. Cornish was an ideal choice for the general agent position. An ordained Presbyterian minister and co-founder and editor (with John Russwurm) of *Freedom's Journal*—the first national black newspaper in the United States—and then co-editor (with Philip Bell) of *The Rights of All,* Cornish brought to the work enormous influence and a wide-reaching network that he had constructed to launch and maintain the two newspapers. He was, as well, already practiced in developing financial support for African-American schools, having served as general agent of the Board of Trustees for the New York City African Free Schools during the 1820s.[31]

As their concluding action, the delegates to the 1831 convention constructed an organizational apparatus for selecting delegates to future conventions, thereby ensuring that the work of the annual meeting(s) would be received and supported at the local level. They mandated the organization of local "Societies" authorized to select up to five delegates to the General Convention. Acknowledging that some areas and towns might be limited by sparse or scattered African-American populations, the delegates stipulated "that in places where it is not practicable at present to form Societies, the people shall have the same privilege, *provided* they contribute to the furtherance of the objects of the convention."[32] The convention did not specify the nature of those contributions.

Once again, in the local public meetings that followed the conven-tion, resistance to African colonization was welded to American nationalism and generational memory. In Rochester, African Americans declared: "This is the land our fathers have tilled before us; this is the land that gave us our birthright." Similarly, in Providence, those who gathered at the African Church resolved that "we will not leave our homes, nor the graves of our fathers." In Hartford, Connecticut, and Wilmington, Delaware, African Americans rejected African emigration in direct and unequivocal language, their forceful protest underscoring the power of American cultural memory in their lives. Those who had gathered at the African Union Church in Wilmington endorsed a resolution that "Africa is neither our nation nor home . . . that our language, habits, manners, morals and religion are all different from those of Africans." In Hartford and Trenton, African Americans condemned the American Colonization Society as "anti-Christian and hostile to our peace, and a violation of the laws of humanity . . . the greatest foe to the free colored and slave population, with whom liberty and equality have to contend." Their discourse also affirmed the bond of race unity that free blacks felt with their enslaved brethren.

In November, 1831, at Trenton's Mount Zion Church, the Reverend Lewis Cork anticipated the impact that Nat Turner's Rebellion of the previous August would have on the lives of free blacks and on the Convention Movement; and he attempted to distance "the free people of color [who] have lived peaceably and quietly in these United States . . . and have never been the cause of any insurrectionary or tumultuous movements" from the Southampton County violence, still horribly and terrifyingly fresh in the memories of white Americans.[33] The 1832 meeting of the American Society of Free Persons of Colour convened at Benezet Hall in Philadelphia on June 4, but moved its proceedings at the close of the first day's session to the First African Church. As Lewis Cork had anticipated, white tolerance of African-American gatherings had deteriorated. Driven by memories of Nat Turner's Rebellion the previous fall (an event that continued to evoke a violent and bloody specter of black insurrection), white Philadelphians had voiced strong objections to and fears about the nature of the gathering. Given the long-standing history of white violence against African-Americans, however, the move to the First African Church probably was necessary as much to assure the physical safety of the convention participants as to assuage white fears, for white Philadelphians were not exceptional in their reactions that year. Nat Turner's Rebellion had fired deeply held fears and racist sentiments, and for two years after the bloody events in Southampton County, Virginia, a wave of race riots and repressive legislation swept the country.[34] In white minds, any gathering of African Americans held the potential for violence and slaughter. In an act of appeasement, the convention delegates appointed a committee of three to invite "our white brethren to Philadelphia as [they] may feel disposed" to attend the convention as observers. Although the convention proceedings do not indicate whether or not the invitation was accepted, they do reveal the depth of the impact that the prevailing racial climate had on the "interests and prospects" of free African Americans.

Following established ritual in the Convention Movement and in public gatherings, the 1832 delegates once again condemned the work of the ACS. Yet the texture of the language had changed. The zealous flavor of moral reform dominated what previously had been carefully phrased appeals to the spirit of democracy. The doctrines and programs of the American Colonization Society were "at enmity with the principles and precepts of religion, humanity, and justice" and the society was characterized as "an evil for magnitude unexcelled." At the same time, the delegates' energies necessarily were focused on domestic issues. Their concerns about heightened race prejudice and discrimination, and the potential for increased racial oppression, dominated the convention proceedings. Following the annual Canadian report more than one delegate agreed with the general observation that "rigid oppression [is] abroad in the land." Turner's Rebellion continued to fuel white fear throughout the nation, and some believed many more might be forced to "fly from the graves of their fathers and seek new homes in a land where the roaring billows of prejudice are less injurious to their rights and privileges." Under these conditions, continued financial support for the Canadian refugee settlements was crucial. Anticipating that many might be unable to finance a move to a more "advantageous environment," as the Cincinnatians had three years earlier, the delegates urged that the general convention continue to "collect moneys through their auxiliaries . . . and contribute to the wants of the free colored population of this country generally."[35]

Race prejudice became an explicit and immediate force in the matter of the national college. The committee charged with raising funds for the institution reported that "in consequence of some hostility, manifested by some of the inhabitants of New Haven," fund-raising activities had been suspended. The delegates must have been deeply discouraged. Some suggested that plans for the national College be abandoned, but in the end the optimism that had informed the initial vision prevailed.

The effort to provide African-American youth with an opportunity for advanced education would continue. "If we ever expect to see the influence of prejudice decrease, and ourselves respected," they explained in the *Conventional Address to the Free Colored Inhabitants of these United States,* "it must be by the blessings of an enlightened education." Accordingly, the convention appointed "provisional committees" for each state then represented in the society to continue fund-raising activities and identify a suitable location for the college that they believed would provide the antidote to "moral degradation" among African-American youth and construct a bridge of respect and tolerance between black and white Americans.[36]

The concluding remarks in the *Conventional Address* foreshadowed the future direction of the national movement. While the 1830 and 1831 national conventions had adhered to the agenda crafted at the first Bethel Church meeting, by 1832 that agenda had been revised. The 1832 delegates offered heavily moralized advice to the African-American public under the rubric of the national movement: "In recommending to you a path to pursue for our present good and future elevation, beware of that bewitching evil, that bane of society, that curse of the world, that fell destroyer of the best prospects, and the last hope of civilized man—INTEMPERANCE." Anticipating eventual protest against equalities such as representation in state legislatures and the acquisition of full citizenship, the delegates to the 1832 convention urged free African Americans to prepare for that moment not by political action but by demonstrating their readiness for equality through lives circumscribed by the virtues of prudence, frugality, and purity.[37] The agenda of morality had diluted the power of the civil religion Richard Allen had promoted.

By 1833 the National Convention Movement had shifted the focus of the national agenda from political concerns to matters of moral reform, and particularly to temperance. From 1833 through 1835, when the final national convention met, coverage of the annual meetings and proceedings by the abolitionist press had declined to pro forma listings of the delegates who were present, a clear signal of the waning third-party interest and involvement in the national movement. The "Colored American Conventional Temperance Society," established in 1833 as an adjunct to the annual national meeting, made clear the extent to which the moral-reform agenda had subsumed the focus of the national movement. Many of the causes that had dominated earlier conventions—aid for Canadian refugee settlements, the ongoing struggle for full and unconditional citizenship, the development of educational facilities and opportunities—would be taken up by a wave of state conventions during the 1840s and 1850s, and the moral-reform agenda would be subsumed under the aegis of the American Moral Reform Society. In 1836, the first year in which the American Society of Free Persons of Colour did not meet, William Whipper, who had participated in all of the annual conventions from 1830 through 1835, published a call in *The Liberator* for the first annual meeting of the American Moral Reform Society, which invited delegates "from those places that have formerly been represented in the 'Colored Convention.'" Concurrently, James Forten, his son-in-law Robert Purvis, and other prominent African-American Philadelphians who had provided unwavering support for the national movement launched an investigation into potential misuse of funds collected by Cincinnatian Israel Lewis and others on behalf of the Canadian refugee settlements.[38]

IDENTITY AND POLITICAL AGENCY

In 1830 a loose confederation of African-American clergy, entrepreneurs, teachers and journalists mobilized national public opinion and material resources in support of displaced black Cincinnatians. Local, racially motivated violence had provided the catalyst for the organization and mobilization of material resources and personnel necessary to form a mass social movement. As would be the case in the 1960s, a successful effort to counter community-based racism fueled a national civil rights movement informed by broad structural goals and an ambitious agenda of social and economic reform. In the 1830s, that agenda included the mobilization of economic support for African-American refugees who had fled to Canada, the creation of the College for the Education of Young Men of Colour, and political reforms intended to bring African Americans into full civic participation.

In contrast to the pattern of the twentieth century Civil Rights Movement, however, the organizational center of the National Convention Movement shifted away from the initial site of violence, probably crucial in the case of the Convention Movement, given the historical moment and circumstances—in particular, the enslavement of the bulk of the African-American population, a relatively weak national press, and the concentration of the free African-American population and economic resources in the urban Northeast. At the same time, the shift away from Cincinnati raises questions about the relationship between the physical location of a movement's organizational center and the formulation of realistically defined and articulated movement goals. In the case of the National Convention Movement, broad and ambiguously defined goals quickly supplemented and eventually supplanted the concrete goal that had initiated the movement—the mobilization of economic support for displaced black Cincinnatians. This shift in the original movement goals, in turn, redirected the movement's energies and resources away from African-American immigrants to Canada and toward an agenda of economic and political change for African Americans in the United States that may have been historically premature and required greater material resources and more personnel than the small and generally impoverished antebellum free black population could supply.

To be sure, at the outset the leaders of the National Convention Movement brought a broad range of organizational experiences within local and regional African-American communities to the enterprise. At the same time, free black communities in the urban Northeast had been organized for half a century or more around African environments of memory, whether autobiographical or culturally reconstructed. As a result, the movement's leaders faced a critical dilemma as they mobilized personnel around American violence and racism. In order to successfully mobilize a free African-American public, movement leaders drew on a repertoire of collective action underscored by New World environments of memory, thereby forging a social movement uniquely suited to advance a New World racial identity.

History and the Politics of Memory, 1835–1860

INTRODUCTION

The bifurcation of the National Convention Movement after 1835 signaled a hardening of the divisions in African-American public opinion regarding the question of emigration and the increasing tension between loyalties to nation and loyalties to race. Those who believed that it was, indeed, possible to be both an American and a Negro gravitated to the moral reform and anti-slavery movements, giving over their considerable energies to promoting structural change in the United States.[1] Many, however, believed it impossible, particularly after the enactment of the 1850 Fugitive Slave Law, to be both an American and a descendant of Africa, and an estimated 20 percent of the free black population left the United States to establish permanent residence in Canada, Hayti, or Africa between 1820 and 1860.[2]

The impact of this antebellum diaspora on African-American consciousness and identity was profound, for while the majority of those who emigrated went to Canada and were fugitives from slavery, driven from the country by fear of capture and reenslavement, the mass migration represented much more than a fear-driven relocation. Many among the Canadian refugees would never entirely relinquish their identity as Americans, and some would return when slavery had been abolished and try, once again, to claim for themselves the promises of American democracy. The migratory "pull" to Hayti remained cultural reunification and political agency, and those who went to Africa were drawn by the promise of economic independence and by an elusive but persistent image of a lost homeland and an ancestry reclaimed. The Haytian emigrants, like the Canadians, maintained various kinds of connections to their American homeland, their persisting concern anchored in the politics surrounding U.S. slavery. As is the case with all diasporas, physical separation from families, neighborhoods, communities, and homeland did not eradicate the psychosocial ties of identity that bound people to each other and to place. At the same time, those who did not migrate gained a heightened awareness of distant places and experienced a freshened connection to symbols of race unity. Representations of that interconnected impulse permeated African-American literature and fueled the historical accounts African Americans told of their lost ancestry and their American nationalism.

African Americans would remember this era through the biographical sketches of African-American "genius, capacity, and intellectual development" William Wells Brown produced in his publication of *The Black Man, His Antecedents, His Genius and His Achievements* (1863). Frederick Douglass hailed Brown's book as "an additional installment of the black man's reply to the damning charge of natural and permanent inferiority."[3] It was that, and more. Designed to counter the "colorphobia" of the times by presenting irrefutable evidence of a legacy of African-American civic, cultural, and political achievement, Brown's biographical dictionary also sketched a transnational map of African-American identity and cultural memory.[4] While U.S. citizens constituted the center of that map, the people who had built Hayti and Liberia and those who had guided the Canadian refugee settlements also stood alongside Crispus Attucks, Denmark Vesey, Charlotte Forten, and William Cooper Nell as publicly claimed and celebrated race heroes. Reflecting an ongoing struggle by African Americans to make real the promises of the American Revolution, *Black Man* also traced the contours of race solidarity and popular historical consciousness that informed African-American identity. The core of that identity was vested in reconstructing and reconvening a people fractured by slavery. Ironically, however, both cultural identity and historical memory transcended the nation's geographical boundaries, the unintentional result of a persistent African-American emigration from the United States between 1820 and 1860.

CHAPTER SIX

Haiti, Canada, and a Pan-African Vision

I came here to escape the oppression of the laws upon the colored man.

—Thomas Hedgebeth, 1856
Chatham, Canada West [1]

BETWEEN 1820 AND 1860 approximately 20 percent of the free African-American population quit the United States, an estimated thirteen thousand emigrating to Hayti and more than sixty thousand to Canada, driven away by fear of reenslavement and an abhorrence of the racial oppression that circumscribed and limited their lives.[2] This antebellum diaspora tells us much about the resonant power of the African-American civic culture at mid-century, and about expectations African Americans held for their lives that could not and would not be met in the United States. Extending the bonds of psychosocial identity, the recurrent waves of migration from the United States to Hayti and Canada over this forty-year period also illuminate the strength of a race bond that transcended time and place, gaining the status of moral authority and fostering movements for cultural autonomy both within and beyond the United States.

Canada was not unfamiliar to African Americans at the onset of the antebellum diaspora. The country had been serving as a refuge for African Americans for a quarter of a century when the refugees from Cincinnati established the Wilberforce settlement in 1829. Largely as a result of efforts by William Wilberforce and his colleagues, the Canadian provinces had been slave-free since 1793, and the government had provided land grants in Upper Canada to African Americans who served in the British army and navy during the War of 1812. Fugitives, primarily from Kentucky and Virginia, had followed the African-American Loyalists, and by 1819, African Americans were cultivating tobacco in the Amherstburg area of Canada West. As the distance between the Revolutionary Era and real time increased, the tiny population of Afro-Canadians had receded in the African-American consciousness, displaced and replaced by more immediate and pressing concerns. Although the Amherstburg settlement received occasional passing notice in the abolitionist press—for exporting their crops to Montreal markets in 1821, for example—the circumstances of its six hundred or more inhabitants had been of no more than casual concern to the reading public in the United States prior to 1829.[3] The Cincinnati crisis brought into clear focus the potential importance of slave-free Canada to the African-American milieu.

Like Canada West, Hayti, the New World republic created and ruled by people of African descent that promised an opportunity for African Americans to live in a climate of freedom and dignity not possible in the United States, was a relatively familiar place to many African Americans. Toussaint's remarkable overthrow of French rule in Saint Domingue elevated the Caribbean nation and those who had created it to a mythic stature in the collective consciousness of African Americans. Representing a model of race unity and political agency, Hayti both offered personal opportunities for resettlement and presented a material New World challenge to the ideology of Anglo-European world supremacy. The slaves-turned-revolutionaries who had defeated Napoleon's army, and the succession of rulers who had guided the young nation into the international political arena, epitomized the exercise of "genius, capacity, and intellectual" development denied African Americans in the United States.[4]

African Americans probably first had learned about the Haytian Revolution in much the same manner as they and other Americans had learned in general about life in the West Indies. A regular drift of people and a vigorous trade in coffee, sugar, and rum between the United States and the Caribbean fostered a steady flow of information about the Caribbean milieu. Details about daily life and customs, embedded in more nebulous images of the political and cultural environment, probably had filtered into African-American communities primarily through black sailors and others who had direct and routine contact with the region. From the outset, the image of a nation created and ruled by people of African descent offered a resonant *lieu de memoire* for African Americans. Slave uprisings in Northampton, York, and Powhatan Counties and in the areas around Norfolk and Petersburg, Virginia, during 1792 and 1793—the years immediately following the initial 1791 Haytian slave insurrection—were believed to have been influenced if not inspired by the Haytian revolt, and the Haytian influence seems unmistakable in the case of Gabriel and Nancy Prosser's Rebellion in 1800.[5] Additionally, refugee *affranchis,* or free people of color who had fled to the United States during the early years of the nineteenth century, brought firsthand accounts of the Haytian Revolution to the African-American communities where they settled.[6] Their story of dispossession born of a revolution, however, did little to diminish the radiance of the black nation in the perceptions of African Americans, for by 1815, the year Paul Cuffe sailed for Sierra Leone with the first small wave of African-American emigrants, Henri Christophe, who had fought in the American Revolution and served under Toussaint during the early stages of the Haytian Revolution, had set into motion the international alliances that would foster the first of several waves of African-American immigration to Hayti.[7]

From 1806 through 1818, a period of intense political turmoil in Hayti, Henri Christophe controlled the northern region of the divided island, while Alexandre Petion, a French-educated mulatto, remained in control of the southern region. Hayti had been the pride of the French colonial empire, but it collapsed in post-revolutionary economic and political chaos. Particularly in the area under Christophe's control, plantations that had been models of prosperity under the French regime ceased production. The country's labor force was unreliable. There was little revenue for a government already near bankruptcy, and illiteracy was widespread. In conjunction with a larger economic development plan Christophe initiated a public school system and, with William Wilberforce, the English abolitionist and philanthropist acting on his behalf, solicited English teachers to staff that system.[8]

That same year, Prince Saunders had traveled to England as a delegate of the Prince Hall Masonic Lodge (Lodge No. 459) in Boston. In the course of his visit to London, perhaps because of his friendships with Paul Cuffe, William Ellery Channing, and William S. Shaw, Saunders was invited into British abolitionist social circles. There he came to the attention of Wilberforce. Saunders was an experienced schoolteacher who had taught in schools for African-American children in Colchester, Connecticut and then in Boston. Wilberforce, ever the philanthropist, working within his own evangelical agenda, drew Saunders into the Hayti project, charged him with two tasks, and dispatched him to Hayti and to a meeting with Christophe: Saunders was to organize Christophe's school system and change Haytian religion from Catholic to Protestant.[9]

Christophe and Saunders developed a solid alliance during that initial trip. Under Wilberforce's guidance, Saunders created the framework for an educational system, and he also introduced smallpox vaccination into Hayti by personally inoculating Christophe's children. Christophe ultimately engaged Saunders as an agent of the Haytian government and, in that prestigious capacity, Saunders returned to London in 1816 to recruit teachers for the Haytian school system. During that return to London, Saunders published *Haytien Papers. A Collection of the Very Interesting Proclamations and Other Official Documents . . . of the Kingdom of Hayti.* In the collection of documents, intended to legitimize the Haytian government to an international audience, Saunders declared Hayti to be in "an improved state" as a result of its liberation from European oppression. Directly challenging contemporary charges that Afro-Haytians had been able to form their own nation only because of their contact with "civilized" Europeans, Saunders declared the Code Henri, the Proclamation of the First Consul to the Inhabitants of St. Domingo, and Christophe's Proclamation of the State of Hayti all to have been "written by those whose names they bear . . . black men, or men of colour."[10] Saunders probably intended the *Haytien Papers,* which was reissued in Boston two years after its initial publication, would inform the British and American publics about the ideological contours of Haytian political philosophy. In this capacity, the collection of documents would gain support for the emigration plan Christophe and Saunders intended to promote and at the same time counter popular charges that black Haytians, like African Americans, were handicapped by inherent racial inferiority. *The Haytien Papers,* Saunders believed, provided concrete evidence of Hayti's dedication to unconditional personal liberty and political equality "whatever be your origin or your colour."[11]

Saunders returned from London to the United States in 1818 and settled in Philadelphia through 1820. Perhaps because there already was a nucleus of Haytian immigrants well integrated into the Philadelphia African-American community, or perhaps because of the longstanding connections many had with the maritime trades, Saunders found in Philadelphia a community particularly receptive to Haytian emigration. James Forten, who vigorously opposed the African emigration program being promoted by the American Colonization Society, took an equally strong public position in support of Haytian emigration. For Forten, as for many other African Americans, the republic promised to make real African Americans' dreams of nationalism and autonomy.

Competing with the ACS, Saunders advanced Hayti to American audiences, both black and white, at every opportunity. In Philadelphia he consistently and repeatedly portrayed Hayti as a potential place of asylum for African Americans. In other cities along the eastern seaboard, perhaps following Cuffe's Sierra Leone recruitment pattern, Saunders repeated his message.[12] Unlike Africa, Hayti was not a mysterious and removed place for African Americans living in the cities along the eastern seaboard of the United States. Many had a long history of contact with the Caribbean island. For those who had not been born in the United States, one of those islands had been their first stop in the New World, their terminus of the middle passage from the African west coast. Those who worked in the maritime trades traveled frequently and freely throughout the Caribbean. The Haytian *gens du couleur* who had fled to the United States during the initial stages of the revolution were an immediate and influential presence in African-American urban life, particularly in New Orleans and Philadelphia. As a result, many African Americans listened with more than passing interest as Prince Saunders, a young New Englander believed to be "of pure African blood," described the Haytian emigration program during the final years of the Christophe reign. Some made personal preparations for resettlement there, for Christophe had promised to provide a ship for their passage and a sum of money for their resettlement. However, internal Haytian politics—Christophe's incapacitating stroke and subsequent suicide in 1820, followed by renewed internal political turmoil—imposed a temporary delay on Haytian emigration.

A PREFERENCE FOR HAITI

In 1818 Jean Pierre Boyer, a French-educated mulatto, assumed the presidency of Hayti and, following Christophe's suicide two years later, unified the country. Despite fourteen years of nominal independence, however, Hayti remained economically unproductive, impoverished, and unrecognized by the world community.[13] Throughout Toussaint's generalship, from 1793 through 1804, the United States continued the lucrative trade in rum, sugar, and coffee while avoiding outright diplomatic recognition of the nation. Despite the economic advantages that would have followed diplomatic recognition—particularly, a firm political legitimacy and autonomy that would strengthen Hayti's position in the world economy—this New World nation born of a slave revolt challenged fundamental Anglo-European assumptions about social order vested in racial distinctions. As a result, at the official level Hayti remained unacknowledged.[14]

For African Americans, Hayti represented quite a different immigration choice from the ACS settlements in Liberia. Hayti was the political manifestation of African military supremacy in the New World. In contrast, Liberia was the creation of white American politicians, and while there were few white Americans who lived permanently in the Liberian settlements, until Liberia declared its independence in 1847 those settlements remained politically subordinate to and economically dependent upon the American Colonization Society and, indirectly, the U.S. government. Thus, while African emigration represented opportunities for economic self-sufficiency and symbolized the reclamation of a lost homeland and a lost ancestry, Hayti represented cultural autonomy and political agency in the lived moment in a New World milieu.

When Loring Dewey, a white agent for the ACS, initiated a correspondence with Boyer in 1824 asking whether Hayti might be willing to receive African-American immigrants, the new president seized upon the inquiry as an opportunity to remedy Haytian economic and political problems and to strengthen the nation's ties with the United States. Both Boyer and the ACS would gain from the proposed arrangement. For Dewey and the ACS, who were finding enormous resistance among African Americans to Liberian emigration, the logic of a Haytian emigration program derived from "a preference of Hayti over Africa frequently expressed . . . among the Coloured People themselves."[15] For Boyer, an affiliation with the ACS offered an advantage similar to that enjoyed by the Liberian settlements: indirect alliance with the United States government. The prospect of African-American emigrants—both unskilled laborers who could revitalize the plantation economy and skilled artisans who could renew the urban economy—held enormous promise to the president. Yet, in the end, Boyer proved unwilling to accept de facto United States colonization.

Initially Boyer negotiated openly with Dewey concerning the details of the emigration program, and while he seemed eager to capitalize on the society's resources and political contacts, the Haytian president also clearly intended to protect Haytian political and cultural autonomy. He had no intention of allowing the ACS to colonize Hayti as it had Liberia. He insisted that the society and the Haytian government share the expenses of the voyage and that the immigrants "submit themselves to the laws of [Hayti]" rather than a legal system constructed by the ACS separate and apart from the host society, as had been the arrangement in

Liberia. Boyer assured Dewey that Hayti could provide adequate educational facilities and all immigrants would be provided "nourishment, tools, and other things of indispensable necessity until they shall be sufficiently established to do without this assistance." Artisans would be "exempted from the law of patent" for their first year of residence, allowed to practice their trade without a license otherwise required by the Haytian government. Boyer placed no numerical limit on either the number of immigrants who would be accepted nor on the amount of agricultural land allotted to them. Farm land, "as much as each family can cultivate," would be provided to the immigrants "in fee simple, to those who will cultivate it," and farmers would be settled near each other so as to foster "neighborhoods" among the immigrants, but on one point Boyer remained firm. The American Colonization Society would not be allowed to establish a territory in Hayti as it had in Liberia. Land would be provided in the form of grants direct to individual immigrants. No land would be sold to the ACS.[16]

Boyer acted quickly to put the administrative apparatus for the emigration program in place. He dispatched Jonathas Granville to the United States in May 1824 to serve as his agent for the emigration that would follow, and he charged General J. B. Inginac with responsibility for resettlement of the African-American immigrants once they had arrived in Hayti.[17] As Granville departed for the United States, Boyer simultaneously shipped "fifty thousand weight of coffee" to a New York agent. The president of the struggling republic had devised a bold and shrewd plan for financing his impoverished government's share of the emigration expenses. He instructed his New York agent to create a fund for paying the emigrants' passage from the United States to Hayti from the profits from the coffee sale. As the emigration program continued, Boyer intended to replenish the fund through additional shipments of commodities; a plan, he believed, that would, "facilitate the emigration of such individuals of the African race, who, groaning in the United States under the weight of prejudice and misery, should be disposed to come to Hayti and partake, with our citizens, of a liberal constitution." Jean Pierre Boyer had designed a scheme in which middle-class American consumers would finance the Haytian government's share of the emigration expenses.[18]

For Jonathas Granville, as for Prince Saunders, promotional efforts began in Philadelphia. There, and then in Boston and New York, Granville presented an appealing portrait of the opportunities African Americans would find in Hayti. He cited the successes of "children of

Africa, who have [already] come from the United States," probably under the agency of Prince Saunders, as material evidence of the opportunities he promised. Immigrants from that sporadic and brief emigration, he told those who gathered at the churches and in the halls of fraternal and mutual-aid societies, had already "fixed themselves . . . in the country, where cultivation repays their toil with interest, [and] others in our cities, where they are engaged in a lucrative trade, or pursue with advantage some mechanical profession."[19] With the assistance and the support of the Haytian Government, Granville assured his audiences, economic prosperity would be possible for all emigrants.

African Americans responded immediately and favorably to the Haytian emigration plan, which also received support and endorsement from a number of prominent white abolitionists. At the Elm Street Presbyterian Church in New York City, Peter Williams, Jr., and Samuel Cornish led a meeting of African Americans who favorably entertained President Boyer's proposal. Benjamin Lundy lent the voice of *The Genius of Universal Emancipation* to the enterprise, and some who entertained the prospect of emigration must have been reassured about the veracity of Granville's promotional promises by correspondence from previous African-American emigrants that appeared in Lundy's paper. Among the earliest was a letter posted by an African-American emigrant from Port-au-Prince on November 5, 1823 to a friend in New York City, reporting in detail that the Haytian government had supplied him all necessary farming equipment and implements. All that were printed confirmed safe arrivals and satisfactory initial settlement.[20]

During 1824 and 1825, the momentum for Haytian emigration steadily increased in the urban Northeast. In Philadelphia, under the leadership and guidance of Richard Allen, representatives of various churches formed a "committee to take into consideration the propriety of calling a public meeting" at which the merits of a renewed Haytian emigration might be openly debated.[21] At that meeting black Philadelphians endorsed Haytian emigration with the same fervor they had expressed in condemning the American Colonization Society's African emigration plan. In both Philadelphia and New York City, African Americans organized Haytian Emigration Societies and made clear their intentions to manage their own emigration plans to the (white) Society for Promoting the Emigration of Free Persons of Colour to Hayti.[22] In Boston, Baptist minister Thomas Paul vigorously supported and promoted emigration, declaring Hayti "the best and most suitable place of residence which Providence has hitherto offered to emancipated people of colour for the enjoyment of liberty and equality, with their attendant blessings."[23] Paul had lived in Hayti during 1823 and his personal familiarity with the country probably strengthened the credibility of his positive recommendation.

Richard Allen made independent inquiries, writing directly to General Inginac for confirmation of the Haytian government's promises to African-American emigrants and sending his son, John, to Hayti to conduct a personal inspection of conditions there. John Allen reported back to his father that he had been well received and looked forward to the arrival of his brother, Richard. Inginac, at the same time, advised the elder Allen that all emigrants who had arrived were settled in an appropriate fashion.[24] In Philadelphia, Richard Allen began to compile names of families who intended to make the voyage. With endorsements from Peter Williams, Jr., Samuel Cornish, John Summersett, Joseph Casey, and Russell Parrott, Haytian emigration began. (Summersett and Parrott were Haytian expatriates and their support for the emigration program makes its own statement about the powerful pull of memory.) By the spring months of 1825, approximately 700 African Americans were resettled in Hayti.[25]

Those who had gone out wrote back from Port-au-Prince, Santo Domingo, and Cape Haytian to friends and relatives in the United States, reporting their initial safe arrival and first impressions. Richard Allen sent Daniel Copeland's letter to Lundy. Others wrote to the editor directly. George Flower, who lived in Albion, Illinois, received news from his former neighbors, Arthur Jones and George Jann. They were settled in Port-au-Prince. Charles W. Fisher wrote to his father, who forwarded the letter on to Lundy for publication in the *Genius of Universal Emancipation*. Other African-American emigrants were making plans to move about ten miles out of town, Fisher reported, and he planned to go with them. The agriculturists were generally pleased. Some believed the prospect for cultivating fruit trees to be quite good, noted prompt delivery of materials and supplies the Haytian government had promised, described abundant vegetables and scarcity of meat in local markets, and commented on the relatively high prices of staple foods. Some promised to send coffee and fruit to their friends and kinspeople in the United States. All seemed satisfied with the circumstances surrounding their new lives.[26]

During the 1820s, an estimated 13,000 African Americans emigrated to Hayti. Some grew discouraged by the difficult conditions and moved on—generally to Jamaica—or returned to the United States. By mid-century, while the majority of the African-American emigrants remained "in the condition of day laborers, or worse," there were prosperous successes among those who had gone out to Hayti. In Port-au-Prince a Philadelphia artisan had become the proprietor of one of the finest cabinet-making shops in the city; the most skilled local sailmaker had apprenticed under James Forten; and an emigrant from New Orleans was reported to own a thriving bakery.[27]

SHAPING PAN-AFRICAN IMAGES

Before 1827 African Americans who stayed in the United States learned about the destinies of those who had emigrated to Hayti or to Liberia in only a limited fashion. Lundy's *Genius of Universal Emancipation* provided some coverage of the Haytian emigrants, and the American Colonization Society's annual reports and its *African Repository,* intended as much for recruitment as for any other purpose, were available to African-American audiences through churches and fraternal and benevolent societies. But prior to 1827, the bulk of the information African Americans received about their friends, neighbors, and kin who had quit the United States and gone out to Africa or Hayti probably came through erratic correspondence, the news in those letters home passed informally from person to person by word of mouth.

Samuel Cornish and John Russwurm were largely responsible for initiating a formal expansion of the African-American cultural map in the pages of *Freedom's Journal,* which began publication in 1827. The co-editors were predisposed to consider the Haytian and Liberian emigration ventures in a relatively positive fashion. Cornish had endorsed Haytian emigration as early as 1824. That year he and Peter Williams, Jr., had been delegated by New York City African Americans to act on behalf of black New Yorkers interested in Haytian emigration and to mediate with the Society for Promoting the Emigration of Free Persons of Colour to Hayti.[28] Russwurm, a native Jamaican, brought an implicitly transnational identity and consciousness to his editorship of the paper. As a result, while *Freedom's Journal* did not offer unconditional or uncritical endorsement of emigration, from the outset it brought a blend of history and current events concerning both Hayti and Liberia to the popular classes.

Freedom's Journal provided a wide range of journalistic and ethnographic information about Africa in general, ranging from reports of the continuing slave trade to descriptions of tribal life and lion hunts.[29] While

Cornish and Russwurm generally were critical of the ACS and cautious in their comments about Liberia's climate, they also were relatively generous in their coverage of the Liberian colonies, offering limited praise for their successes and relating reports of satisfaction among those who had settled there. By 1828 the paper's readers had followed the Americanization of Liberia for two years. They knew that cows had been introduced into the colony and that butchery and shipbuilding industries had been established in Monrovia. They were advised that Francis Devaney, high sheriff of the colony and the first black elected official from Liberia to visit the United States, had brought a horse into the colony and that several other colonists were awaiting the arrival of horses they had ordered. The bulk of the settlers, living along the coast, were involved in maritime trades but were "beginning to add both to their comfort and their independency by agriculture." Yet, the editors did not bypass the problems and difficulties of life in Liberia. They made note of houses not completed and limited financial resources, particularly among newer arrivals, and they described the conditions of those who were still living in "public houses" because they had not adjusted to the tropical climate and were unable to work.[30]

Throughout 1827 *Freedom's Journal* published a serialized column, *The Scrapbook of Africanus,* a richly textured narrative of Haytian history and culture. *Africanus* traced the "rapacity and insolence" of European colonization on the island and described the pre-Revolutionary circumstances of the *gens du couleur,* strikingly similar to the conditions endured by African Americans living in the Northern United States: they were "forbidden to hold any public trust or employment . . . not allowed to defend themselves against personal assaults . . . [and] could not enter into the priesthood, nor any of the professions."[31]

The column's readers could not have failed to make the connection between expectations engendered among the black Haytians by the 1789 French Revolution and the internal revolt that followed when those expectations were not met, and their own condition in the United States. *Africanus* traced the outline of the Haytian revolt from the initial outbreaks in 1791 through Rochambeau's withdrawal and Dessalines's proclamation of Haytian independence on January 1, 1804. Detailing the governmental structure of post-Revolutionary Hayti Dessalines had created, *Africanus* gave particular attention to the state-supported educational system and protections of citizens' civil rights. These changes were "most interesting and remarkable" because they had derived from the "energies of a people deemed but a step above the brute creation."

Africanus characterized contemporary Hayti as an island paradise where "winter never shows his hideous head" and a tropical climate kept all vegetation "in perpetual movement." Additionally, the columnist gave voice to a sense of political triumph probably current among many readers of *Freedom's Journal.* "The Republic of Hayti," *Africanus* declared, "exhibits a spectacle hitherto unseen in these modern and degenerate days: it is now demonstrated that the descendants of Africa are capable of self-government."[32]

Concurrent with the *Africanus* column, *Freedom's Journal* reprinted a biographical sketch of Toussaint L'Ouverture and an article that aimed to refute a contemporary New York *Enquirer* characterization of Mme. Christophe as "a fat, greasy wench . . . who would find it difficult to get a place as a Cook in this city." The *Freedom's Journal* editorialist, who claimed a personal friendship with Mme. Christophe, found her to be "a good and virtuous wife, an affectionate mother, and . . . a hospitable and charitable lady, who sought for and improved every opportunity of exercising these good qualities to all the foreigners at the Cape [Haytian]."[33]

The paper reported in detail the departure of a ship from Norfolk, Virginia, carrying some one hundred emancipated slaves who would be resettled in Hayti under a three-year sharecropping agreement arranged through Benjamin Lundy with the Haytian government. The agreement had been designed to reimburse the government for the expense of their passage. Despite the three-year indenture, *Freedom's Journal* declared, the men and women would be "emphatically free the moment they touch the soil of Hayti—under the protection of a republican government composed of their brethren."[34]

Over the paper's two-year life, its coverage of Hayti shifted gradually from the historical to the contemporary and spanned a wide range of issues: Mme. Christophe's exile to Florence; the state of public education; treaty negotiations with England and France; the plot to overthrow Jean Pierre Boyer; a summary of the nation's political and economic problems. A four-part fictional serialization of the Revolution that appeared during the 1828 issues cast a woman in an heroic role.[35] Regular readers gained a familiarity with the republic that strengthened its symbolic importance. Hayti had been firmly imprinted on the African-American cultural map, its history and heroes welded to the popular historical consciousness of African-American memory—a memory that now included an explicitly political story. On January 16, 1829, already making preparations for his own departure to Liberia that spring, John Russwurm declared Hayti favorable for African-American emigration.

While there are no circulation statistics for *Freedom's Journal*, the listing of agents carried on the masthead of each issue suggests the paper reached a relatively wide public. In the Southern, slave-holding states, with the exception of Charleston, the paper listed agents in all urban areas where free African Americans tended to cluster, as well as in Virginia and North Carolina Quaker communities. The press maintained agents in all major urban areas along the eastern seaboard from Washington to Boston, where David Walker represented *Freedom's Journal*; and agents in Albany and Rochester, New York, suggest the western edge of the paper's circulation. Agents also received issues of *Freedom's Journal* and provided the editors with local news from more removed locations in the Northern states: Princeton and Trenton, New Jersey; Hudson, Troy, and Utica, New York; New London, New Haven, and Norwich, Connecticut; Salem, Massachusetts; Portland and North Yarmouth, Maine; and Carlisle, Pennsylvania. *Freedom's Journal* also circulated in Port-au-Prince, Liverpool and Upper Canada during its brief life. The paper reached across the rigid if invisible line between slave and free states to provide a uniform body of images and information about everyday life in places geographically removed but spiritually immediate for many African Americans in the United States, places to which many had been and more would be drawn in subsequent decades by the promises of personal freedom and civic equality.

THE CANADIAN REFUGEES: "THICK AS BLACKBIRDS"

In the years after 1829, whether they settled in the Amherstburg area or in Wilberforce, in Dawn or in Elgin, the African Americans who emigrated to Canada during the antebellum period arrived as refugees, and prior to 1850 they were generally without resources and destined at least during the first generation to lives of poverty. The communities they built, often utopian in design—without support from the Canadian government or the colonization societies in the United States—reflected that poverty. To be sure, in Canada African Americans were free, but their freedom had been bought with great misery. Impoverished and with limited resources, drawn by the bonds of race and relying on the overarching principle of mutual aid that reinforced those bonds, the refugees turned to black communities in the United States for the financial support they needed to meet their basic daily needs. In turn, free African Americans traveled routinely and regularly to the Canadian settlements, and their reports of conditions there kept the Canadian refugee communities firmly located on the African-American cultural map. After 1850, when the Fugitive Slave Law drove an estimated fifteen to twenty thousand refugees into Canadian sanctuaries, concrete ties of friendship and kinship elaborated and strengthened the moral and spiritual bonds of race.

The Wilberforce settlers, like all refugees, were at a grave disadvantage from the outset of their arrival in Upper Canada. Greatly handicapped by a lack of financial resources, they issued a public appeal for financial support. The strategy they employed to advance that appeal, devised and directed by Rochester grocer Austin Steward, gave birth to the widely disputed and often corrupted "begging system." In its perfected form, agents for various Canadian settlements traveled through the United States representing the refugees, often quite accurately, as starving and suffering and raising sums of money on their behalf from African-American churches and mutual-aid societies. While the "begging system" fostered a certain level of transnational race unity, its success in terms of the benefits accrued by the refugees depended not only upon the charity and philanthropy of African Americans in the United States, but also upon the often problematic integrity of the soliciting agents.

Steward had first learned about the Wilberforce settlement and the desperate circumstances of the people who lived there at the 1830 Philadelphia convention, but the immediate force driving his move from Rochester to Wilberforce lay in a visit Israel Lewis made to Rochester. In a public appeal for money, Lewis gave a compelling account of suffering and poverty among the Cincinnatians then living on the Canadian lands they had purchased. Steward attended that meeting and, counting himself among the "more favored brethren in New York, felt a deep sympathy" for his outraged brothers and sisters. In Rochester, as elsewhere, that sympathy found expression through a formal declaration of solidarity with the Cincinnati refugees. Steward was especially moved by the conditions Lewis described, he explained, because "I had at that time just made a public profession of my faith in the Christian religion and . . . I felt for the distressed and suffering everywhere."[36]

His missionary zeal ignited, Steward went north to Toronto and then by hired wagon struck for the west, traveling through the Huron Trace, "one unbroken wilderness," to the Wilberforce settlement in Kent County, London District. He found a collection of a few rude log cabins, bordered on the south by an Irish community and on the west by a township of Welsh immigrants. Perhaps recalling his own enslavement, certainly moved by a people who had chosen poverty in order to obtain liberty, he determined to unite with the settlement "in the enterprise of building up an asylum for the oppressed." Steward envisioned a model community, "guiding by its beacon light of liberty, the destitute and oppressed everywhere, to home and plenty."[37]

Toward that idealized and romantic end, Steward founded and chaired the Free Colonization Board, an organization designed to raise money for the settlement and to encourage emigration to and resettlement in Wilberforce. The community appointed Israel Lewis and Benjamin and Nathaniel Paul, Baptist preachers in Boston and Albany and advocates of Haytian emigration, as agents for the board. The three men ultimately squandered most of the money they raised and were the source of an embarrassing scandal that publicly discredited the settlement. Yet their fund-raising activities created a public awareness about Wilberforce that probably solidified the ties many African Americans in the Northern states felt with the Canadian exiles. Benjamin Lundy and Samuel Cornish both made personal inspections of the community and reported the conditions they found there, and for a time many in the abolitionist community regarded Wilberforce as a model community built by "human fortitude and heroism, a haven for fugitives from slavery."[38]

In 1837, disillusioned and exhausted, Steward quit Wilberforce and returned to Rochester, where he resumed his grocery business. Under the editorial control of Samuel Cornish, *The Colored American* condemned the settlement and disavowed its efforts to raise money among African Americans in the United States. Putting the Wilberforce experiment behind him, Steward aligned with Cornish and served as the paper's Rochester agent. Reentering black politics, he presided over the 1840 Convention of the Colored Inhabitants of the State of New York and the 1841 State Convention of Colored Citizens. Both conventions organized African Americans' demands for suffrage in the state of New York. Neither addressed the matter of emigration in general nor the situation of the Canadian refugees in particular.

Even as the Wilberforce disgrace was made public, other attempts to construct utopian communities in Canada proceeded. The Dawn settlement near Chatham, Canada West, as well as the Elgin-Buxton and Windsor settlements, derived from intentional and philanthropically motivated efforts at community-building. Dawn grew out of biracial collaboration, Elgin-Buxton from white philanthropy, and Windsor from African-American initiatives.

The community at Dawn grew up around a manual-labor school established in 1840 through joint efforts by the American Anti-Slavery

Society and the British-American Institute. While Dawn did not suffer from the corruption that had stained Wilberforce in the perceptions of African Americans living in the United States, the refugees who had settled on rented farms in the area before the school was opened were inexperienced in the details and nuance of agricultural management. They tended to "hire wild land on short terms" or concentrate on a single cash crop, usually tobacco. As a result, many had been unable to produce a profitable crop within the limited terms of their leases or, if they did manage to clear the land and get a crop within the terms of their leases, they then artificially glutted the market and unintentionally depressed the price of their crop.[39]

As Austin Steward had held a vision for Wilberforce, fugitive slave Josiah Henson held one for Dawn. Emphasizing the crucial importance of economic self-sufficiency and working within a structural framework that consigned African Americans to the least-skilled and lowest-paid jobs, Henson combined land ownership with a manual training school: "where boys could be taught . . . the practice of some mechanic art, and the girls could be instructed in those domestic arts which are the proper occupation and ornament of their sex." A similar educational philosophy would guide the education of emancipated slaves in the Southern states during Reconstruction. In collaboration with Hiram Wilson, one of the Lane Rebels who had traveled to Canada during 1836 to investigate the circumstances of the refugees, Henson guided the development of the school and the surrounding lands.[40] By the early 1840s refugee settlers in the area had acquired title to some 1,500 acres of land "covered with a beautiful forest of noble trees" that the settlers cleared by cutting and burning. Henson recognized the market potential of the forest and raised money for a sawmill. The settlers at Dawn entered into the Canadian lumber industry with an "astonishing" sale of milled black walnut in Boston that earned both a substantial monetary profit and the support of Boston abolitionists.[41]

Despite management problems at the school, the Dawn settlement continued to attract African-American fugitives, who virtually streamed into the Chatham area in the years after 1850. At times the new arrivals seemed "thick as blackbirds" to long-term Dawn residents. Connected by steamboat to Detroit and Buffalo, the Chatham area grew rapidly after the enactment of the Fugitive Slave Law, and its resources were limited. But the community had a strong sense of self-sufficiency and despite the stresses associated with absorbing the new arrivals, the established residents at Dawn rejected the "begging system." The Chatham "True Band"—a refugee organization popular throughout the Canadian settlements that promoted local autonomy through school development, moderated local disputes, raised funds for poor and sick relief, and unconditionally condemned the "begging system"—had 375 members at Dawn. Relying on the principles of mutual aid and self-help, the Dawn community, while never particularly prosperous, managed to absorb many of the refugee immigrants who arrived after 1850. Frederick Douglass, invited by the Dawn "Friends of Freedom" to speak at the community's 1854 First of August celebration—the celebration of the abolition of slavery in the British West Indies that was also commemorated by African Americans in the United States—reported productive and thriving fields and well-tended livestock on land equivalent to that in western New York.[42]

The Elgin Association and Buxton Mission was the product of (white) William King's philanthropic and Christian vision. During the 1840s King inherited and then emancipated fifteen slaves. Ohio laws prohibited their permanent resettlement there, and King made plans to relocate the group to Canada. The fifteen spent their first free winter on King's Ohio farm learning the artisanal and mechanical skills that King believed would ease their resettlement. The fifteen ultimately formed the core of a community that, within a decade, had grown to one hundred fifty families. A school, grist and sawmills, brick and potash manufactories, a savings bank, a Baptist church, and prosperous farms raised Elgin and Buxton well above the subsistence level typical of other Canadian refugee settlements.[43] The bulk of the settlers at Elgin, like those in other parts of Canada, were refugees from slavery, but some were free-born Northerners who, like Henry Johnson, had been attracted to Elgin in order to "educate my children." Johnson had lived twenty-three years in Massillon, Ohio and made a decent living there draying and carting. But when his children were "thrust out of the schools" he packed up his family and moved to Elgin. Still, Henry Johnson and his family were the exception rather than the rule among the Canadian emigrants.

Like Austin Steward and William King, Henry Bibb, the architect of the controversial Refugee Home Society, had a vision of African-American self-sufficiency. He organized the Refugee Home Society in Michigan in 1851 with a single agenda: to purchase and redistribute Canadian lands to "refugees from American slavery."[44] An escaped slave, Bibb brought to his vision and his plan twelve years of personal freedom and eight years of experience on the western Ohio abolitionist lecture circuit. During the 1850s the society purchased and redistributed some three thousand acres of land in the area around Windsor, Ontario, well short of a declared 30,000-acre purchase. Perhaps recalling the details of the Wilberforce scandal, African-American leaders criticized Bibb deeply for his use of the "begging system" to raise funds for the land purchase and for his segregationist philosophy. Mary Ann Shadd charged that Bibb's agents withheld 20 to 25 percent of their collections for personal use.[45] Shadd and Bibb conducted a war of words through their respective newspapers, *The Provincial Freeman* (Shadd) and *The Voice of the Fugitive* (Bibb), and Bibb created a wider audience for the work of the Refugee Home Society through his correspondence with the American abolitionist press, publicly criticizing both Frederick Douglass and William Lloyd Garrison, reporting the settlement of fugitives on society lands, and otherwise countering his critics at every opportunity. Bibb's community, Windsor, was incorporated in 1854, the year of his death. Many of the local families were known to "entertain as boarders a number of fugitives from bondage."[46] Bibb's widow maintained a private school established by the Refugee Home Society. While the community did not achieve the level of prosperity that marked the Elgin settlement, the families who settled there eventually forged an enduring community.

Despite widespread controversy and public criticism, Windsor, the community that grew up around the Refugee Home Society lands, received its share of the post-1850 African-American emigrants seeking asylum and sanctuary in the Canadian settlements. Bibb reported constant arrivals throughout 1851 and 1852. Chester, Pennsylvania agents for the Underground Railroad made a personal visit to Windsor in preparation for forwarding a particularly large group of fugitives. Bibb reported that many who arrived in the community fleeing the new repression surrounding the Fugitive Slave Law were "men of capital with good property, some of whom are worth thousands." This new group of refugees reflected the tenor of the times. In Pittsburgh "nearly all the waiters in the hotels fled to Canada" and the Columbia, Pennsylvania African-American population dropped from 943 to 487 in 1850. Like the *gens du couleur* half a century earlier, the new Canadian refugees were a part of a New World Diaspora as the descendants of Africa continued their search for a stable home in a stable place. Many had left what had once been secure homes in Northern cities to escape the threat posed by the fugitive slave legislation.[47]

Windsor was not alone in experiencing this heartrending population explosion. After 1850 tens of thousands of refugees poured into Canada

West, to the Wilberforce, Dawn, Elgin, and Buxton settlements. Some arrived in groups, others "one-by-one," dropping by in a deceptively casual fashion, all driven by a fear far more powerful than the pull of opportunity that had drawn Henry Johnson to Elgin. At the United States–Canadian border some found temporary housing in government barracks, but many simply encamped along the waterways and waited for transportation inland. "Each boat up the river carried as many as could stand upon its decks" and those who could not find a space struck out on foot through the Canadian woods in search of one of the agricultural communities they knew to be there. At Elgin they generally found the residents "as busy as bees, chopping, burning, boiling, singing, [and] talking," and many decided they had found a new home.[48]

The Elgin community was well known throughout Northern white abolitionist and African-American circles and it was highly respected. In large measure, that respect derived from the order and productivity King had fostered through the Elgin Association. The stock company provided the apparatus for financing land ownership—an approach to self-sufficiency Wilberforce and Dawn organizers had rejected, but that would serve as a model for Henry Bibb's Refugee Home Society—and it administered local affairs. Through regulations attached to land ownership embedded in the financing agreement, the Elgin Association established and maintained housing standards for land purchasers. Lands purchased through the association would not be resold to a white person for ten years, nor could those lands be rented or sharecropped until the mortgage had been paid in full. The association also required that houses built on lands the organization had financed measure eight by six meters, be four meters high, and be set back from the road eight meters. All front yards had to be enclosed by a picket fence. Each house lot had to have a drainage ditch, and residents were required to maintain a garden inside the required picket fence.

King's design had the desired effect. Frederick Douglass observed a pride and self-assurance among the Elgin residents that set them apart from other Canadian refugees:

> There the people have thrown off the bowed down look of slaves and menials. They bear themselves like free men and women . . . the evidences of material progress do not surpass those showing a solid moral and intellectual growth.

King's experiment in philanthropy had succeeded, and while the community never entirely freed itself of King's benevolent and removed guidance, Elgin residents elected a representative to Parliament in 1856.[49] Despite their Canadian citizenship, however, the Elgin and Buxton residents never entirely relinquished their American identity. When Lincoln called for the recruitment of black troops in 1863, forty Elgin men enlisted immediately and an additional thirty followed them into the ranks of the Union Army within weeks. Organized as the 24th Kent Regiment of Militia, the men joined Union troops at Detroit. Two years later word reached the community that the Freedman's Bureau would be selling plantation lands to blacks. Acting on an essentially American identity, the community voted to return to the United States and to recreate Elgin on a grand scale. Each resident would purchase several hundred acres of cotton land and the purchases would be made on contiguous tracts. While they were unable to translate that dream into a reality, the men and women at Elgin had nonetheless made clear the tenacious and enduring nature of their national identity.[50]

THE NEW EMIGRATIONISTS

John Russwurm and Benjamin Roberts quit the United States in 1829 and went out to Liberia. Russwurm edited the *Liberian Herald* for a time and then took his place in the political structure of the new republic, serving as governor of Cape Palmas until his death in 1851. Roberts, a successful merchant and trader, advanced through several political posts to president of the republic. He held the office through five reelections, from the moment of Liberian independence in 1847 until 1876. Reverend Alexander Crummell emigrated to Liberia in 1852, fully a generation after Russwurm and Roberts went out to build a nation. During the intervening years more than seven thousand other African Americans had gone out to Liberia.

The colony spread out from Monrovia to settlements in Edina and Bossa Cove. The Maryland Colonization Society settled the Cape Palmas Region. Gradually, Paul Cuffe's vision had become a reality, although Cuffe probably would not have fully recognized Liberia as the offspring of Christian benevolence he had envisioned. Still, African Americans had settled on the African west coast, had built schools and churches where they carried out their Christian mission to educate and evangelize, and had established trading and mercantile centers that, at times by force, disrupted then brought to a slow and grinding halt the hideous traffic in slaves. Martin Delany enjoyed a restful stop at Monrovia before he moved on to his rendezvous with Robert Campbell.[51]

Hezekiah Grice quit the United States and went to Hayti in 1832. Working for a time as a gilder and carver, he, like other African Americans there, survived Boyer's forced resignation and flight into Jamaican exile and several subsequent political regimes. Grice served as director of Public Works for Port-au-Prince from 1843 through 1854. African Americans continued to emigrate to Hayti through the antebellum period, their numbers rising and falling with the country's internal political stability.

The National Emigration Convention met at Cleveland in 1854. The delegates developed an eight-point proposal for emigration to Hayti, which they presented the following year to Faustin I. They requested: private homesteads; guarantees of civil, political, and religious equality; a seven-year exemption from military service; government assistance to develop private enterprise, with promises of reimbursement through anticipated profits; duty-free importation of tools, machinery, and personal goods; and Haytian citizenship. The work of that convention revived interest in Haytian emigration, and following six years of negotiation James Redpath was appointed chief agent of the Haytian Bureau of Emigration. *Douglass' Monthly* carried full-page advertisements paid for by the Haytian government to attract emigrants for the program. William Wells Brown approved the plan. Emigrants massed at Ripley, Ohio, Lewiston, Pennsylvania, New Haven, Connecticut, and Rochester, New York. In the pages of the *Weekly Anglo-African* Hezekiah Grice reported that in Port-au-Prince there had been public mourning at the moment of John Brown's execution.

Henry Highland Garnet organized the African Civilization Society. Delany proposed emigration for the most talented. David Christy published his *Lectures on African Colonization,* reviewed in *The Aliened American,* published in Cleveland, as containing "many truths and untruths." Reverend George Thompson, a missionary to the Mendi Mission, wrote *Letters to Sabbath School Children,* a book that described the geography and animals of Africa as well as the social conditions of Africans. The book was readily available at Thomas Hamilton's bookshop in New York City. The pages of *The Anglo-African Magazine* were filled with tales of the now-ended slave trade and poetry extolling the beauties of an African sunset. The 1839 revolt of kidnapped Africans on the schooner *Amistad,* which became a cause célèbre in the United States, brought a fresh infusion of African images and memories into the United States milieu. The 1839-1841 campaign to free the *Amistad* Africans raised for public review the specter of slavery and the glories of an unspoiled Africa, as embodied in Joseph Cinque, the leader of the revolt and primary spokesperson for the group while they were imprisoned. John Quincy Adams, then in his seventies, pled their case before the United States Supreme Court, which freed them in February 1841. During the time the *Amistad* Africans were imprisoned, the abolitionist press made much of the captives, who then helped in the campaign to raise money for their return to Sierra Leone by speaking and making public appearances throughout the New England states, New York, and Pennsylvania.[52]

The memories of half a century crystallized in African-American literature and politics after 1850. William Wells Brown characterized Toussaint, the Liberator as "dignified, calm . . . [and] endowed by nature with high qualities of mind." In Brown's invented past, Boyer had been "a brave man, a good soldier, and . . . a statesman of no ordinary ability." Of the Liberians, all were lost except Roberts, a man Brown described tepidly as "thoroughly devoted to the interests of the rising republic." Yet Brown praised the controversial Henry Bibb for his brave battle "against tremendous odds" and for his rise "from an ignorant slave . . . to an educated freeman." Brown noted only in passing Garnet's "interest in behalf of emigration to Africa" and Delany's concern with African civilization, but made special note of Theodore Holly's devoted effort to develop a "Negro Nationality."

Biography, Narrative, and Memory: The Construction of a Popular Historical Consciousness

. . . if you give a people a thorough understanding of what it is that confronts them, and the basic causes that produce it, they'll create their own program: and when the people create a program, you get action.
—Malcolm X, 1965[1]

IN 1841 THE REVEREND J. W. C. PENNINGTON (1809-1870), fugitive slave, Presbyterian minister, abolitionist, and political activist, published *A Text-Book on the Origins and History . . . of the Colored People.* Pennington intended the slim, vest-pocket-sized volume, regarded by some as the first effort by an African American to trace and record the history of Africans and their descendants in North America, to be more than the illumination of a lost past. The *Text-Book* had immediate and practical applications. "We suffer much," Pennington wrote in the introduction, "from the want of a collocation of historical facts so arranged as to present a just view of our origin." Suffering had assumed many forms in antebellum America: enslavement; physical violence; social segregation; political disfranchisement; economic marginalization. In constructing a common and heroic African ancestry that transcended and preceded New World enslavement, Pennington had created an intellectual apparatus he believed would render impotent the assumptions of racial inferiority that shaped the contemporary contours of African-American sufferings.

The volume could not and did not counter white racial attitudes. It did, however, formalize an African-American intellectual tradition that redefined the boundaries as well as the content of a collective past by grounding that past in historical consciousness rather than autobiographical memory and by subordinating the particularized and individualized to larger explanations of events and processes. In this manner, individual fate—"good" fortune and "bad" luck—could be reinterpreted and understood as products of larger historical and cultural patterns of normative behavior, of socially structured arrangements of power. Similarly, outcomes—human successes and failures—could be interpreted as the evidence of human agency rather than of foreordained destiny. Historical consciousness is a way of understanding and interpreting individual biography, a process whereby the individual and the autobiographical is collectivized and generalized.[2]

Responding to a complex set of contemporary political and cultural circumstances, African Americans in the antebellum North were, by 1840, a people reaching for a new body of tradition and myth. Pennington wrote for that generation in transition from autobiographical memory to a broader cultural and historical consciousness that could authenticate personal identity through affiliation with collective representations anchored in the moral authority of a legitimized ancestry. Atomized memories of an African homeland and personal experiences of American slavery had faded for many African Americans living in the Northern United States by the time Pennington published the *Text-Book*. Those who had enjoyed the marginal benefits that followed from the abolition of slavery in the North sought an explanation of their collective past that welded African ancestry to a New World heritage accumulated across many generations. The popular historical consciousness that emerged from that milieu after 1840 fused the particularized memories of the past to a politicized vision of the future.

The welding of past to present and the crafting of a political agenda informed by that union took place at a revolutionary intersection of social movements and demographic shifts in antebellum America. In particular, the numerical growth of the free African-American population in the Northern states, and the expansion of a literate public within that population, combined with two great civil rights movements— the (biracial) anti-slavery movement and the (African-American) Convention Movement. The resulting political climate nurtured an intellectual and literary tradition that Pennington formalized with the publication of the *Text-Book*.

Neither Pennington nor the others who shaped and elaborated this tradition were trained in techniques of formal historical inquiry. They often omitted, distorted, and combined events and details in ways that would be dismissed if subjected to current standards of scholarly evaluation. Nevertheless, their writings trace the terrain between individual memory derived from a "lived" past and the self-consciously constructed historical myth of a collectively "remembered" past, and their work illuminates how a people reshapes its corporate identity for specifically political or ideological purposes. Anticipating the meticulous historical study of George Washington Williams and the critical social commentaries of W. E. B. DuBois, Pennington constructed a collective African-American past that incorporated a common, if distant, African homeland, but more directly focused on African-American involvement in the post-Diaspora, New World political arena. William Cooper Nell and William Wells Brown, also members of that generation in intellectual transition, contributed their own relocations and redefinitions of African Americans on the American cultural map.

In *Colored Patriots of the American Revolution* William Cooper Nell Africanized American military heroism, lifting individual recollections from the repository of the particular and framing those recollections as representations of a race. Explaining that "a combination of circumstances has veiled from the public eye a narrative of these military services [that] are generally conceded as passports to the honorable and lasting notice of Americans," Nell intended to counter antebellum racism by expanding the historical realities of the Revolutionary Era. By documenting the military heroism of African Americans, Nell claimed that passport for them and formalized the central element of the antebellum African-American political agenda: the demand for full and unconditional citizenship. Nell's inventory of African-American military service in the Revolutionary Era stretched from New England to the Carolinas and made formal and public the connection between a collective American past and the contemporary American political climate. Locating the origins of that past in a specific historical and geographical setting, *Colored Patriots* established the symbolic connection between past and present in American ancestral heroism and patriotism and rendered public a body of memories that previously had been contained and preserved in the more private loci of personal recall. In the pages of *Colored Patriots,* Nell legitimized African-American claims on the American Revolution as a site in which historical consciousness and memory crystallized.

Like Nell, William Wells Brown created sites of historical consciousness and memory in a series of individualized and particularized pasts that, while anchored in heroic historical moments, fueled a clearly contemporary political agenda. Brown intended *The Black Man: His Antecedent, His Achievements, and His Genius* to serve two interconnected functions. First, the text broadened the African-American remembered past both geographically and structurally. The figures Brown selected for inclusion in his first biographical dictionary reflected a Pan-African impulse that had emerged and matured in New World milieux. Henry Bibb represented the Canadian refugee settlements and Alexander Crummell, Joseph Cinque, and J. J. Roberts described the spectrum of connections between African Americans and Africa. Henri Christophe, Andre Rigaud, Jean Jacques Dessalines, Edward Jordan, Alexandre Petion, and Toussaint L'Ouverture were publicly declared African-American heroes, and the Haytian Revolution and the republic that resulted were drawn into the domain of African-American historical consciousness. The sketches of Charlotte Forten, Frances Ellen Watkins Harper, and Phillis Wheatley reflected the vigorous presence of African-American women in the public arenas of antebellum life and illuminated a major cultural distinction between the white middle-class ideal of womanhood and the African-American middle-class reality of women actively and publicly engaged in community-building.

Second, Brown, like William Cooper Nell, had employed the broadened African-American memory he had constructed as a direct attack on the prevailing assumption of African and African-American inferiority. The collection of biographical sketches would, Brown believed, "aid in vindicating the Negro's character, and show that he is endowed with those intellectual and amiable qualities which adorn and dignify human nature." As they expanded African-American identity, the heroic figures in *Black Man* would also revise the contours of white Americans' attitudes toward race.[3]

Memory—private as well as cultural—is shaped within both historical context and cultural milieu; African-American perceptions of slavery and freedom, dominant themes in both personal and cultural African-American memories, varied widely during the antebellum period. John Marrant, Oladuduh Equiano, Lemeul Haynes, and Jarana Lee, for example, writing in real time rather than reconstructed time, reflected both the ordeal of Africans and their descendants and a broader autobiographical tradition that prevailed during the late eighteenth and early nineteenth centuries.[4] As autobiographers, they wrote of singular and unique spiritual experiences. As Africans and African-Americans, they generally credited their religious awakening to Christian salvation within a Euro-American cultural tradition. Whether or not they were African-born, the spiritual autobiographers implicitly portrayed enslavement as the vehicle for their salvation.

Not all African-American writing from this period, however, had such an intensely personal focus. Concurrent with the autobiographers, a small group of clergy and other community leaders of mutual-aid societies and fraternal organizations produced a body of writing that critically commented on the condition of Africans in the New World.[5] Their sermons and addresses, published in pamphlet form, were printed and distributed primarily in the urban centers along the Northeastern seaboard—Philadelphia, New York City, and Boston. Circulation was circumscribed by the limitations of both literacy and demography. These imprints contrasted sharply with the writings of the spiritual autobiographers. Addressing larger African-American audiences, they assumed Christianization even as they drew on images of a common African heritage to shape a moral community of Africans and their descendants in the New World. Jupiter Hammon, for example, began his *Address to the Negroes of New-York* with a warm, fraternal greeting, "My Beloved African Brethren," and Prince Hall used similar language—"Dear African Brethren"—in private correspondence.[6] Within the protected terrain of that moral community, the sermons and addresses reflected, both slaves and the quasi-free would find the spiritual strength and resources to survive with dignity in a fundamentally hostile environment.

Neither the spiritual autobiographers nor the pamphleteers advanced explicit protests against enslavement. To the contrary, they advocated acceptance and emphasized spiritual and moral development within the limitations that had been imposed on Africans in the New World. Even as the sermons were preached and the addresses delivered, however, the audience for African-American writings began to broaden considerably. A complex educational apparatus constructed by Free African Societies and African churches separate and apart from white society elevated the literacy levels in Northern African-American communities. At the same time, African Americans, like their white neighbors, had pushed back the boundaries of the American frontier. By the early decades of the nineteenth century increasing numbers of African Americans lived in the towns and cities radiating out from the urban centers of the eastern seaboard, and the ranks of those communities had been swelled by Southern slaves who had slipped across the Ohio and Delaware Rivers, eager for personal freedom.

This population, which had expanded both demographically and educationally, sought more than survival with dignity, and it embraced the timely intellectual perspective advanced by Samuel Cornish and John Russwurm, the editors of *Freedom's Journal*. Cornish and Russwurm openly challenged the notion of survival through subordination and segregation. In contrast to the spiritual autobiographies and pamphlets that issued from churches and mutual-aid societies, the editors of *Freedom's Journal* initiated a tradition of critical social commentary that informed African-American journalism throughout the antebellum period and beyond. From the outset, the two journalists invoked the common African ancestry on which the earlier pamphleteers had drawn to shape a moral community. Yet the African-American press pursued an explicitly political rather than implicitly moral agenda, manipulating the symbolism of common ancestry to unify public opinion and mobilize collective action. Pennington, Nell, Brown, and William Still helped shape the contours of that press.

When Pennington's *Text-Book* appeared in 1841, however, the most popular contemporary printed accounts of an African-American past recalled the tradition of Equiano and Marrant. These autobiographical narratives, written by fugitive slaves in real time rather than remembered, or reconstructed time, circulated widely, their production fueled and financed by British and American abolitionists. In these texts personal experiences of enslavement and escape were transformed into politicized condemnations of slavery through the vehicle of memoir. From Equiano to Douglass, from the Revolution to the Civil War, the heroes who emerged through the pastiche of life events were victims who had triumphed, first spiritually, then materially, over the adversity of enslavement.

Like the eighteenth-century autobiographies, these personal accounts of tragedy and triumph were rhetorical devices, and although they were widely read by African Americans, they were intended primarily for white readerships: the British and American politicians who debated the legality of slavery; the zealots of the transatlantic abolitionist movement; the pious Protestants who held forth to still-enslaved African Americans a promise of spiritual salvation in lieu of physical freedom. There was in these narratives a poverty of formal knowledge about the shared African heritage that predated the African Diaspora, perhaps reflecting the stigma attached to that heritage—particularly after the organization of the American Colonization Society in 1817—as well as the political agenda of the anti-slavery movement.

In contrast to the earlier spiritual autobiographies, the fugitive autobiographies routinely embraced American rather than African ancestry and claimed an American birthright. They aimed not to interpret a common heritage but to condemn a common fate. J. W. C. Pennington would, himself, produce such an autobiography, *The Fugitive Blacksmith* (London, 1849), as would William Wells Brown. But the *Text-Book,* which preceded Pennington's autobiography by eight years, stretched across time and space to ancient Africa, forging a heritage from the raw material of popular belief, mythology, and Biblical lore.

The generation of African Americans to whom Pennington, Nell, and Brown belonged, writing half a century or more after the spiritual autobiographers and the pamphleteers, similarly reflected a cultural mandate that was tied to a particular historical moment. They shaped and nurtured race pride through constructed historical memory. Informed by the principles of the early-nineteenth-century moral community and the ideas of the Enlightenment that had been taught in African schools and preached from the pulpits of African churches for two generations, they advocated a political community that rejected racial separatism in favor of a pluralistic society.

POLITICS, CONSCIOUSNESS, AND MEMORY

At the onset of the 1840s, the white-dominated abolitionist movement, the African-American Convention Movement, and the flow of emigrants to Canada, Hayti, and Africa offered competing solutions to the increasingly troublesome and controversial dilemma African Americans presented to a democratic society. Like many free blacks in the North, J. W. C. Pennington bitterly opposed the efforts of the American Colonization Society, aligned himself with the abolitionist cause, and was actively engaged in the politics of the Convention Movement.[7] These two affiliations were a common combination among the African American elite: abolitionism provided the organized connection between the free and slave populations, and the Convention Movement served as the vehicle through which African Americans throughout the North established and maintained translocal political coalitions. Yet, for Pennington as for others—participants in a moral crusade that included but went well beyond the slavery issue—the frequent contradictions between the two movements were not easily reconciled. Pennington's *Text-Book* vividly illustrates the nature of those contradictions.

The *Text-Book* mirrored the Convention Movement's emphasis on a racial unity that included the slaves even as it simultaneously transcended slavery. While the *Text-Book* defined that unity in terms of a common African ancestry and the Convention Movement did so in terms of a common New World heritage, both Pennington's book and the movement contrasted sharply with the abolitionist emphasis on slavery and the not altogether benign neglect of the economic and political disadvantages free African Americans endured. Additionally, although both the Convention Movement and the abolitionists aimed to eradicate slavery, the abolitionists were only nominally committed to securing the civil equality that the Convention Movement advocated and demanded. Pennington's *Text-Book* buttressed that demand by disclaiming the barbarism of an African heritage with evidence of pre-Diaspora African achievements in religion, science, and nation-building.

Still a fugitive when the *Text-Book* appeared, Pennington had escaped from his Maryland master in 1827, at the age of eighteen, but would not be purchased and manumitted by Connecticut abolitionists until 1851. Like many other fugitives, he had found sanctuary in the North and there became an active and visible public figure through his anti-slavery work.[8] Had his public career followed a more standard path, Pennington's autobiography would have preceded the *Text-Book*. Yet it did not.

While the full range of forces that inspired Pennington will never be known, his focus on Africa had many precedents in African-American cultural imagery. The names of churches, schools, mutual and fraternal societies—many initially organized during the decades immediately following the Revolution—made public a self-proclaimed bond with Africa. Whether or not Pennington drew consciously from this symbolism, the *Text-Book* thematically followed a well-established tradition of affiliation with African environments of memory.

At the same time, Pennington probably had been sensitized to the African issue through his involvement with the thirty-nine kidnapped Africans who had revolted against the captain of the Cuban ship *Amistad*. The group, led by Joseph Cinque, attempted to return from Cuba to the African west coast but, having no knowledge of navigation, ended up in shallow water off the Long Island–Connecticut coast. The *Amistad* was impounded by the U.S. Coast Guard and the Africans were jailed as mutineers and pirates. Their situation became an abolitionist movement cause célèbre when Louis Tappan and others formed the "*Amistad* Committee" to raise money for the Africans' legal defense against claims by the Spanish government that both the boat and the "mutineers" were property of Spanish citizens. The case, eventually decided by the U.S. Supreme court in 1841, freed the Africans but affirmed the legal claims of one person on another.

As the pastor at the Talcott Street (Presbyterian) Church in Hartford, Pennington had ministered to the Africans while they languished in the Hartford jail from their initial imprisonment in 1839 until the 1841 Supreme Court decision that freed them; he had helped raise the moneys to resettle them in Sierra Leone following their release. Perhaps through his work with the kidnapped and then imprisoned Africans he had gained fresh understanding of the historical continuities linking African Americans to contemporary Africa during that period.[9]

Self-educated and unrestricted by the conventional rules of evidence that inform the inquiry of academic historians, Pennington arranged the *Text-Book* like a catechism, in a question and answer format, and the book, as the title suggests, had a clear instructional, or educational purpose. It could be used, Pennington explained in his preface, as a quick and ready reference by "families and students and lecturers," presumably black, who might be called on to discuss any number of potentially controversial issues: the racial and cultural origins of African Americans; the slave trade, and its connection to Western Christendom; the intellectual potential and capacities of Africans and African Americans, as compared to Americans of European descent; American race prejudice.

Pennington may have intended his *Text-Book* as an aid to rhetorical exchanges between informed African Americans and whites who lacked a "just view" of the origins of African Americans, or as an educational tool to be used within the black community, or both. In either case, he had crafted a popular and well received book. The *Text-Book* ran through three editions during its first year of publication. It filled an enormous knowledge vacuum among a people whose ancestral memories had been deformed by the middle passage, seasoning in the island, enslavement, and half-freedom on the North American continent.

The state and regional conventions that began in 1840 foreshadowed the formal break between a number of black abolitionists and William Lloyd Garrison. Opposition to Garrison's doctrine of moral suasion erupted publicly when, against his counsel, Frederick Douglass moved to Rochester in 1847 and began publishing *The North Star*. Emphasizing race unity between free and enslaved African Americans, the political climate of state and regional conventions became the catalyst for intensified professional coalitions and personal alliances among African Americans who worked in the biracial anti-slavery movement.

The public careers of William Wells Brown, William Cooper Nell, William Still, a young African-American employee of the Pennsylvania anti-slavery society who would become the first chronicler of the Underground Railroad, and Frances Ellen Watkins Harper, anti-slavery lecturer, political activist, poet, and reformer, clearly illustrate this process. Born within a few years of each other, the four lived distinctly different lives until the 1840s, when they were drawn to black radicalism and a developing intellectual tradition that profoundly influenced their thinking and shaped their writings. While they differed in historical focus, each elaborated the theme of racial unity that centered the movement ideologically. As a result, through their writings they shaped a richly textured sense of race pride that established continuity with an African-American past and anticipated an African-American future.

William Cooper Nell (1816-1874) was born and raised in Boston, the son of Revolutionary War veteran William G. Nell. He probably learned his first lessons about black soldiering from his father, and his first lessons about slavery and social activism from both the elder Nell and David Walker. Nell's father, a tailor by trade, maintained a shop on Brattle Square during the 1820s only a few doors removed from David Walker's used-clothing store. Both men were members of the General Colored Association of Massachusetts, a regional abolitionist society that predated but in 1833 sought and received auxiliary affiliation with Garrison's New England Anti-Slavery Society. In 1830, the year Walker was murdered, he and the Nell family were neighbors, both living on Bridge Street. William Cooper Nell was fourteen that year.[10]

Nell's formal education came at Boston's African School. There he was an excellent student, eligible to receive the prestigious Franklin Medal, an award given by the Boston School Committee each year for outstanding scholarship. Nell was denied that honor because of his race. In his adulthood he recalled the incident as a primary motivating factor in his campaign to achieve racial equality in the Massachusetts school system.[11]

William Wells Brown (1814-1884) spent his slave childhood on a Missouri farm working as a field hand. Taken to St. Louis in 1827, he received his education by working as a physician's assistant, a hotel servant, a slave trader's assistant, and, briefly, a printer's assistant for

Elijah P. Lovejoy. He attempted to escape slavery twice, the first time unsuccessfully with his mother in 1833, when he was nineteen. After mother and son were recaptured, Brown watched as his mother was sold to a slave trader and shipped down the Mississippi River. Two years later, while working as a boat hand, Brown accomplished alone that which he and his mother together had been unable to do. He casually walked off a steamboat in Cincinnati in 1835 and made his way to Cleveland on foot. He was twenty-one that year. From Cleveland, Brown moved on to Buffalo, where he organized a local temperance society in 1836, and in 1840 he traveled to Hayti and Cuba. During his first five years of freedom Brown made a remarkable transition from slave to political activist. By the age of twenty-six he had become an established figure in the anti-slavery movement, a popular and entertaining lecturer as well known for his ability to rouse a crowd with song as for his fiery oratory.[12]

William Still (1821-1902) also had a rural childhood, and while Still had been free-born, his family had been fractured by slavery. His parents, two sisters, and two brothers had been slaves in rural Maryland. His father bought his own freedom and moved to New Jersey to make a new life for himself. His mother had followed as a fugitive, bringing the four children with her to join her free husband. She had been recaptured and returned to Maryland with the children, only to make a second, successful escape by leaving her two sons—Still's older brothers—in the care of her slave mother. William Still was the youngest of the fifteen children his parents produced in their freedom.[13]

Frances Ellen Watkins (1825-1911) was born free in Baltimore, orphaned at the age of three, and educated in Baltimore at a private school organized by her uncle, the Reverend William Watkins. Watkins published her first volume of poetry, *Forest Leaves,* at the age of twenty-one, in 1846. In the early 1850s, faced with a state law that put free African Americans at risk for sale into slavery if they entered or reentered Maryland, Watkins left Baltimore for the North. There she began her public career in the anti-slavery movement lecturing for the State Anti-Slavery Society of Maine.

While both Brown and Still were largely self-educated, and Watkins's formal education was limited to the years she spent in her uncle's Baltimore academy, Nell's formal education continued after his years at Boston's African School. As a young man he entered the biracial abolitionist world, first reading law in the offices of William I. Bowditch and then joining the anti-slavery movement. He lectured acceptably, organized anti-slavery meetings, and worked in the offices of Garrison's

Liberator. Many in the movement considered him in line for the position of general agent at the paper, a job to which Garrison appointed a white man. While Nell remained silent about his failure to obtain the position, it must have been fresh in his thoughts when the twenty-five-year-old Bostonian, still employed in the offices of the *Liberator,* went down to New Haven in 1840 to attend the National Reformed Convention of Colored People. There he met J. W. C. Pennington and was catapulted into the arena of black radicalism.

Throughout their deliberations, the delegates who had gathered in New Haven emphasized the importance of African-American initiative in the struggle against racial oppression. They targeted both Southern slavery and Northern disfranchisement.[14] Nell must have been struck by the sentiments he heard there. When he returned to Boston he initiated a petition campaign to end racial segregation in the Massachusetts public schools. (That campaign would continue until 1855, when the state acceded to black citizens' demands for legislative reform and revoked the school segregation laws.[15])

RADICAL POLITICS AND POPULAR HISTORICAL CONSCIOUSNESS

William Cooper Nell, William Wells Brown, William Still, and Frances Ellen Watkins Harper all came to political maturity within the context of the anti-slavery and Convention Movements, and the imprint of those movements is reflected in their public activities as well as in the political issues that informed their writings. Representative of a generation of African-American political activists, all began their political careers in late adolescence and early adulthood, when they joined with white abolitionists in the fight to end Southern slavery. Equally representative of that generation, their visions of race unity ranged broadly during the course of their careers, shaped in part by personal and particularistic experiences, but also by the variations in perspective embedded within the anti-slavery movement.

Given his family background and the political climate in Boston, Nell's entry into the anti-slavery movement had marked a logical transition from adolescence to adulthood. Brown, as well, had joined the anti-slavery movement at a moment of personal transition, in his case both from adolescence to adulthood and from slavery to freedom. From the outset, however, there were contrasts between their experiences within the movement. Nell began his abolitionist career with a solid Garrisonian affiliation, while Brown's initial ties to the movement were established with the Western New York Anti-Slavery Society, a group that tended throughout the quarter century preceding the Emancipation to resist Garrison's guidance and dominance. Accordingly, Nell's and Brown's philosophical foundations were differently shaped; while the Convention Movement drew them both into the common arena of black radicalism, throughout his public career Nell remained firmly committed to the struggle for equal rights within the Constitutional principles and territorial boundaries of the United States. In contrast, Brown held a more expansive definition of race unity. In much the same manner as these fundamental variations of definition often evoked passionate debates within the convention halls, after 1855 they would profoundly shape the texture of the collective memories Nell and Brown constructed through their historical studies.

In many respects, William Still's vision of race unity merged the points of view Nell and Brown represented. For Still, the journey from rural New Jersey to the center of the African-American political arena began in 1844 when, at the age of twenty-three, he left home armed with three dollars and a deep faith that "neither death, nor life, nor things present, nor things to come" could prevent him from fulfilling the possibilities life held for him beyond his father's farm. His path into the movement was less direct than either Nell's or Brown's. Newly arrived in Philadelphia, still green from the country, Still worked at odd jobs for a time, tried his entrepreneurial hand at a secondhand clothing business, and educated himself. He later would draw on the practical business skills and the philosophy he had developed during these three years when he expanded the definition of race unity to encompass an economic and mercantile dimension. With that future still before him, however, at the age of twenty-six William Still took a position as clerk in the offices of the Pennsylvania Anti-Slavery Society. His formal duties included managing the society's correspondence, maintaining accounts, and distributing the *Pennsylvania Freeman*. His informal, dangerous, and illegal duties involved assisting fugitive slaves. He proved skilled at both labors.[16]

Similarly, Frances Ellen Watkins proved a skilled and energetic anti-slavery worker. A popular and well-received lecturer, Watkins enjoyed both respect and friendship with other African Americans in the anti-slavery movement, particularly with William Cooper Nell and William Wells Brown. In 1854 she published her second volume of poetry, *Poems on Miscellaneous Subjects,* a well-received work that was reprinted eight times and sold an estimated 12,000 copies by 1858, although throughout the antebellum period Watkins devoted the bulk of her energies to the anti-slavery movement. In 1860, at the age of thirty-five, Watkins married Fenton Harper, an Ohio farmer, and lived with Harper on his farm outside Cincinnati until his death in 1865. At Harper's death, Frances Ellen Watkins Harper moved to Philadelphia and resumed her anti-slavery work, with William Still as her mentor.

Fragments of evidence suggest an intersection of Pennington's, Nell's, Brown's, Still's, and Walker's lives during the 1840s and 1850s. All wrote for the abolitionist press, Pennington and Nell at various times for *Frederick Douglass' Paper,* Nell consistently for Garrison's *Liberator,* and Still for the *Pennsylvania Freeman.* Walker's first fiction was published in *The Anglo-African Magazine* and she regularly published poetry and essays in Garrison's *Liberator* and *Frederick Douglass' Paper.* All four were paid anti-slavery workers, and all were involved in the work of the Underground Railroad. All moved freely through abolitionist circles, and Nell—in Boston—and Still—in Philadelphia—were deeply involved in the work of local Vigilance Committees. To the horror of his white abolitionist employers, Still kept case histories and meticulous records of his activities, which he secreted from time to time in the loft of a building at Lebanon Cemetery. "I knew the danger of keeping strict records," he later would write, "and while I did not then dream that in my day slavery would be blotted out, or that the time would come when I could publish these records, it used to afford me great satisfaction to take them down fresh from the lips of fugitives on the way to freedom."[17] Still's records would be the only documentation of an invisible network of abolitionists, black and white, who directed fugitives ever northward toward freedom and safety for a quarter of a century.

William Wells Brown had moved from Buffalo to Boston in 1844, but apparently retained his ties with the western abolitionists, at least for a time. He joined with other African Americans who remained friendly with the western branch of the movement in their increasingly organized demands for suffrage. During preparations for the 1845 New York State Free Suffrage Convention the thirty-one-year-old fugitive was selected by the organizing committee to formally invite William H. Seward to attend the proceedings.[18]

From his new location in Boston, the scope of Brown's political activities expanded. While he continued to lecture widely, he also began writing for the abolitionists, producing first his slave autobiography, *The Narrative of William Wells Brown* (1847) and then a collection of abolitionist songs, *The Anti-Slavery Harp* (1848). He proved as popular an author as he had a platform lecturer. The first edition of the *Narrative,* three thousand copies, sold out in six months. In 1849, Brown joined the transatlantic movement, attending the Paris Peace Congress as a delegate from the American Anti-Slavery Society. Following the conclusion of the congress, the "eloquent fugitive" toured England, Ireland, and Scotland, lecturing widely in the abolitionist cause, an experience he recounted in his travelogue, *Three Years in Europe; or, Places I Have Seen and People I Have Met* (1852).

Even as the emigrationists and anti-emigrationists, the moral suasionists and the radical abolitionists debated within the Convention Movement, on the suffrage issue African-American activists were unified. Nell's *Colored Patriots of the American Revolution,* which appeared in 1855, marked a crucial moment in the suffrage campaign. The book clearly departed from the white anti-slavery agenda. Focusing on what was in 1855 a strictly Northern cause among African Americans, *Colored Patriots* established a formal and public connection between a collective New World past and contemporary civil issues. Nell inventoried the military heroism and patriotic acts of African Americans from New England to the Carolinas. There was no question that black soldiers had fought bravely and died for political freedoms now denied their children and grandchildren, and in a lengthy appended essay, *Conditions and Prospects of Colored Americans,* Nell described the circumstances of African Americans who lived in the nominally free states of the North during the early decades of the nineteenth century. The relationship between historical fact and contemporary political agenda at mid-century was clear: "We claim our enfranchisement," Nell wrote bluntly, "upon the ground that we are patriotic." Nell's radical colleagues responded immediately and with enthusiasm to the publication of *Colored Patriots.* Samuel Ringgold Ward heralded the book as the only "history of our unhappy people" and John Mercer Langston declared that *Colored Patriots* placed Nell "among the savants of this country."[19]

The Convention Movement continued to press the claim to citizenship Nell had asserted in *Colored Patriots.* An earlier generation had organized "African" churches, schools, and fraternal societies, and from those institutions that generation had built a moral community. Through the "Colored" associations and conventions of subsequent decades, African Americans had declared their respectability in the belief and hope that embourgeoisiement would lead to acceptability. At mid-century, new and expanded organizational labels announced a new level of conscious and intentional politicization. Nell and Brown served as officers of the 1858 Convention of Colored *Citizens* of Massachusetts (emphasis added) and Nell sat on the Committee on the Dred Scott Decision and the Committee on Publication. The following year all three men attended the 1859 New England Colored *Citizens'* Convention (emphasis added) in Boston. Brown delivered the Convention Address and Nell entered comments on the military service of Crispus Attucks into the convention proceedings. Both served on the Publication Committee. William Still attended the convention as the Pennsylvania delegate, and while less prominent in the proceedings than either Brown or Nell, he must have received both guidance and instruction from his colleagues while he was in Boston that year. When Still returned to Philadelphia he initiated a drive against racial segregation on the city's streetcar system, reminiscent of Nell's campaign nineteen years earlier to end racial segregation in the Boston public schools.[20] That same year Watkins received a special invitation to participate in the 1858 Convention of the Colored Men of Ohio in Cincinnati and was one of five participants to the convention who signed a petition to the General Assembly of the State of Ohio requesting that the state "take the steps necessary to strike, from the Constitution, the word 'white,' wherever it occurs; and to repeal all laws, or part of laws, making distinction on account of color or race."[21]

Despite the claims to citizenship and demands for suffrage that issued from African American activists throughout the 1850s and 1860s, the public attitudes of white Americans toward those cries for equality between the races remained at best quietly neutral in the Northern states as well as in the Southern ones. Even among the most ardent white abolitionists, opposition to slavery did not imply acceptance of political or social equality. Louis Agassiz, himself an abolitionist and the founder and director of Harvard's Museum of Comparative Zoology, had popularized the doctrine of inherent biological (rather than theological) inferiority. After the 1840s, white Americans of various political persuasions easily partitioned the political issue—slavery—from the "scientifically" established biological inferiority of non-Europeans in general and Africans in particular.[22] William Wells Brown issued a direct attack on the Agassiz doctrine in 1863 when he published *The Black Man: His Antecedents, His Achievements and His Genius.* The biographical sketches in *Black Man,* Brown wrote, would "aid in vindicating the Negro's character, and show that he is endowed with those intellectual and amiable qualities which adorn and dignify human nature."[23]

Nell had turned to historical documentation of African-American claims to the same civil rights enjoyed by all citizens. Brown turned now to historical documentation to refute the prevailing myth of racial inferiority that blocked African-American access to those rights. The geographical spread of Brown's entries makes clear the continuing conflict between race and national identity that had informed the debates on emigration throughout the nineteenth century and that prevailed in the African-American collective consciousness at mid-century. Despite William Cooper Nell's assertion that "the colored people of the United States have no destiny separate from that of the nation of which they form an integral part," 25 percent of Brown's entries were Haytian and West Indian.[24] Brown placed his friends and colleagues, Nell and Still, alongside Nell's hero Crispus Attucks; the "Negro Philosopher," Benjamin Banneker; the enslaved African muti-neer, Joseph Cinque; and J. W. C. Pennington.

In the text of *Black Man,* Henri Christophe, Andre Rigaud, Jean Jacques Dessalianes, Edward Jordan, Alexandre Petion, and Toussaint L'Ouverture were publicly claimed as African-American heroes. The Haytian Revolution and the ongoing governance of the black island republic remained a glorious example of the political and administrative abilities of Africans in the New World. Brown included three women in his dictionary: Charlotte Forten, Frances Ellen Watkins, and Phillis Wheatley. Henry Bibb represented the Canadians, Alexandre Dumas the Europeans, and Nat Turner and Denmark Vesey the slaves in rebellion and resistance. Largely as a result of Brown's compilation, by the onset of the Civil War, revolutionaries, actors, artists, educators, abolitionists, journalists, clergy, and politicians had been firmly embedded in the popular historical consciousness of African Americans as race leaders and race heroes.

Emancipation, Reconstruction, and Empire-Building

THE CIVIL WAR BROUGHT NEW DEMANDS to the anti-slavery apparatus. In the most immediate sense, African Americans who had worked for the ending of slavery put aside their claims to political equality and asserted their right to participate, once again, in a holy war of liberation, this time not for nation, but for race. Those who could shouldered arms and others recruited soldiers for the regiments they had helped to create. Nell and Brown, both approaching fifty, were too old to march into battle, and too removed for direct involvement in the war effort, but William Still, forty when war was declared, left a successful stove and coal delivery business and joined the Union Army, serving as Post Sutler—selling food and liquor to the soldiers—at Camp William Penn, near Philadelphia, until the end of the war.

Many of the anti-slavery societies continued on for a time after 1865, often working in cooperation with the Freedman's Bureau to provide the freed people in the Southern states with the educational and social services they so desperately needed. Eventually, however, the anti-slavery machine disbanded. In May, 1871, at the final meeting of the Pennsylvania Anti-Slavery Society, William Still received a mandate to "compile and publish his personal reminiscences and experiences relating to the Underground Railroad."[1] *The Underground Rail Road* resulted from this mandate, a book that consciously and intentionally constructed a historical record preserving the most recent chapter of the African-American lived past. Still transformed a multitude of personally lived pasts into a collectively remembered history of "the heroic fugitives [from slavery] who would endure the yoke no longer" and those who had guided their flights to freedom.[2]

Still self-consciously intended *The Underground Rail Road* as a memorial that would permanently preserve the memory of an era and its people, and he envisioned that the book would become the centerpiece of an African-American publishing empire. The *Rail Road* would serve as an educational tool bringing to the four millions newly emancipated the history of "their" protest against enslavement. The publishing empire would produce and distribute "works on various topics from the view of colored men." Sales for the book never achieved the levels Still initially had projected, and his plans for future publications were not realized. Nevertheless, his vision of a national publishing company unified by race reflected a sense of community among African-American intellectuals that had expanded dramatically over the century separating the abolition of slavery in the North and Emancipation in the South.[3] The transition from a lived to a remembered past anchored firmly in New World environments had been completed, and the political and economic agendas that would inform African-American community-building into the twentieth century had crystallized in the *lieux de memoire* constructed by Nell, Brown, Still, and their generation.

Immediately following that final meeting of the Pennsylvania Anti-Slavery Society, Still began his work, bringing to the task a rich combination of resources. His own meticulous records and case histories, compiled during his years at the Pennsylvania Anti-Slavery Society and the Philadelphia Vigilance Committee, provided the cornerstone of documentation. But Still sought a broader portrait of the secret and clandestine railroad. In the fall months of 1871 he began soliciting narratives from his old abolitionist friends, the stationmasters and conductors who had labored silently and secretly to maintain the invisible railroad. He faced a formidable task and must have felt an urgency of time as he began his work. Some of his former colleagues, like Oliver Johnson, flatly declined his request for information. For Johnson, the anti-slavery days had passed. He advised Still that "my duties in the [New York] *Tribune* overtax my strengths, while my health is not as good as it once was." There is no mention of Johnson among the stationmasters and conductors in Still's stunning history of the secret organization.[4]

Others, however, responded more favorably to Still's request, though at times reluctantly, and at times with great difficulty. John Hunn, whom Still described as the chief engineer of the Southern End of the Rail Road (in North Carolina), initially felt "unwilling to comply with thy request, not from any false modesty . . . but because I have done nothing in the cause worthy of public record." Still must have persisted in pressing his request for information, because Hunn eventually sent several different sketches, being careful even in 1871 to disguise individual identities. "Thy will know who is meant in the account," Hunn confided to Still, "but others will not be likely to recognize the individual except they were intimately acquainted with the family."[5]

The organized Vigilance Committees in various Northern cities had played especially vital roles in the resistance movement. Still turned to Lewis Tappan, the most senior member of the New York Vigilance Committee, for a personal narrative. In failing health when Still's request arrived, Tappan responded through his son, who advised Still that his father "would willingly furnish you with the statement that you request, if he were able to write, or to dictate. Even the dictation of an ordinary letter," J. A. Tappan explained to Still, "is now too fatiguing to him." Nevertheless, in the end Tappan must have laboriously dictated the material Still had requested. A lengthy article appeared in *The Underground Rail Road* over Tappan's signature, dated a month after he initially declined Still's request.[6]

By early December 1871, the text Still had been commissioned to compile was taking form. Luck McKim Garrison supplied a sketch of William Lloyd Garrison. Later in the month, James Miller McKim, who had hired Still as an office clerk for the Pennsylvania Anti-Slavery Society when he had been a hungry greenhorn from rural New Jersey, proofed and returned his material as well as the Garrison entry, sent first to Wendell Phillips for his comments.[7]

Still negotiated a printing agreement with Porter and Coates in January 1872 and became the first African-American author to have his work produced by a major American publishing company. The contractual agreement, which could be terminated by either party with twelve months' written notice, was mutually beneficial. Because the book would be marketed by subscription, with Still responsible for all publicity, there was very little financial risk involved in the venture for Porter and Coates. For Still, who had exercised and refined his entrepreneurial skills over thirty years' time, and who envisioned *The Underground Rail Road* as the centerpiece of an African-American publishing company, the agreement offered a near-ideal opportunity. He retained the copyright on the electroplates and secured the right to purchase an unlimited number of copies of the book at a 40 percent discount.[8]

By late spring of 1872, Still had begun distributing promotional copies of the *Rail Road* through his Republican and abolitionist connections. Like all authors, he needed reviews, and in his case, because *The*

Underground Rail Road would be sold by subscription, reviews were an immediate and vital concern. Despite Oliver Johnson's initial rebuff of his request for a narrative, Still once again appealed to his former anti-slavery colleague, seeking this time a favorable review of his book in the *Tribune.* "My Dear Sir," Johnson haughtily responded, "I am not permitted to write book notices for any edition of the *Tribune,* daily, semi-weekly, or weekly." James McKim frankly told Still that he "was a good deal disappointed" in a review of the book that appeared in the *Nation.* African-American journalists were more cooperative and supportive. Philip A. Bell wrote from San Francisco, requesting engravings that he intended to use as illustrations for a planned series of weekly extracts from the *Rail Road.* Still sent Bell the plate of *The Runaway,* asking only that it be returned as soon as possible, explaining that it would be needed for "a new edition of 5,000" copies that he intended to publish in the near future.[9]

Public reviews were not Still's only problem as he prepared to put the book on the market. Although McKim reported that Garrison had been pleased with the final copy, Lewis Tappan's wife Sarah, writing for him, reported that while Tappan had received and read his advance copy "with deep interest" and had been "much pleased" with the work on the whole, he objected to his portrait. Sarah Tappan listed her husband's complaints in detail: "The shape of the head is not right—the face too long for the width; the nose is too broad & the under lip too short. But the greatest objection is that the hair is made to look as if he wore a wig." Tappan, too frail to write for himself, asked through his wife that the faults in his image be remedied. Henry Bleby, another of Still's anti-slavery colleagues, wrote from the Bahamas requesting a free copy of the *Rail Road,* as did a former colleague from the Pennsylvania Anti-Slavery Society office who had gone west to Montana. "I suppose I could buy it," Still's former coworker wrote, "but I want you to send me an author's copy and write in it that it is to a friend who will never forget the old days."[10]

Still began marketing *The Underground Rail Road* in 1873, soliciting the names of "our most intelligent and influential" men and women from the network of African-American abolitionists, educators, and clergy who spanned the southern and western states and might be interested in selling the book on commission. Ellen Craft reported from Savannah that prospects for sales there were positive and promised to provide Still with a list of potential agents in her area. T. F. B. Marshall at the Hampton Institution supplied Still with "a list of reliable agents" from among his students. W. H. Stanton, publisher and editor of *The Freeman's Journal* in Brookfield, Missouri, advised Still that he was "advertising the book extensively" in anticipation of a rush of sales in his area during the spring months.[11]

Salespeople were the linchpin in Still's plan, and he queried sharply concerning the character and personality of the women and men who were recommended to him: "Is he wide awake?" he asked about William Perry. "Does he feel the need of an education amongst us?" he asked of another potential agent. Still sought people willing to do the difficult work of door-to-door canvassing, and he looked for the same entrepreneurial spirit and driven determination that informed his own labors. Simply put, he solicited "male or female, white or colored . . . who have some knowledge of canvassing, are active and industrious, and can enter fully into the work." Negotiating an agency in Delaware, Still challenged one potential applicant by asking if he was one "who will put his feet down and say, 'if one man can sell *The Underground Rail Road* and make money, so can I.'"[12]

Still sought more, however, than a willingness to work hard and a desire to make money in the people he accepted as agents. He specifically wanted women and men "who comprehend the dreadful oppression that rested upon the race a little while ago, and who now comprehend the great value of freedom." He expected an ideological commitment to racial uplift and mutual aid, a belief "that we as a race have got to work our way up the literary, scientific, mechanical, agricultural world by hard work and steady plodding." He wanted people who mirrored his own philosophy, who were "willing to work to promote each others' elevation—encourage business enterprises springing up amongst us, the works of our own brains."[13]

Still took several shrewd steps to foster cooperation rather than competition among his agents. They received exclusive sales rights to assigned territories, generally beginning with a township and a promise of a larger area, "one or two other adjoining counties, providing you succeed," he explained to one applicant. He offered liberal terms on sales commissions, an initial 50 percent discount on the listed sales price, and no shipping costs on prepaid orders. In return, agents were required to invest $3.75 in an "outfit" that included a sample copy of *The Underground Rail Road* in English cloth binding, a canvassing book for recording orders and payments, and advertising circulars and posters. For an additional charge, agents could have their names printed on the advertising material. "Equipped with this outfit," Still explained, "an agent is prepared to go to work and get subscribers." When agents had proved themselves in an initial territory, Still offered an additional incentive, a pyramiding sales strategy. "If you can get any good agents, allow them forty percent, and for all the books you may order for them, I will allow you a fifty-five percent discount on your own [orders]." Still aimed to sell books, and he believed his sales strategy offered an "excellent chance for young men and women of intelligence to make money faster than by the old methods."[14]

Still provided ongoing marketing and financial advice to his sales force. "This is the best time in the whole season for selling books," he wrote encouragingly to a Tennessee agent during the summer months, a time when the farmers he hoped would buy *The Underground Rail Road* were selling their crops and had cash on hand. To a North Carolina agent who reported a lack of ready money among the impoverished farmers in his territory, Still suggested installment payments, explaining that "white agents do a large business amongst our people in some of our Northern cities in this way." He described the system: potential buyers could pay "one or two dollars down and the balance on a fixed date," while agents fixed the details of the arrangement. He also guided his agents toward financial resources for their own needs, suggesting to one that he secure a loan from the Freedman's Bank to finance his own initial investment in a sales outfit. "These institutions were first started to encourage our people in the ways of making and saving money," he reasoned. "I hardly think it would be against their principles to do a favor of this kind if they could be guaranteed that they would not lose in the operation."[15]

From the outset Still worked to build a network of reliable and successful door-to-door canvassers who would saturate the vast new Southern market created by the Emancipation with the sale of *The Underground Rail Road* and then be "ready to sell any books that I might publish" in the future. Yet, while he was an ardent advocate of entrepreneurial capitalism, William Still was equally concerned with the intellectual and material advancement of the race. "We have no books produced by colored men," he observed to William Wells Brown, and he believed there was a need for "works on various topics from the view of colored men to represent the race intellectually." He provided guidance and other assistance to Sojourner Truth as she planned her autobiography, and he encouraged Frances Ellen Watkins Harper in her literary project. When Mary Ann Shadd Carey appealed to him for assistance in publishing her writing, he forwarded her work to Brown for comments and promised to try to help her locate "a paying place on some newspaper." To Brown, then completing *The Rising Son,* he offered advice on developing a subscription sales program and warned Brown of the attendant "trials, vexations and delays" of such an undertaking. Perhaps thinking of Oliver Johnson, he also cautioned Brown against depending on their white anti-slavery colleagues, telling him that since the Emancipation their old friends had "not been so hearty as they should have been" in providing support for his own enterprise. The time had come, Still believed, when African Americans should sever the bonds of economic dependence on whites. "We Colored men," he wrote to Brown, "must do business [with each other] and we must be governed by the principles that govern honorable business men."[16]

The Underground Rail Road never achieved the sales record Still had projected. His market collapsed in the depression of the 1870s. Agents grew discouraged with slow sales and, especially in the South, many abandoned their work in midstream. Some absconded with funds and books. Dismayed, Still wrote to William Wells Brown that the "period has not yet arrived when colored men are going to do much to promote enterprises being controlled by men of their own numbers. We are too selfish for such nobleness and efforts as these." Brown, too, had been disillusioned. There had been difficulty arranging promotional advertising for *The Rising Son* in Fred Douglass' *New National Era.* For these two old comrades, feeling the pressure of the passing years, further discouragement came with the death of William Cooper Nell. Brown wrote to Still that with Nell's death he had been forced to acknowledge that "thus the old guard, one after another, fall and leave us with the assurance that we, too, are on the downward road."[17]

In the 1870s the economic community that Still had envisioned remained a promise for the future rather than an achieved reality. Nevertheless, Still's understanding that "we Colored men must do business [with each other]" in order to achieve "more independence than has here to fore been possible" could have emerged only from the expanded connection between self and others, between past and present, that was constructed by Pennington and his generation. The moral community that was constructed by the spiritual autobiographers and pamphleteers had laid the foundation for the political community and historical consciousness that nurtured that vision through the difficult times of Reconstruction, Redemption, and the beginning of the twentieth century.[18]

In 1893, in her sixty-eighth year, Frances Ellen Watkins Harper would produce *Iola Leroy, or Shadows Uplifted,* a novel that carried forward William Still's explicit mandate for "works on various topics from the view of colored men to represent the race intellectually." At a time when the Plantation School was producing romanticized rememberings of the antebellum South and embedding racial stereotypes of happy and contented slaves into the texture of post-bellum culture, Still had encouraged Harper to take up the challenge through the fiction genre. In his introduction to the first edition of the novel, Still declared his unconditional endorsement of the book, praising its "grand and ennobling sentiments which have characterized all her utterances in laboring for the elevation of the oppressed."[19] Perhaps only in retrospect can the full depth of *Iola Leroy* be understood: it is both a work that served particular political and cultural purposes when it was written, and a book that claimed the Reconstruction Era as an African-American *lieu de memoire*.

During the 1860s and 1870s Harper had toured the South, lecturing and teaching among the emancipated African Americans. She wrote to Still during that time. From Darlington, South Carolina, on May 13, 1867: "I here read and see human nature under new lights and phases. I meet with a people eager to hear, ready to listen." And from Cheraw, South Carolina, the following month: "The South is to be a great theatre for the colored man's development and progress. There is brain-power here. If any doubt it, let him come into our schools, or even converse with some of our Freedman either in their homes or by the way-side."[20] The characters she crafted in the pages of *Iola Leroy*, a novel that begins with the arrival of the Union troops in North Carolina, certainly were conceived during that time; but they were equally formed during Harper's dialogue with Still and the other abolitionists of her generation. Robert Johnson, who will prove to be Iola Leroy's long-lost uncle as the plot unfolds, is a man who had been lost in the fracturings of families that were so common among the enslaved. Johnson explains the meaning of race unity in conversation with a fellow slave: "Tom, if ever we get our freedom, we've got to learn to trust each other and stick together if we would be a people."[21] The words could as easily have been William Still's. At times Harper's characters transcend the boundaries that race had imposed on psychosocial perspective in post-bellum America. While another author might have chosen an African-American character to represent her vision of race unity, race leadership, and race achievement, Harper chose Dr. Gresham, a white Army physician who falls in love with Iola. In a conversation with Iola, Gresham declares: "out of the race must come its own defenders. With them the pen must be mightier than the sword. It is the weapon of civilization, and they must use it in their own defense."[22]

While Harper's novel ranges across contemporary issues, predictably, the enduring evils of slavery constitute a core theme. As Iola and Dr. Gresham discuss the schools opening up throughout the South, for example, Gresham again becomes the vehicle for Harper's opinions on and understandings about education among the freed people. Gresham believes it will be "uphill work. I believe it will take generations to get over the duncery of slavery." But Iola believes that the army of teachers, "a new army that had come with an invasion of ideas," would be an effective antidote against the dulling effect of slavery, and that belief informs her own decision to become, as had Harper, a teacher among the freed people.

Slavery also had torn families apart, and the pain of those forced separations as well as the reunification of African-American families drives the plot of *Iola Leroy*. As Aunt Linda testifies in a church meeting, the mother's loss of her children brings enduring pain: "Bredren an' sisters, it war a drefful time when I war tored away from my pore little chillen." But the evils are being remedied. In the course of Reconstruction, families will be reunited "after years of patient search through churches, papers, and inquiring friends." For Robert Johnson, as for many others recently freed from slavery, Harper understood that "to bind anew the ties which slavery had broken and gather together the remnants of his scattered family became the earnest purpose of Robert's life."[23] Those ties were renewed in the pages of *Iola Leroy*.

Frederick Douglass had written eloquently about the immorality of slavery in his autobiographies, and Harper's discussion of the irrational and corrupting power of the institution strongly paralleled Douglass' argument. Both were concerned with the way in which slavery distorted class-based interests in favor of race loyalties. Douglass used autobiographical memory as his vehicle, recounting his apprenticeship in the Baltimore shipyard during the 1840s and from within that experience identifying the labor competition and ultimately the violence between Irish immigrants and African-American slaves as the result of the "conflict of slavery with the interests of white mechanics and laborers. . . . The slaveholders, with a craftiness peculiar to themselves, by encouraging the enmity of the poor laboring white man against the blacks, succeeded in making the said white man almost as much a slave as the black slave himself."[24] Similarly, Harper's character Colonel Robinson, commander of the Union Army post in the Carolinas, observes: "It surprises me to see how poor white men who, like the negroes, are victims of slavery, rally around the Stripes and Bars. . . . What, under heaven, are they fighting for?" Agreeing with his commander, Captain Sybil adds: "these ignorant white men have been awfully deceived. They have had presented to their imaginations utterly false ideas of the results of Secession, and have been taught that its success would bring them advantages which they had never enjoyed in the Union." While varying the historical context, Douglass and Harper conveyed a shared understanding of the power of slavery, "a deadly cancer eating into the life of the nation," to foster false consciousness among poor whites.[25] Few white writers would locate the irrationality of slavery in that false consciousness.

Anticipating DuBois's careful analysis of the African-American yeomanry that emerged in the South during Reconstruction, Harper describes at some length the group of "colored men [who] have banded together, bought [Gunderson's] plantation, and divided it among themselves." Perhaps drawing on her own experiences in South Carolina at a time when that state had attempted a government-financed land redistribution program, Harper easily conveyed the resonant power of land ownership in the lives of the freed people: "the gloomy silence of those woods was broken by the hum of industry, the murmur of cheerful voices, and the merry laughter of happy children" among the families who had settled on their own farms. A community emerged that revolved around the ownership of land. "Where they had trodden with fear and misgiving, freedmen walked with light and bounding hearts. The schoolhouse had taken the place of the slave-pen and auction-block."[26]

Considered as interrelated productions, *Colored Patriots, Black Man, The Underground Rail Road,* and *Iola Leroy* trace the passage of African-American collective consciousness from a focus on personal experiences recounted in real time through autobiographical memory to an emphasis on collective experience recalled through cultural memory and reconstructed in historical time. An examination of that process illuminates how a people reshaped their collective identity. The popular historical consciousness that resulted from these *lieux de memoire*—a body of shared beliefs, myths, and images—connected a New World past to an American present and validated a vision of the future that would inform the African-American political and cultural agenda into the twentieth century.

NOTES

PROLOGUE

1. William Cooper Nell, *Property Qualifications or No Property Qualifications, A Few Facts on the Record of Patriotic Services of Colored Men of New York, During the Wars of 1776-1812* (New York, 1860).
2. *Boston Massacre, March 5th, 1770: The Day Which History Selects as the Dawn of the American Revolution.* Broadside, American Antiquarian Society.
3. *The Liberator* (Boston), March 5, 1858, 39.
4. John Daniels, *In Freedom's Birthplace* (1905; New York, 1969 reprint ed.), 14, 36, 449.
5. See especially: John Bodnar, *Remaking America: Public Memory, Commemoration, and Patriotism in the Twentieth Century* (Princeton, 1992); Susan G. Davis, *Parades and Power: Street Theatre in Nineteenth-Century Philadelphia* (Philadelphia, 1986); Lawrence Levine, *High Brow/Low Brow: The Creation of Social Hierarchy in America* (Cambridge, 1988); George Lipsitz, *Time Passages: Collective Memory and American Popular Culture* (Minneapolis, 1990); Mary Ryan, "The American Parade: Representations of the Nineteenth-Century Social Order," *The New Cultural History,* ed. Lynn A. Hunt (Berkeley, 1989), 131-53; *Memory and American History,* ed. David Thelan (Bloomington, 1990); William H. Wiggins, Jr., *O Freedom: African-American Emancipation Celebrations* (Knoxville, 1987); Shane White, "'It Was a Proud Day': African-American Festivals and Parades in the North, 1741-1834," *Journal of American History* (June 1994), 13-50.
6. See: Arthur M. Schlesinger, Jr., *The Age of Jackson* (Boston, 1945) for descriptions of Fourth of July celebrations during the early years of the republic. Leonard I. Sweet, *Black Images of America, 1784-1920* (Unpublished Ph.D. dissertation, University of Rochester, 1974) provides an extended treatment of African-American attitudes toward this national holiday.
7. Although there is no biography for William Cooper Nell, the following sources are helpful in reconstructing the details of his life: George W. Forbes, *Biographical Sketch of William Cooper Nell* (typescript, n.d., Boston Public Library); William Wells Brown, *The Rising Son* (Boston, 1874), 485-86; James Oliver Horton, *Black Activism in Boston* (Unpublished Ph.D. dissertation, Brandeis University, 1973); Daniels, *In Freedom's Birthplace*; Carter G. Woodson, *The Mind of the Negro* (Washington, D.C., 1926); *Triumph of Equal School Rights in Boston*: Proceedings of the Presentation Meeting Held in Boston, December 17, 1855 (Boston, 1855); *The Liberator,* November 4, 1842, June 28, 1844, February 15, 1850, December 10, 1852, January 25, 1856, August

13, 1858; *Proceedings of the Colored Convention, Held in Rochester, July 6th, 7th, and 8th, 1853* (Rochester, printed at the office of *Frederick Douglass' Paper,* 1853). Nell did not write an autobiography. His published writings include: *Services of Colored Americans in the Wars of 1776 and 1812* (Boston, 1851); *Colored Patriots of the American Revolution* (Boston, 1855); and *Property Qualifications or No Property Qualifications, A Few Facts on the Record of Patriotic Services of Colored Men of New York, During the Wars of 1776-1812* (New York, 1860).

8. In my use of *lieux de memoire* I am indebted to: Pierre Nora, "Between Memory and History: *Les Lieux de Memoire*," *Representations,* 26 (spring 1989), 7-25. For discussions of parallel reform and protest movements, see especially: Nancy F. Cott, *The Grounding of Modern Feminism* (New Haven, 1987); Leon Fink, *Workingman's Democracy: The Knights of Labor and American Democracy* (Urbana, 1983); Gary Gerstle, *Working Class Americanism: The Politics of Labor in a Textile City, 1914-1960* (Cambridge, 1989); Herbert G. Gutman, "Historical Consciousness in Contemporary America," *Power and Culture, Essays on the American Working Class,* ed. Ira Berlin (New York, 1987), 395-412; Sean Wilentz, *Chants Democratic: New York City and the Rise of the American Working Class, 1788-1850* (New York, 1984).

9. Nora, "Between Memory and History," 7.

10. Adin Ballou, *The Voice of Duty. An Address Delivered at the Anti-Slavery Picnic at Westminster, Massachusetts, July 4, 1843* (Milford, Massachusetts, 1843), 3; Leonard I. Sweet, "The Fourth of July and Black Americans in the Nineteenth Century: Northern Leadership Opinion Within the Context of the Black Experience," *Journal of Negro History,* 61 (January 1976), 256-75 provides an excellent overview of the structural tension surrounding white and African-American definitions of the Fourth of July.

11. James Forten (1766-1842) of Philadelphia was a Revolutionary War veteran, a leader among African-American and white abolitionists, the owner of a successful Philadelphia sail loft, and a supporter of various social reforms, including abolitionism, women's rights, temperance, peace, and equal rights for African Americans. Forten opposed African colonization and convinced William Lloyd Garrison of the evil embedded in the scheme. Garrison's American Anti-Slavery Society was organized in Forten's Philadelphia home in 1833, and he is generally regarded as among the most influential African Americans of the antebellum period. For additional information see: Esther M. Doughty, *Forten the Sailmaker, Pioneer, Champion of Negro Rights* (Chicago, 1968); *The Journal of Charlotte Forten,* ed. Ray Allen Billington (New York, 1953).

12. James Forten, *A Series of Letters by A Man of Color* (Philadelphia, 1813).

13. Frederick Douglass (1817-1895), born a slave on a Maryland, eastern shore plantation, raised in Baltimore and on the Maryland eastern shore, escaped slavery in 1838, joined the anti-slavery movement in the New Bedford area, and rose to leadership as an abolitionist, journalist, and diplomat. Douglass wrote three autobiographies: *Narrative of the Life of Frederick Douglass* (Boston,

1845); *My Bondage and My Freedom* (Boston, 1855); and *The Life and Times of Frederick Douglass* (1881; revised and updated, 1892; New York, 1962 reprint). Douglass is of enduring interest to biographers. See: Phillip S. Foner, *The Life and Writings of Frederick Douglass* 2 Vols. (New York, 1950); Waldo Martin, *The Mind of Frederick Douglass* (Chapel Hill, 1980); William S. McFeely, *Frederick Douglass* (New York, 1991); Benjamin Quarles, *Frederick Douglass* (Washington, D. C., 1948).

14. Frederick Douglass, "The Meaning of July Fourth for the Negro" as reproduced in: Foner, *The Life and Writings of Frederick Douglass,* vol. II, 443.

15. Carl L. Becker, *The Declaration of Independence, A Study in the History of Political Ideas* (New York, 1942), 135-6. I am indebted to Genevieve Fabre, "Commemorative Celebrations Among African-Americans in the 19th Century" (Unpublished paper, W.E.B. DuBois Institute, Harvard University, 1988) for her preliminary summary of African-American freedom celebrations. Neither Fabre nor others, however, have included the intriguing "Bobalition" (abolition) ceremonies that occurred in Boston during the 1820s in their considerations of freedom celebrations. A dialogue between "Scipio Smilax" and "Mungo Meanwell" printed on one of the Bobalition broadsides suggests that the rather grand exercises, which were sponsored by Boston's African Society, were probably not-so-subtle condemnations of the Fourth of July excesses, disguised by the same cultural mask that invented Br'er Rabbit. Scipio declared: "no sooner dey get sober arter deir Independence, den dey begin to brackguard our Independent Day fore we sellybrate." *Grand Bobalition, or great annibersary fussible.* African Society (Boston, 1821); *Reply to Bobalition , A Dialogue between Scipio Smilax and Mungo Meanwell.* African Society (Boston, 1821); *Grand and Splendid Bobalition of Slavery.* African Society (Boston, 1822); *Splendid Celebration of the "Bobalition" of Slavery.* African Society (Boston, 1823). Broadsides. American Antiquarian Society.

16. R. W. Emerson, *Address in Commemoration of the Great Jubilee (New York, 1836); An Address Delivered in the Courthouse in Concord, Massachusetts, on the First of August, 1844, on the Anniversary of the Emancipation of the Negroes in the British West Indies.* (Boston, 1844); *Weekly Anglo-African* (New York) July 23, 1859, October 15, 1859. First of August Emancipation Day celebrations have an enduring appeal. In Providence, the Rhode Island Black Heritage Society reintroduced the holiday in the 1970s, and there Emancipation Day is a popular and well attended, community-wide festival that incorporates folk crafts and visual and performing arts reflecting the multinational cultural legacy of African Americans in the Rhode Island–Southeastern Massachusetts region. After the 1865 General Emancipation in the Southern United States, African Americans universally acknowledged the nation's day of emancipation as the First of January, the date the Emancipation Proclamation went into effect in 1865.

17. Edward [Edwin] Bannister (1828-1901) was born at St. Andrews, New Brunswick. As a youth he shipped as a cook on a coasting vessel and throughout

his life enjoyed sailing in the Narragansett Bay in the area around Newport, Rhode Island. As a young man Bannister moved to Boston and studied drawing and anatomy under Dr. Rimmer. During the 1850s and 1860s Bannister shared a studio in Boston with Edwin Lord Weeks, married Christiana Carteaux, and largely through her influence became involved in anti-slavery and reform activities. In 1871 Bannister and Carteaux relocated to Providence, where Bannister continued his painting and was a founding member of the Providence Art Club. His first major artistic success came in 1876 when his landscape, *Under the Oaks,* received a first-class medal at the Centennial Exhibition in Philadelphia. The painting subsequently was sold in Boston for $1500. Bannister is best known for his landscape paintings, particularly *After the Storm, Narragansett Bay, The Ship Outward Bound,* and *Dusk.* All reflect Bannister's lifelong enchantment with the sea and sailing ships. See Bannister's obituary in the *Providence Journal,* January 11, 1901; W. Alden Brown, *Edward Mitchel Bannister* (typescript, n.d.), Rhode Island School of Design.

18. William L. Simpson. See: William Wells Brown, *The Black Man, His Antecedents, His Genius, and His Achievements* (Boston, 1865; 1969 reprint edition), 199-202. Although William Wells Brown wrote about Simpson with both warmth and enthusiasm, the later historical record is remarkably silent on the details of Simpson's life and his artistic production. Neither the William Graham Sumner nor the John Hilton portraits seem to have survived, although Simpson's portraits of Bishop Jermain Wesley Loguen and his wife, Caroline, are at the Howard University Gallery of Art, Washington, D.C.

19. George L. Ruffin (1834-1886) graduated from Harvard Law School in 1869 and was admitted to the Suffolk County, Massachusetts bar and elected to the state legislature that same year. In 1883 Ruffin was appointed a Boston city court judge for the Charlestowne district. Ruffin's wife, Josephine St. Pierre Ruffin (1842-1924), daughter of an English woman and an Afro-Martinique man, enjoyed a public career as a club woman and reformer, provided guidance and leadership to a variety of racial-uplift activities during and after the Civil War, and served as an editor for the Boston newspaper *Courant* during the 1880s. See: Brown, *The Rising Son;* Daniels, *In Freedom's Birthplace,* 100-2, 209-10; and William Simmons, *Men of Mark* (1887; New York, 1968 reprint ed.). All contain biographical sketches of George L. Ruffin. For Josephine St. Pierre Ruffin see: *Lifting as They Climb: An Historical Record of the National Association of Colored Women* ed., Elizabeth Lindsay Davis (Washington, D.C., 1933); Eleanor Flexner, *A Century of Struggle: The Woman's Rights Movement in the U.S.* (Cambridge, 1959).

20. John S. Rock (1825-1866) was born to free parents in Salem, New Jersey, taught school in the Philadelphia area during 1844-1848, and, when denied admission to medical school because of his race, studied dentistry under Dr. Harbert Hubbard. In 1850 Rock opened a dental practice in Philadelphia. (The following year Rock received professional recognition for creating artificial teeth.) In 1852 Rock was awarded the M.D. from the short-lived American

Medical College in Philadelphia. Believing opportunities for a person of his education, skin color, and political persuasion were greater in the Northern states, Rock emigrated to Boston in 1853. He was a vigorous opponent of African colonization during the 1850s and would be an active recruiter for the 54th and 55th Massachusetts Infantry Regiments after the U.S. Congress authorized the raising of African-American troops in 1863. In 1864, following the death of Roger B. Taney, Rock was admitted to practice law before the United States Supreme Court. See: Charles Sumner Brown, "Genesis of the Negro Lawyer in New England," *Negro History Bulletin* 22 (May 1959), 171-76; Brown, *The Black Man;* George A. Levesque, "Boston's Black Brahmin: Dr. John S. Rock," *Civil War History* 25 (December 1980), 326-46; Eugene P. Link, "The Civil Rights Activities of Three Great Negro Physicians (1840-1940)," *Journal of Negro History* 52 (January 1967), 169-84; "John Sweat Rock, M.D., Esq., 1825-1866," *Journal of the National Medical Association* (May 1976), 237-42; Benjamin Quarles, *Black Abolitionists* (New York, 1969).

21. Charles Lenox Remond (1810-1873) was born in Salem, Massachusetts, to John Remond, an immigrant from Curaçao, and Nancy Perry Remond, daughter of a Revolutionary War veteran. John and Nancy Remond enjoyed considerable financial success as caterers, restaurateurs, and suppliers of foodstuffs. Both were active in anti-slavery activities and forged a legacy of social consciousness for their eight children. Charles Lenox Remond's early schooling was matched by the vital social and political climate in the Remond home. By 1832 he had become an agent for Garrison's *Liberator* and by 1837 he also represented *The Weekly Advocate* and *The Colored American.* Throughout the 1830s and 1840s Remond lectured throughout New England on the anti-slavery cause and in 1840 was selected by the American Anti-Slavery Society as a delegate to the World's Anti-Slavery Convention in London. Following the conclusion of the convention and an eighteen-month lecture tour in the British Isles, Remond returned to the United States and resumed his anti-slavery work. He was primarily known as a lecturer with a "crisp, vehement, and dreadful" style.

    With William Wells Brown and Frederick Douglass, Remond recruited soldiers for the Massachusetts 54th Regiment, and after the Civil War he opened a temperance Dining Room for Ladies and Gentlemen, an alcohol-free family restaurant. See: Dorothy Burnett Porter, "The Remond Family of Salem," *Proceedings of the American Antiquarian Society* 95, part 2 (October 1985), 259-96; Quarles, *Black Abolitionists;* William Edward Ward, *Charles Lenox Remond: Black Abolitionist, 1838-1873* (Unpublished doctoral dissertation, Clark University, 1977); Miraim L. Usery, "Charles Lenox Remond, Garrison's Ebony Echo," *Essex Institute Historical Collections* 106 (April 1, 1970), 112-25; Carter G. Woodson, "Letters of Charles Lenox Remond," *Journal of Negro History* 10 (July 1925), 477-512; *The Mind of the Negro as Reflected in Letters Written during the Crisis, 1800-1860,* ed., Carter G. Woodson (Washington, D.C., 1926).

22. A full analysis of the role of women in the anti-slavery movement has yet to be written. For partial studies see: Ira V. Brown, "Cradle of Feminism: The

Philadelphia Female Anti-Slavery Society, 1833-1840," *Pennsylvania Magazine of History and Biography* 102 (April 1978), 143-66; Flexner, *Century of Struggle*; Alice Kessler-Harris, *Women Have Always Worked* (New York, 1981), 106-07; Charles H. Wesley, "The Negroes of New York in the Emancipation Movement," *Journal of Negro History* 24 (January 1939), 65-103; Dorothy Burnett Porter, "The Organized Educational Activities of Negro Literary Societies, 1828-1846," *Journal of Negro Education* 5 (September 1936), 556-76.

23. From an American Peace Society pamphlet as quoted by Kessler-Harris, *Women Have Always Worked,* 107.

24. Frances Ellen Watkins Harper (1825-1911) was a popular poet, speaker, and novelist whose work and writings spanned the abolitionist, temperance, and woman suffrage movements. An 1853 Maryland law that put free African Americans from the North who entered the state at risk of sale as slaves drove her from Baltimore. Early contact with William Still, the Philadelphia anti-slavery activist, drew her into the anti-slavery movement. Her "clear and melodious voice," coupled with a graceful platform style, made her a popular speaker in an era when respectable women generally were discouraged from public speaking. According to Still, *The Underground Rail Road,* she spoke "without notes, with gestures few and fitting. Her manner is marked by dignity and composure. She is never assuming, never theatrical." Her essays and poems were published regularly in the *Liberator, Frederick Douglass' Paper,* and *Anglo-African Magazine.* She did not marry until the age of thirty-five, in 1860, was widowed in 1864, and resumed an active life as author, speaker, and reformer until her death in 1911 at the age of eighty-five. See: William Still, *The Underground Rail Road* (Philadelphia, 1872); *A Documentary History of the Negro People in the United States,* ed., Herbert Aptheker (New York, 1951); Frances E. W. Harper, *Iola Leroy* (1893; New York, 1988 Schomburg reprint ed.), especially the "Forward" by Henry Louis Gates, Jr. and the "Introduction" by Frances Smith Foster.

25. Charlotte Forten Grimke (1837-1914), granddaughter of James Forten of Philadelphia, was born in Philadelphia, educated by private tutor in her grandfather's home, and spent her childhood in the company of Forten family members and their friends and associates in the anti-slavery movement. Two aunts, Margaretta and Sarah Forten, were outspoken anti-slavery activists. In 1854 Forten was sent to the Remond home in Salem, Massachusetts, where she attended and graduated from the Higginson Grammar School and then completed a one-year course at the State Normal School at Salem. In 1856 Forten began teaching at Epes Grammar School, where she held the distinction of being the first African-American to instruct white children. Throughout her years in the Remond home, Forten combined education and anti-slavery work and by 1858, the year of the Commemorative Festival, exhausted and ill, she had resigned her teaching post and was preparing to return to Philadelphia. For a brief period during Reconstruction, Forten would teach in the school Laura Matilda Towne had established on St. Helena Island, South Carolina, live for

a time in Philadelphia and then Washington, and marry Henry Grimké in 1878, when she was forty-one years old. Her marriage marked the end of her public life. See: Ray A. Billington, "Introduction," *The Journal of Charlotte L. Forten* (New York, 1953); Charlotte Forten, "Life on the Sea Islands," *Atlantic Monthly* 13 (May-June 1864), 587-96; Willie Lee Rose, *Rehearsal for Reconstruction* (1964; Indianapolis, 1984 reprint ed.).

26. Jupiter Hammon (1711-1806) is discussed extensively in chapter 2, "Sons and Daughters of Distress," A Theology of Liberation.

27. Nancy Gardner Prince (1799-1856) was born to free parents in Newburyport, Massachusetts. Her maternal grandfather, a slave, had fought at Bunker Hill. Her young life was made difficult by extreme poverty and homelessness. A devout religious reformer, Nancy Gardner married Nero Prince, a founding member of the Prince Hall Freemasons, in 1824. The couple lived for a time in Russia, where Nero Prince held a servant position in Russia's imperial court, and then in Jamaica, where Nancy Prince believed she could convert and enlighten newly emancipated Afro-Jamaicans. Prince had some contact with Garrison, protested racist treatment aboard a steamship, led an attack on a slave-catcher, and participated in the 1854 National Woman's Rights Convention. See: Nancy Prince, Letter to William Lloyd Garrison, *The Liberator* (September 17, 1841); *A Narrative of the Life and Travels of Mrs. Nancy Prince* (Boston, 1853); *Sisters of the Spirit: Three Black Women's Autobiographies of the Nineteenth Century,* ed. William L. Andrews (Bloomington, Indiana, 1986); William H. Grimshaw, *Official History of Freemasonry Among the Colored People in North America* (1909; New York, 1969 reprint ed.).

28. Harriet Tubman (1820?-1913) was a Maryland slave, a fugitive from slavery, a rescuer of slaves, an associate of William Still and John Brown, and a Union spy. See: Sarah H. Bradford, *Harriet Tubman: The Moses of Her People* (New York, 1886); Earl Conrad, *Harriet Tubman* (Washington, D.C., 1943); Still, *The Underground Rail Road;* Wilbur H. Siebert, *The Underground Rail Road* (New York, 1898). The memory of Tubman's exploits is further commemorated in an opera—*Harriet, The Woman Called Moses,* by Thea Musgrave—and in a thirty-minute animated videocassette, *Harriet Tubman,* produced by Arthur Luce Klein and directed by Paul Kresh for Warner-NEST Animation. The video promises opportunities to "witness the daring exploits of the most famous 'conductor' on the Underground Railroad."

29. Horton, *Black Activism,* 39; Sweet, *The Fourth of July and Black Americans,* xx.

30. Daniels, *In Freedom's Birthplace,* 9; Nell, *Colored Patriots,* 15-17; Benjamin Quarles, *The Negro in the American Revolution* (Chapel Hill, 1961), 6. George Washington Williams, *The History of the Negro Race in America from 1619 to 1880: Negroes as Slaves, as Soldiers, and as Citizens,* 2 Vols. (New York, 1882); Joseph T. Wilson, *The Black Phalanx: A History of the Negro Soldiers of the United States* (Hartford, 1892). See the (Boston) *Gazette,* October 2, 1750, for an advertisement placed by his master in Framingham for Attucks's apprehension.

31. *The Liberator,* October 3, 1851.

32. William J. Watkins, *Our Rights As Men—An Address Delivered in Boston, Before the Legislative Committee on the Militia* (Boston, February 24, 1853).

33. *The Liberator,* April 10, 1857.

34. Woodson, *The Mind of the Negro,* 348. J. W. C. Pennington's *Text-Book of the Origin and History of the Colored People* (Hartford, 1841), addressed "to families, and to students and lecturers in history" as a pocket reference, had preceded the publication of *Colored Patriots* by fourteen years, and often is described as the first attempt by an African American to write a history of the race. While the arguments Pennington set forth were "collected with a right state of feeling on the total subject of human rights," they were, nonetheless, grounded more in theological assumption than historical evidence. *Colored Patriots* set the standard by which subsequent African-American historians, especially George Washington Williams and Joseph T. Wilson, would, as Pennington had advocated, collect "historical facts so arranged as to present a just view of our origin."

35. The formula worked in other contexts. Nell's twenty-four-page pamphlet, *Property Qualifications or No Property Qualifications* (New York, 1860) commissioned by African-American New Yorkers who were seeking an end to the property qualifications attached to suffrage eligibility in that state, called again on the memory of Attucks to advance claims for political equality.

36. Nell, *Colored Patriots,* xx.

37. Dred Scott, known as a "quiet and unobtrusive man, an affectionate father and a faithful husband," died on September 17, 1858, at the age of sixty-three. Irving Dillard, "Dred Scott Eulogized by James Milton Turner," *Journal of Negro History* 26 (January 1941), 1-12; Don E. Fehrenbacher, *The Dred Scott Case: Its Significance in American Law and Politics* (New York, 1978).

38. *Convention of the Colored Citizens of Massachusetts, August 1, 1858,* in *Proceedings of the Black State Conventions, 1840-1865,* Philip S. Foner and George E. Walker, eds., Volume II (Philadelphia, 1980), 100.

39. Wilson, *The Black Phalanx,* 29-30.

40. Daniels, *In Freedom's Birthplace,* 58-59; *Address of the Committee Appointed by a Public Meeting held at Faneuil Hall, September 24, 1846, for the Purpose of Considering the Recent Case of a Kidnapping from Our Soil, and of Taking Measures to Prevent the Recurrence of Similar Outrages* (Boston, 1846); *The Boston Slave Riot, and Trial of Anthony Burns, Containing the Report of the Faneuil Hall Meeting* (Boston, 1854); Charles Emery Stevens, *Anthony Burns: A History* (Williamston, Massachusetts, 1973).

41. William C. Nell to William Lloyd Garrison, *The Liberator,* December 10, 1852.

42. The details of the 1858 Commemorative Festival are abstracted from the account of the event in *The Liberator,* March 12, 1858.

43. Pennington, *Text-Book,* 1.

44. The literacy of Africans prior to their enslavement is a problematic topic. Autobiographical writings in Arabic and mathematical and engineering skills applied to the counting houses of Boston and Newport as well as in the

construction of rice fields in the Carolinas provide a range of evidence that documents the literacy of African captives.

45. The oratorical texts delivered at the Commemorative Festival are reprinted in *The Liberator,* March 12, 1858.

46. Boston City Directories, 1847-1860.

47. *Boston Massacre, March 5th, 1770.* Broadside, American Antiquarian Society.

48. Thomas Wentworth Higginson (1826-1911), writer, abolitionist, and feminist, was born into a thoroughly New England family, educated at Harvard, and ordained a Unitarian minister at Newburyport, Massachusetts. Higginson ran for Congress in 1848 as a Free Soiler and served for a time on the Boston Vigilance Committee. There he worked directly with Nell, Rock, and Remond, protecting anti-slavery meetings from disruption and assisting fugitives from slavery in their attempts to escape from slave-catchers, in direct violation of Federal law. His essays, *A Ride Through Kansas* and *Assorted Lots of Young Negroes,* chronicled and protested slavery on the frontier in the 1850s. Higginson was among those who supported John Brown as Brown designed his raid on Harper's Ferry, and he plotted to rescue the survivors of the failed raid. In 1862 Higginson would be appointed commander of the First South Carolina Volunteers, a regiment composed of newly emancipated African Americans charged with protecting the area around Port Royal Sound, South Carolina, after the withdrawal of regular army troops from the area. (Those troops were needed to reinforce George McClellan in the Potomac area.) Thomas Wentworth Higginson, *Army Life in a Black Regiment* (1869; New York, 1984 reprint ed.), 9-25.

49. The split between the moral suasionists and those who advocated more direct (and violent) political action against slavery and slaveholders had its roots in the National Negro Conventions of the 1830s, but became more explicitly focused at the 1843 Buffalo Convention when Henry Highland Garnet called for armed slave uprisings. Frederick Douglass, who began his anti-slavery career as a moral suasionist, shifted to a political-action stance in the early 1850s, and while there were a number of disputes and conflicts among African-American advocates of political action, there was a general agreement on the efficacy of direct, confrontational and, if necessary, armed attack on slaveholders. James Brewer Stewart, *Holy Warriors, The Abolitionists and American Slavery* (New York, 1976) and Peter Walker, *Moral Choices, Memory, Desire and Imagination in Nineteenth-Century American Abolition* (Baton Rouge, 1978) offer excellent broad discussions of moral suasion and the ideological schisms within the anti-slavery movement. Martin, *The Mind of Frederick Douglass,* provides detailed discussion of African-American abolitionists and their rejection of moral suasion.

50. *Boston Massacre, March 5th, 1770.* Broadside, American Antiquarian Society.

51. See: Thomas P. Slaughter, *Bloody Dawn: The Christiana Riot and Racial Violence in the Antebellum North* (New York, 1991).

52. *Boston Massacre, March 5th, 1770.* Broadside, American Antiquarian Society.

CHAPTER ONE

1. Letter from a colored servant in camp, September 3, 1777. Folder V:3. Box C. *Spooner Manuscripts,* Pilgrim Society Archives, Plymouth, Massachusetts.

2. Ephriam Spooner (1735-1818), a lifelong and highly respected Plymouth resident, had been visibly active in the Patriot cause during the Revolution, was commissioned by Washington during the war, and held a variety of official positions after the war, including: first Postmaster in the town, U.S. Collector at the Port of Plymouth, and (elected) Town Clerk for fifty-two years. Spooner was a deacon in the church and an "exemplary professor of religion." See: James Thacher, *A History of the Town of Plymouth,* 3rd ed. (Yarmouthport, 1972), 229-30.

3. William Cooper Nell, *Colored Patriots of the American Revolution* (Boston, 1855), 21. See also Benjamin Quarles, *The Negro in the American Revolution* (Chapel Hill, 1961).

4. Joseph T. Wilson, *Black Phalanx, A History of Negro Soldiers of the United States* (Hartford, 1892), 33.

5. Robert Middlekauff, *The Glorious Cause* (New York, 1982), 361ff. Dunmore hoped to demoralize the Virginia planters by depriving them of their labor force, and he expected to strengthen the ranks of his fighting force. He accomplished both. Some two hundred Virginia slaves joined him immediately, and rumors and fears of slave rebellions circulated through Virginia and the Carolinas, diverting the Patriots' energy from the Revolutionary cause.

6. William H. Grimshaw, *Official History of Freemasonry Among the Colored People of North America* (New York, 1903; 1969 reprint ed.), 67-96; Harry E. Davis, *A History of Freemasonry Among Negroes in America* (The United Supreme Council, Ancient and Accepted Scottish Rite of Freemasonry, Northern Jurisdiction, U.S.A., 1846), 14-20.

7. Quomony Quash and Cato Howe, *Fact Sheets* (mimeo, n.d., n.p.) Parting Ways, The Museum of Afro-American Ethnohistory, Plymouth, Massachusetts.

8. William Cooper Nell, *Property Qualifications or No Property Qualifications, A Few Facts on the Record of Patriotic Services of Colored Men of New York, During the Wars of 1776-1812* (New York, 1860).

9. Theopholis Cotton (1717-1782), Revolutionary leader and member of the influential and prestigious Cotton family. See: Thacher, *A History of the Town of Plymouth,* 177-78, 206, 207.

10. Plymouth Notary Public Records, Book 4 (1768-1830), 106. By 1777, as pressures to fill local militia quotas increased, masters routinely sent their slaves as substitutes for their own military service, often exchanging freedom for military service. In February 1778, when the Rhode Island General Assembly enacted legislation allowing African Americans, slave and free, to enlist in the state militia, those pressures had become acute and manumission offered a powerful incentive to enlistment for African Americans. Rhode

Island attempted through the legislation to stabilize the economic dimension of the exchange. Rather than masters receiving their slaves' bounty money, in Rhode Island slaves were to be "immediately discharged from the service of [their] master or mistress" upon enlistment and owners were, in turn, "compensated" for the loss of their property at the fixed rate of four hundred dollars. (In Rhode Island, free African Americans who enlisted under this program for the duration of the war received wages equivalent to those of white soldiers.) In neighboring Massachusetts, however, the exchange remained a personal one. See: Lorenzo Greene, *The Negro in Colonial New England* (New York, 1942), 143.

11. Revolutionary War Pension Claims, File #R18097, National Archives; *Massachusetts Soldiers and Sailors of the Revolutionary War,* Vol. XII, 885; Revolutionary War Rolls, Pilgrim Hall Archives, Plymouth, Massachusetts.

12. Quarles, *The Negro in the American Revolution,* 19-32.

13. Jack Foner, *Blacks and the Military* (New York, 1974), 6-15.

14. Plymouth Registry of Deeds, Book 60:165; 68:210.

15. Revolutionary War Pension Claims, File #W2354, National Archives. Nell, *Colored Patriots,* 21ff; Cato Howe *Fact Sheet* (mimeo, n.d.) Parting Ways, The Museum of Afro-American Ethnohistory, Plymouth, Massachusetts.

16. Cato Howe to Ephriam Spooner, January 30, 1781. Folder IX:3, Box C. *Spooner Manuscripts.* Pilgrim Society Archives, Plymouth, Massachusetts. Cushing is not among the family names common in the Plymouth area. The document may have misspelled the more common name, Cushman.

17. William D. Pierson, *Black Yankees, The Development of an African-American Subculture in Eighteenth Century New England* (Amherst, 1988), 14-22. U.S. Bureau of the Census, *Negro Population, 1790-1915* (New York, 1918; 1968 reprint ed.), especially 21-57; Carter G. Woodson, *Free Negro Heads of Families* (Washington, D.C., 1925), xx.

18. By 1790, a surplus of adult women over men in the region reflected the extent on this primarily young, single male migration. *Negro Population, 1790-1815*; Evarts B. Greene and Virginia Harrington, *American Population Before the Federal Census of 1790* (New York, 1932); James A. Henretta, *Evolution of American Society, 1700-1815* (Lexington, 1973).

19. For discussions of English precedents for popular claims on common lands see especially: E. P. Thompson, *Whigs and Hunters* (New York, 1976), 31-2; E. P. Thompson, "The Grid of Inheritance," in eds. Jack Goody, Joan Thirsk, and E.P. Thompson, *Family and Inheritance: Rural Society in Western Europe* (Cambridge, U.K., 1976), 340ff.

20. For broad analyses of the intersection of physical ecology and culture see: Elizabeth Rauh Bethel, *Promiseland* (1981; Columbia, South Carolina, 1997 revised ed.); Edward Mark Cook, *Fathers of the Town* (Baltimore, 1976); Charles S. Grant, *Democracy in a Connecticut Frontier Town* (New York, 1961): Philip Grevin, *Four Generations: Population, Land, and Family in Colonial Andover* (Ithaca, 1970); George Hesslink, *Black Neighbors: Negroes in a Northern*

Rural Community (Indianapolis, 1968); William L. Montell, *The Saga of Coe Ridge* (New York, 1972).

21. Records of the Town of Plymouth, Massachusetts, Vol. 1 (1636-1705), 314.

22. Old Plymouth Colony Proprietors Book, Vol. 1:190-1.

23. For discussions of the social structure in Old Plymouth Colony and the importance of landholding within this structure see: John Demos, *A Little Commonwealth* (London, 1970); John Demos, "Notes on Life in Plymouth Colony," *William and Mary Quarterly,* 3rd series, XXII (1965):264-86; George D. Langdon, "The Franchise and Political Democracy in Plymouth Colony," *William and Mary Quarterly,* 3rd series, XX (1963): 513-26; Darrett B. Rutman, *Husbandmen of Plymouth* (Boston, 1967); George Willison, *Saints and Strangers* (New York, 1945).

24. Marcus W. Jernegan, "Slavery and Conversion in the American Colonies," *American Historical Review* 21 (April 1916), 507; Lester B. Scherer, *Slavery and the Churches* (Grand Rapids, Michigan, 1975), 35; Robert C. Twombley and Robert H. Moore, *Black Puritans, The Negro in Seventeenth Century Massachusetts* (Indianapolis, 1969); Jules Zanger, "Crime and Punishment in Early Massachusetts," *William and Mary Quarterly,* 3rd series, XXII (1965), 471-77.

25. Greene, *The Negro in Colonial New England,* 125-67. Importantly, this legislation did not provide for the status of the children of slaves, although a 1670 revision of the code would provide for children of slaves to be sold *into* slavery. Children, according to English common law, held the same status as their father. This convention, while generally ignored, never was altered by legislation in New England as it had been in the Southern colonies. During the Revolutionary Era African Americans would capitalize on this flaw in the New England slave codes. See the discussions of the Slew and Somersett freedom suits in this chapter.

26. See especially: Jay Coughtry, *The Notorious Triangle* (Philadelphia, 1982).

27. Gary Nash, *Red, White, and Black* (New York, 1970); Winthrop D. Jordan, "Enslavement in America to 1700" in ed. Stanley N. Katz, *Colonial America* (Boston: Little Brown, 1976 ed.), 229-70. For details of trade route and cargo patterns for ships sailing from Plymouth see: *Barnes Family Collection,* Isaac Barnes File, "Miscellaneous Shipping Papers, 1787-1806," shipping papers for schooners *Sally, Little Lucy, Polly,* and *Laura;* William Davis Collection, Business papers of William and Thomas Davis, Ships Merchants, both in Pilgrim Society Archives, Plymouth, Massachusetts. For King Philip's War, see: Douglas Leach, *Flintlock and Tomahawk: New Negland in King Philip's War* (New York, 1958).

28. For cases of eighteenth-century slaveholders providing posthumously for the manumission of their slaves see: Plymouth Registry of Deeds and Probate, Vols. I:202-3; IV:120-1; IV: 239-40; XIV:334, 336; Justin Winsor, *History of Duxbury, Massachusetts: with genealogical registers* (Boston, 1849), 71; Thomas Weston, *History of Middleboro, Massachusetts* (Boston, 1906), 105, 429. Colonial legislation stipulating the conditions under which slaves might be freed

first appeared in New England around 1680, generally combined with other codes related to the regulation of slaves.

29. Plymouth Registry of Deeds, Vol. 9:433-4.

30. Plymouth Registry of Deeds, Vol. 25:37; Nahum Mitchell, *History of Bridgewater* (Boston, 1840), 207-10.

31. Plymouth Registry of Deeds, Vol. 52, 199-200; Mitchell, *History of Bridgewater*, 127.

32. Plymouth Colony Records, Vol. XI, Laws (1623-1682), 17, 188. The legislation anticipated later homesteading provisions, allowing for the allocation of five-acre tracts at the satisfactory conclusion of a term of service "if they be found fit to occupie it for themselves in some convenient place."

33. Twombly and Moore, *Black Puritans*; Louis Ruchmes, "Sources of Racial Thought in Colonial America," *Journal of Negro History* 52 (October 1967), 264-7.

34. Kingston Vital Records, Births, Deaths, and Marriages, Book 1:51, 94. Plymouth Records of the General Sessions of the Peace, Vol. 2:165. Japheth Rickard, a descendent of Joseph Rickard, whose earliest known residence was Middleboro, had married Martha Mitchell of nearby Kingston in 1751. Japheth and Martha's first child, Susannah, was born in Middleboro four months after their marriage, and shortly after her birth the family faced a series of crises common among the impoverished of colonial New England. Repeated cross-references to the Plymouth sheep pasture as "The Parting Ways" make clear that by mid-century the tract of land on the Carver Road had been identified in popular thought by its ecological and spatial location rather than by its originally designated use as common grazing lands.

35. Plymouth Records of the Court of Common Pleas, Vol. 11:98, 218. Problems within their marriage probably compounded the Rickards' marginal economic and social circumstances. In January 1756, Japheth Rickard "blacklisted" his wife, placing public notice with the town of Plymouth that "I denye paying any thing that any Bodey shall Trust her, on my Acco^t." See: Plymouth Town Records, Vol. 3: 687.

36. Plympton Vital Records to 1850:104, 107, 293, 312, 323, 446. Fuller, a native of Plympton, was born at about the same time that the sheep pasture had been laid out. Fuller married twice, first to Sarah Wright of Plympton in 1720 and then to the widow Deborah Edwards Cole in 1726. Fuller's son Archippus was born in 1721, settled in Middleboro, and is described as a wheelwright. He later would dispose of the interest his father acquired in the sheep pasture lands.

37. Plymouth Records of the Court of General Sessions of the Peace, Vol. 2:170.

38. Plymouth Records of the Court of General Sessions of the Peace, Vol. 3:55, 99, 142, 172.

39. Plymouth Town Records, Vol. 3:250; Plymouth County Registry of Deeds, Book 53:260.

40. Plymouth Records of the Court of General Sessions of the Peace, Vol. 3:364.

41. Plymouth Registry of Deeds, Book 57:186.
42. Plymouth Registry of Deeds, Book 58:113. After Archippus Fuller had paid his father's debt to Samuel Bartlett, the sale of Seth Fuller's homestead yielded a profit of 12 pounds.
43. Several of his children had died in infancy. During the 1760s Elijah Leach had been involved in three lawsuits, once as the plaintiff and twice as the defendant. All involved trespassing and nonpayment of debt and none of the suits were resolved in his favor. Perhaps shamed by the publicity, or perhaps discouraged with his diminished status in Bridgewater, in 1765 Leach sold his 26-acre farm that he had owned for only three years. During 1765 Leach also had been reprimanded by the Plymouth court twice for public misbehavior (indecent exposure and irreverent speeches). In March 1767, Leach and his household—his mother, wife, son, daughter, and his wife's niece—were warned out of the hamlet of Halifax. The whereabouts of Leach and his family are not known from 1767 until 1773, when Leach purchased Seth Fuller's dwelling house, building, fencing, and right to the unimproved land at The Parting Ways. Bridgewater Vital Records, Vol. I:206, 207, 209, 210; Vol. II:235, 236, 513, 515, 517; Records of the Court of General Sessions of the Peace, Vol. 3:155-56. Records of the Court of Common Pleas, Vol. 12:483; Vol. 13:6, 64. Plymouth Registry of Deeds, Book 50:176. At mid-life, an outcast, gone to live on the former sheep pasture, Leach was still living a life of wandering. His son enlisted in the Continental Army, his daughter warned out of Pembroke in April 1777 and convicted of fornication in 1780 before she finally married and settled in Bridgewater in 1786, Leach sold his Parting Ways tract and moved to Westmorland. Plymouth Registry of Deeds, Book 57:186. General Sessions of the Peace, Vol. 3:511-12.
44. General Sessions of the Peace, Vol. 3:511-12.
45. Plymouth Registry of Deeds, Book 60:165; 68:210, 258.
46. Lazarus LeBaron (1699-1773), was the son of French surgeon Francis LeBaron. After being shipwrecked in Buzzard's Bay, Francis LeBaron had been granted the right to settle in Plymouth. Lazarus LeBaron studied medicine and maintained a large and successful practice in Plymouth, and his sons emigrated to the West Indies.
47. Elizabeth Rauh Bethel, *Life Events as Indices of Social Status: Mate Selection and Reproduction Among Afro-Americans in Southeastern Massachusetts, 1650-1780*. Unpublished paper presented at the Southern Sociological Society Annual Meeting (1984).
48. The details of Quashey Quandey's life are distilled from a number of sources. See especially: Jane G. Austin, *Dr. LeBaron and His Daughters* (Boston, 1890); Plymouth, Massachusetts *First Church Records* (1620-1859), 420; Plymouth, Massachusetts *Births, Deaths, Marriages and Publishments* Vol. 1A:281; Kingston, Massachusetts *Vital Records to 1850*:396; Quashey Quandey *Fact Sheet*, (mimeo, n.p., n.d.), Parting Ways, The Museum of Afro-American Ethnohistory, Plymouth, Massachusetts. There is no record of manumission for either

Quashy or Phillis Quash, and the timing of Phillis's arrival at The Parting Ways remains problematic.

49. Austin, *Dr. LeBaron and His Daughters,* 441.

50. Miscellaneous House Documents and Papers, Box 74: No. 4488, Massachusetts State Archives; Bridgewater, Massachusetts; *Vital Records,* Vol. 4 (1785-1808):60, 104, 154 Plympton, Massachusetts *Town Records* (1802-1815), 460; Scituate, Massachusetts *Town Records,* Vol. C-8B:106; Scituate, Massachusetts *Town Meetings* Vol. 8(1782-1796), 129, both in Scituate, Massachusetts Town Archives; *Warnings Out of Town Files,* Parting Ways Museum; Gary Nash, *The Great Fear* (New York, 1970), 25

51. For discussions of regional and temporal variations in American slavery see especially: Ira Berlin, "Time, Space, and the Evolution of Afro-American Society on British Mainland North America," *American Historical Review* 85 (February 1980):44-78.

52. Greene, *The Negro in Colonial New England,* xx; Leon Litwak, *North of Slavery* (Chicago, 1961); Orlando Patterson, *Slavery and Social Death* (Cambridge, Massachusetts, 1962); David Brion Davis, *The Problem of Slavery in Western Culture* (Ithaca, 1966).

53. Raymond A. Bauer and Alice H. Bauer, "Day to Day Resistance to Slavery," *Journal of Negro History* 27 (October 1942), 388-419; Lorenzo J. Greene, "The New England Negro as Seen in Advertisements for Runaway Slaves," *Journal of Negro History* 2 (April 1944), 125-46

54. John Daniels, *In Freedom's Birthplace* (New York, 1969 reprint ed.), 9-10.

55. Records of the Inferior Court of the Court of Common Pleas of Massachusetts (September 1760-July 1776), 520; Records of the Superior Court of Judicature, Commonwealth of Massachusetts, (1776)7:175, as cited in Roger Bruns, *Am I Not A Man and a Brother* (New York, 1983), 106-7.

56. Greene, *The Negro in Colonial New England,* 21-50; Nash, *Red, White and Black,* 282ff; Kenneth W.Porter, *Relations Between Negroes and Indians Within the Present Limits of the United States* (Washington, D.C., 1930), 310-12.

57. E. D. Preston, Jr., "Genesis of the Underground Railroad," *Journal of Negro History* 18 (April 1933), 144, 170.

58. Deposition of Elnathan Samson and John Chaffee, July 9, 1770. Records of the Town of Dartmouth, *Town Meetings* (1674-1787), 455.

59. Receipt to Cuff Slocum from David Brownell, December 15, 1766. Paul Cuffe Collection. New Bedford Free Public Library. New Bedford, Massachusetts.

60. Venture Smith's life is fully recounted in his autobiography, *A Narrative of the Life and Adventures of Venture, A Native of Africa: but resident above sixty years in the United States of America.* Related by himself (New-London, Connecticut, 1798).

61. Massachusetts Historical Society Collections, Series 5, III:439-42; *Massachusetts Historical Society Proceedings* (Series 1, 20 vols, Boston, 1859-84) XIII, 298; Helen T. Catterall, *Judicial Cases Concerning American Slavery and the Negro,* 5

Vols. (Washington, D.C., 1926-37), Vol. IV:481; Litwack, *North of Slavery,* 10-11; Arthur Zilversmit, *The First Emancipation* (Chicago, 1967).

62. Litwak, *North of Slavery,* 9. For examples see: Joseph B. Felt, *Annals of Salem,* 2nd ed, 2 Vols. (Salem, 1849), II:417; George H. Moore, *Notes on the History of Slavery in Massachusetts* (New York, 1866).

63. The following discussion of The Parting Ways residents' lives from the end of the Revolutionary War to the deaths of the veterans is distilled from the Fact Sheets for Prince Goodwin, Cato Howe, Quashey Quandey, Quomony Quash, and Plato Turner compiled by Parting Ways, The Museum of Afro-American Ethno-History, Plymouth, Massachusetts. I am indebted to the Museum for its long effort to preserve this chapter of the story of Africans and their descendants in New England.

64. James Deetz, *In Small Things Forgotten* (Garden City, NY, 1977), 148.

65. Plymouth, Massachusetts *Town Records,* Vol. 4 (1796-1828), 477.

CHAPTER TWO

1. David Walker, *Walker's Appeal, in Four Articles: Together with a Preamble, to the Coloured Citizens of the World, but in particular and very expressly, to those of the United States of America, written in Boston, State of Massachusetts, September 28, 1829* (Boston, 1829).

2. For a review of cases see: Charles H. Wesley, "The Participation of Negroes in Anti-Slavery Political Parties," *Journal of Negro History* 29 (January 1944), 32-74; Charles H. Wesley, "Negro Suffrage in the Period of Constitution-Making, 1787-1865," *Journal of Negro History* 32 (April 1947),143-68.

3. For discussions of nationalism and ethnic identity and comparisons of white and African-American nationalism during the nineteenth century, see especially: Benedict Anderson, *Imagined Communities: Reflections of the Origins and Spread of Nationalism* (London, 1985); Rodney Carlisle, *The Roots of Black Nationalism* (Port Washington, New York, 1975); Michael Fischer, "Ethnicity and the Post-Modern Art of Memory," in *Writing Culture: The Poetics and Politics of Ethnography,* eds. James Clifford and George E. Marcus (Berkeley, 1986); Wilson J. Moses, *The Golden Age of Black Nationalism* (Hamden, Connecticut, 1978); Werner Sollors, "Introduction," *The Invention of Ethnicity* (New York, 1989).

4. The problem of defining the African-American elite/middle class is an enduring scholarly conundrum. While there is little research to guide analysis of early-nineteenth-century African-American class structure, scholars of later periods have struggled with both the contours of class and the nature of relationships among various strata in African-American communities. W. E. B. DuBois, in *The Philadelphia Negro* (New York, 1899) posited parallel class delineators: the

more conventional strata defined by occupation and income, and second, less explicit strata distinguished in socio-moral terms. While their analytic perspectives differ in other important ways, E. Franklin Frazier, *Black Bourgeoisie* (New York, 1957) and St. Clair Drake and Horace Cayton, *Black Metropolis* (New York, 1962) recognize the methodological fragility of socioeconomic criteria for illuminating African-American class structure and, like DuBois, turn to symbolic and ideational delineators.

5. Prince Hall, *Address to African Lodge No. 459* (Boston, 1797).

6. Four of Jupiter Hammon's poems survive: *An Evening Thought: salvation by Christ, with penitential cries* (Long-Island, 1760); *An Address to Miss Phillis Wheatley, Ethiopian Poetess, in Boston* (Long-Island, 1778); *A Poem for Children with Thoughts on Death* (Hartford, 1782); *An Evening's Improvement: Shewing, the necessity of beholding the Lamb of God* (Long-Island, 1790). *The Poetry of Jupiter Hammon* (computer file) (Alexandria, VA, 1995). Three of Hammon's essays survive: *A Winter Piece* (Hartford, 1782); *An Evening's Improvement* (Hartford, 1783); and *An Address to the Negroes of New-York* (New-York, 1787). For a biographical sketch see: Oscar Wegelin, *Jupiter Hammon, American Negro Poet* (New York, 1915).

7. Jupiter Hammon, *A Winter Piece*, 2; *An Evening's Improvement*, 3. His reference to his superiors doubtless refers to his master, John Lloyd.

8. Hammon, *An Address to the Negroes of New-York*, 13-14.

9. For examples of African-American spiritual autobiography see especially: *A Narrative of the Most Remarkable Particulars in the Life of James Albert Ukawsaw Gronniosaw, An African Prince* (Newport, Rhode Island, 1774 reprint ed.); *Narrative of the Lord's Wonderful Dealings with John Marrant, A Black*, ed. William Aldridge, (London, 1785); George White, *A Brief Account of the Life, Experiences, Travels, and Gospel Labours of George White* (New York, 1810); *The Life and Religious Experience of Jarena Lee, A Coloured Lady, Giving an Account of Her Call to Preach the Gospel* (Philadelphia, 1836); *Memoirs of the Life, Religious Experience, Ministerial Travels and Labours of Mrs. Zilpha Elaw, An American Female of Colour* (Philadelphia, 1836). For a broader discussion of spiritual autobiography see: William L. Andrews, "Introduction," in *Sisters of the Spirit* (Bloomington, Indiana, 1986), 1-22; Jerome Hamilton Buckley, *The Turning Key, Autobiography and the Subjective Impulse Since 1800* (Cambridge, Massachusetts, 1984); A. O. J. Cockshut, *The Art of Autobiography in 19th and 20th Century England* (New Haven, 1984).

10. See especially: Hans S. Baer and Merrill Singer, *African-American Religion in the Twentieth Century, Varieties of Protest and Accommodation* (Knoxville, 1992); Randall K. Burkett, *Garvyism as a Religious Movement: The Institutionalization of a Black Civil Religion* (Metuchen, New Jersey, 1978); W. E. B. DuBois, *The Negro Church in America* (Atlanta, 1903); Arthur H. Fauset, *Black Gods of the Metropolis* (Philadelphia, 1971); E. Franklin Frazier, *The Negro Church in America* (New York, 1974); Sara Harris, *Father Divine* (New York, 1971); C. Eric Lincoln, *Race, Religion, and the Continuing American Dilemma* (New York,

1984); Gary R. Peck, "Black Radical Consciousness and the Black Christian Experience: Toward a Critical Sociology of African-American Religion," *Sociological Analysis* 43 (January 1982), 155-69; Robert Weisbrot, *Father Divine and the Struggle for Racial Equality* (Urbana, 1983) Carter G. Woodson, *The History of the Negro Church*, 2nd ed. (Washington, D.C., 1945). Scholarly analysis and popular discussion of Martin Luther King, Jr.'s theology of liberation is extensive. David Garrow, *Bearing the Cross, Martin Luther King Jr. and the Southern Christian Leadership Conference* (New York, 1986) and David L. Lewis, *King, A Critical Biography* (New York, 1970) are excellent biographical studies, but the most concise and accessible personal statement of King's theology of liberation is found in: Martin Luther King, Jr., *Why We Can't Wait* (New York, 1964) and *Where Do We Go From Here?* (London, 1968).

11. Hammon, *A Winter Piece*, 2; *An Evening's Improvement*, 3; *An Address to the Negroes of New-York*, 5-12.

12. Hammon, *A Winter Piece*, 9; *An Address to the Negroes of New-York*, 5-12.

13. Hammon, *Address to the Negroes of New-York*, 6.

14. Hammon, *A Winter Piece*, 9; *An Evening's Improvement*, 3, 8, 20.

15. Hammon, *An Address to the Negroes of New-York*, 9.

16. Ibid., 20.

17. William H. Grimshaw, *Official History of Freemasonry Among the Colored People of North America* (New York, 1903, 1969 reprint ed.), 72 lists Cyrus Jonbus, Bensten Slinger, Thomas Saunderson, Prince Taylor, Cato Spear, Boston Smith, Peter Best, Fortin Howard, Prince Rees, John Cantin, Peter Freeman, Benjamin Tiber, Buff Buform, and Richard Lilly as the group who, with Prince Hall, obtained admission to Masonry from British Lodge No. 58. Grimshaw also speculates that the British Army Lodge that inducted Hall and the others previously had been posted to the British West Indies and had there inducted other men of color, who may have been assigned with the regiment in 1775. Following Grimshaw's logic, the induction of Hall and the other African-American Bostonians probably was not the precedent-setting event that it initially might appear to be.

18. Grimshaw, *Official History*, 67-96; Harry E. Davis, *A History of Freemasonry Among Negroes in America* (The United Supreme Council, Ancient and Accepted Scottish Rite of Freemasonry, Northern Jurisdiction, U.S.A., 1846), 14-29; Hall, *Address to African Lodge No. 459, 1797*, 4.

19. The petition is reprinted in: *A Documentary History of the Negro People*, ed. Herbert Aptheker (New York, 1951), 19-20.

20. Primus Hall and Prince Hall were not kinspeople. Aptheker, *Documentary History*, 19; James Oliver Horton, *Black Activism in Boston* (Unpublished Ph.D. dissertation, Brandeis University, 1973), 18-19. African Americans have continued to struggle with educational inequalities in Boston. See especially: *Report of the Colored People of the City of Boston on the Subject of Exclusive Schools*. Submitted by Benjamin R. Roberts, to the Boston Equal School Rights

Committee (Boston, 1850) and J. Anthony Lukas, *Common Ground* (New York, 1986).

21. Leon Litwak, *North of Slavery* (Chicago, 1961), 121; Carter G. Woodson, *The Education of the Negro* (New York, 1915), 96-101; Edgar McManus, *A History of Negro Slavery in New York* (Syracuse, 1966), 173-4; C. C. Andrews, *The History of the New York African Free Schools from their Establishment in 1787 to the Present Time* (New York, 1830); *Freedom's Journal,* January 11, February 1, 1828.

22. James McCune Smith, "Introduction" in Henry Highland Garnet, *A Memorial Discourse Delivered in the Hall of the House of Representatives, Washington, D.C., 12 February 1865* (Philadelphia, 1865), 22-23; New York City Directories, 1821-1831; Andrews, *History of the New York African Free Schools.*

23. Richard Allen, *The Life Experience and Gospel Labors of the Rt. Rev. Richard Allen, Written by Himself,* Introduction by George A. Singleton (Philadelphia, 1833; Nashville, 1960 reprint ed.), 15-36. See also: Carol V. R. George, *Segregated Sabbaths: Richard Allen and the Emergence of Independent Black Churches, 1760-1840* (New York, 1973); Harry V. Richardson, *Dark Salvation: The Story of Methodism as it Developed Among Blacks in America* (Garden City, New York, 1976); Charles H. Wesley, *Richard Allen: Apostle of Freedom* (Washington, D.C., 1935).

24. George Freeman Bragg, *The Story of the First Blacks, The Pathfinder Absalom Jones* (Baltimore, 1929) provides the most complete biographical information on Jones. See also: William Douglass, *Annals of the First African Church, in the U.S.A., now styled The African Episcopal Church of St. Thomas, Philadelphia* (Philadelphia, 1862); George, *Segregated Sabbaths;* Julie Winch, *Philadelphia's Black Elite, Activism, Accommodation, and the Struggle for Autonomy, 1787-1848* (Philadelphia, 1973).

25. For an autobiographical account see: Allen, *Life Experience and Gospel Labors,* 24-25. See also: Baer and Singer, *African-American Religion in the Twentieth Century, Varieties of Protest and Accommodation,* 18-20; George, *Segregated Sabbaths,* 55; Winch, *Philadelphia's Black Elite,* 9-11.

26. Allen, *Life Experience and Gospel Labors,* 15-36.

27. *Speak Out in Thunder Tones, Letters and Other Writings by Black Northerners, 1787-1865,* ed. Dorothy Sterling (New York, 1973), 31

28. Aptheker, *Documentary History,* 17-18; John Daniels, *In Freedom's Birthplace* (New York, 1969 reprint ed.), 18-22.

29. The self-descriptive phrase is taken from *The Proceedings of The Free African Union Society and the African Benevolent Society, Newport, Rhode Island, 1780-1824,* ed. William H. Robinson (Providence, Rhode Island, 1976), x. In their correspondence with other societies the Newporters described themselves as "strangers in a strange land" as a partial explanation for their African emigration initiative.

30. Robinson, *Proceedings of The Free African Union Society,* 61-62.

31. Mathew Carey, *An Account of the rise, progress, and termination of the malignant fever, lately prevalent in Philadelphia* (Philadelphia, 1793), 28. See also: Mathew Carey, *A desultory account of the yellow fever; prevalent in Philadelphia, and of the present state of the city* (Philadelphia, 1793).

32. Mathew Carey, *An Account of the malignant fever, lately prevalent in Philadelphia* (Dublin, 1794).

33. Carey, *An Account of the rise, progress, and termination,* 28-31

34. Absalom Jones and Richard Allen, *A Narrative of the Proceedings of the Black People, During the Late Awful Calamity in Philadelphia, in the Year 1793, and A Refutation of some Censures Thrown upon them in some late Publications* (Philadelphia, 1793), 4.

35. Carey, *An Account of the rise, progress, and termination,* 28-31.

36. Jones and Allen, *A Narrative,* 22-27.

37. Ibid., 23.

38. Robinson, *Proceedings of The Free African Union Society,* 16-22.

39. William Thornton to Samuel Hopkins, September 29, 1790, in Robinson, *Proceedings of the Free African Union Society,* 33. The Sierra Leone Company made similar promises to African-American Loyalists who had removed to Nova Scotia during the final months of the Revolutionary War and subsequently joined the Sierra Leone venture. The promises were not always kept. See chapter 4 for a more extensive discussion of the Sierra Leone Colony and the involvement of African Americans in the early settlement years there.

40. Bonnar Brown and James McKinzie to Brethren of the Union Society in Newport, January 15, 1794, Charles Chaloner and Newport Gardner to Brethren of the African Society in Providence, n.d., in Robinson, *Proceedings of the Free African Union Society,* 42-45.

41. Floyd J. Miller, *The Search for a Black Nationality, Black Colonization and Emigration, 1787-1863* (Urbana, 1975), 11-20.

42. Some, however, continued to hope for repatriation in their lost homeland. In 1826 Newport Gardner, then in his mid-seventies, "gathered a handfull of similarly frustrated Blacks" and the group traveled to Boston where they boarded the American Colonization Society brig *Vine* and sailed for Liberia. The entire group succumbed to the African fever. See: Robinson, *Proceedings of the Free African Union Society,* 59; Miller, *The Search for a Black Nationality,* 20.

43. Rodney Carlisle, *The Roots of Black Nationalism* (Port Washington, New York, 1975); Theodore Draper, *The Rediscovery of Black Nationalism* (New York, 1970), 14-47. For a more extensive discussion of African emigration see chapter 5. For a more extension discussion of the streams of New World emigration see chapter 6.

44. For biographical treatments see: Sheldon H. Harris, *Paul Cuffe: Black America and the African Return* (New York, 1972); George Salvador, *Paul Cuffe, the Black Yankee, 1759-1817* (New Bedford, Massachusetts, 1969); Henry Nobel Sherwood, "Paul Cuffe," *Journal of Negro History* 8 (January 1923), 153-229.

Cuffe's 1780 petition against taxation without representation is reprinted in Aptheker, *A Documentary History of the Negro People in the United States*, 15-16.

45. Two decades after the initial publication of *Walker's Appeal*, at the 1849 State Convention of Ohio Negroes, forty-one delegates meeting in Columbus, Ohio recommended that five hundred copies of the *Appeal* "be obtained in the name of the convention and gratuitously circulated" among the state's African-American population. *Minutes and Address of the State Convention of the Colored Citizens of Ohio, Convened at Columbus, January 10th, 11th, 12th, & 13th, 1849* (Columbus, Ohio, 1849).

PART II INTRODUCTION

1. W. E. B. DuBois, "The Conservation of the Races." American Negro Academy Occasional Papers, No. 2 (1897),11.

2. The Haytian emigrations are discussed more extensively in chapter 6.

3. For African-American protests against the American Colonization Society see especially: William Lloyd Garrison, *Thoughts on African Colonization: or an impartial exhibition of the Doctrines, Principles & Purposes of the American Colonization Society. Together with the Resolutions, Addresses, & Remonstrances of the Free People of Color*, Part II (Boston, 1832), 62-3; *Minutes and Proceedings of the American Society of Free Persons of Colour, for Improving their Condition in the United States, for Purchasing Lands, and for Establishing a Settlement in Upper Canada* (Philadelphia, 1830), 6. See also: Bella Gross, "The First National Convention," *Journal of Negro History* 31 (April 1946), 435-43. New Yorkers Peter Williams, Jr. and Samuel Cornish had been planning an anti-colonization convention and Allen, eager to upstage their plans, had responded positively to Grice's suggestion and convened the meeting in Philadelphia.

4. *Minutes and Proceedings of the American Society of Free Persons of Colour*, 6.

CHAPTER THREE

1. Absalom Jones, *A Thanksgiving Sermon, Preached January 1, 1808, in St. Thomas's Church, Philadelphia, on Account of the Abolition of the Slave Trade* (Philadelphia, 1808), 26.

2. Absalom Jones (1746-1818) was born a slave in Sussex, Delaware, was brought to Philadelphia at the age of sixteen to work as clerk/handyman in his master's store, attended Anthony Benezet's school for slaves, and married a slave in 1770, at the age of twenty-four. With the assistance of Philadelphia Quakers, Jones

and his wife purchased their freedom in 1784. Jones met Richard Allen in 1786 and joined Allen in his ministry to Philadelphia African Americans. The two, with the aid and cooperation of other leaders in the Philadelphia African-American community, organized the Free African Society in 1787 and, with the aid of Benjamin Rush, The African Church in 1791. In 1793 Jones, Allen, and Rush mobilized the city's African-American population to serve as nurses and undertakers during the Philadelphia yellow fever epidemic. In 1794 Jones was licensed as a lay reader and assumed the duties of rector at The African Church, now renamed St. Thomas African Episcopal Church. He was ordained into the Episcopal priesthood in 1804. Jones held a number of offices in the Philadelphia African Masonic lodge, joined in a variety of efforts to end the slave trade and slavery in the United States and in 1817, the year before his death, helped organize the Philadelphia colonization protest. George Freeman Bragg, *The Story of the First Blacks, The Pathfinder Absalom Jones* (Baltimore, 1929) provides the most complete biographical information on Jones. See also: William Douglass, *Annals of the First African Church, in the U.S.A., now styled The African Episcopal Church of St. Thomas, Philadelphia* (Philadelphia, 1862); Carol V. R. George, *Segregated Sabbaths: Richard Allen and the Emergence of Independent Black Churches, 1760-1840* (New York, 1973); Julie Winch, *Philadelphia's Black Elite, Activism, Accommodation, and the Struggle for Autonomy, 1787-1848* (Philadelphia, 1973); J. H. Powell, *Bring Out Your Dead* (Philadelphia, 1949).

3. W. E. B. DuBois, *The Suppression of the African Slave Trade to the United States of America* (1896, Baton Rouge, 1969 reprint ed.), 95.

4. Peter Williams, Jr., *Oration on the Abolition of the Slave Trade; Delivered in The African Church in New York City, January 1, 1807/8* (New-York, 1807-8), 9.

5. DuBois's, *Suppression of the African Slave Trade* remains a thorough analysis of the 1807-8 and subsequent legislation on the African slave trade.

6. Precise demographic statements for this period are not possible. For various estimates of the composition of the black adult population during the nineteenth century see: Robert W. Fogel and Stanley L. Engerman, *Time on the Cross,* 2 Vols. (Boston, 1974); Lorenzo J. Greene, *The Negro in Colonial New England* (Port Washington, New York, 1942); Evarts B. Greene and Virginia Harrington, *American Population Before the Federal Census of 1790* (New York, 1932); James A. Henretta, *Evolution of American Society, 1700-1815* (Lexington, Massachusetts, 1973).

7. Peter Williams, Jr. (1780?-1840), New York clergyman, abolitionist, and community leader, was born to a slave father who bought his own freedom in 1796 and a free West Indian mother, both said to be of undiluted African descent. Educated in the New York City Free African Schools and licensed as a lay reader in the Episcopal Church, Williams established a separate African-American congregation—St. Phillip's African Church—from which he guided the free African-American community both morally and politically. Williams helped found the first African-American newspaper, *Freedom's Journal,* opposed

African colonization, supported aid to the Canadian refugee settlements, emerged as a leader in the Convention Movement of the 1830s, and traveled to Hayti to assist African Americans in their resettlement there. James McCune Smith, Alexander Crummell, Charles L. Reason, Peter Vogelstand, and George Thomas Downing were among the most prominent members of Williams congregation at St. Phillip's. For additional information see: B. F. DeCosta, *Three Score and Ten: The Story of St. Phillip's Church* (New York, 1889); *Early Negro Writing, 1760-1834,* ed. Dorothy Burnett Porter (Boston, 1971); Joseph Beaumont Wakely, *Lost Chapters Recovered from the Early History of African Methodism* (New York, 1858).

8. Williams, Jr., *Oration on the Abolition of the Slave Trade,* 19-20.

9. Paul Cuffe (1759-1817), the seventh of ten children born to Cuff Slocum (an African who bought his own freedom) and his Wampanoag wife, Ruth Moses, were born and raised in the maritime milieu around New Bedford, Massachusetts and Newport, Rhode Island. Cuffe amassed a fortune in whaling, coastal shipping, and trade with Europe and the Caribbean, and enjoyed warm professional and personal relationships with a number of prominent white American and English Quakers and merchant-philanthropists. Cuffe was active in the early (pre-Garrisonian) abolitionist movement, advanced a plan to colonize Sierra Leone, and built a dynastic economic and political legacy. For biographical treatments see: Sheldon Harris, *Paul Cuffe: Black America and the Africa Return* (New York, 1971); George Salvador, *Paul Cuffe, The Black Yankee* (New Bedford, MA, 1969); Sherwood, Paul Cuffe, *Journal of Negro History,* 153-229. Cuffe's *A Brief Account of the Settlement and Present Situation of the Colony of Sierra Leone in Africa as Communicated by Paul Cuffe (a Man of Colour) to His Friend in New York* (New York, 1812) and his 1780 petition against taxation without representation, reprinted in Aptheker, *A Documentary History of the Negro People in the United States,* 14-16, offers additional insight into the intersection of politics and theology in Paul Cuffe's thought.

10. Williams, Jr., *Oration on the Abolition of the Slave Trade,* 11-12.

11. Ibid., 13-26.

12. Jones, *Thanksgiving Sermon,* 15-16.

13. Ibid., 19.

14. See Joseph Sidney, *An Oration, Commemorative of the Abolition of the Slave Trade in the United States, Delivered Before the Wilberforce Philanthropic Association in the City of New-York, on the Second of January, 1809* (New-York, 1809); Russell Parrott, *An Address on the Abolition of the Slave Trade, Delivered Before the Different African Benevolent Societies, on the 1st of January, 1816* (Philadelphia, 1816); Paul Dean, *A Discourse Delivered Before the African Society, at their Meeting House, in Boston, Mass. on the Abolition of the Slave Trade* (Boston, 1819).

15. Henry Sipkins, *An Oration on the Abolition of the Slave Trade: Delivered in the African Church, in the City of New York, January 2 1809, By Henry Sipkins, A Descendant of Africa* (New-York, 1809); William Miller, *A Sermon on the*

Abolition of the Slave Trade, Delivered in the African Church, New-York, on the First of January 1810, By the Rev. William Miller, Minister of the African Methodist Episcopal Church (New-York, 1810).

16. Sidney, *An Oration, Commemorative of the Abolition of the Slave Trade in the United States,* 4-5, 8-9. At a meeting in April 1809 members of the Electors of Colour in New York City affirmed Sidney's admonition, declaring their support for the Federal Republican Party. See especially: *A Meeting in Mechanics Hall, New York City, 24 April 1809,* a broadside, as cited in Wesley, "Negro Suffrage in the Period of Constitution-Making," *Journal of Negro History,* 143-68; Dixon Ryan Fox, "The Negro Vote in Old New York," *Political Science Quarterly* 32 (1917), 252-75.

17. William Miller is listed in the New York City Directories from 1815 through 1836. Miller had joined with a number of other African Americans, including Peter Williams, Jr., in a withdrawal from the John Street Methodist Episcopal Church in 1796. In 1810 Miller and Thomas Simpkins led a withdrawal from the original African-American congregation and the formation of an African Methodist Episcopal congregation, thereby declaring their theological if not political alliance with Richard Allen in Philadelphia. On more explicitly political concerns, Miller and Simpkins maintained a solid alliance with other New Yorkers against the Philadelphia cabal headed by Richard Allen.

18. Miller, *A Sermon on the Abolition of the Slave Trade* (1810).

19. Joseph Sidney, *An Oration, Commemorative of the Abolition of the Slave Trade in the United States; Delivered in the African Asbury Church in the City of New-York, on the First of January 1814* (New-York, 1814), 10-11.

20. Parrott, *An Address on the Abolition of the Slave Trade on the 1st of January 1816* (1816), 4-8. A Philadelphia printer, Parrott was closely allied with James Forten on a wide range of social and political causes

21. *Resolutions and Remonstrances of the People of Colour against Colonization on the Coast of Africa* (Philadelphia, 1818), 4.

22. See: Alfred N. Hunt, *Hayti's Influence on Antebellum America* (Baton Rouge, 1988), 84-101 for an extended discussion of United States foreign policy toward Hayti and France during this period.

23. Toussaint's role in shaping Hayti and his (untested) policies on trade, political autonomy, the role of Hayti's mulattos in national development, and the revival of the plantation system have led at least one student of Hayti to dub him the "Kenyatta of the Caribbean." See David Nicholls, *From Dessalines to Duvalier, Race, Colour and National Independence in Hayti* (New Brunswick, New Jersey, 1996 ed.), 29. On Toussaint, see: Aime Cesaire, *Toussaint Louveture* (Paris, 1962); Hunt, *Hayti's Influence,* chapter 3, "Toussaint's Image," 84-101; R. Korngold, *Citizen Toussaint: A Biography* (New York, 1942).

24. Hunt, *Hayti's Influence,* 88.

25. Lured into the French camp, arrested, and deported to France, Toussaint died in a French jail in 1803.

26. See especially Sister M. Reginald Gerdes, OSP, "To Educate and Evangelize: Black Catholic Schools of the Oblate Sisters of Providence (1828-1880)," *U.S. Catholic Historian* 7 (Spring/Summer, 1988), 183-200; Nicholls, *From Dessalines to Duvalier,* chapter 2, "Fathers of National Independence, 1804-1825," 33-66; Julie Winch, *Philadelphia's Black Elite: Activism, Accommodation, and the Struggle for Autonomy, 1787-1848,* (Philadelphia, 1988), 49-69.

27. See especially Sterling Stuckey, *Slave Culture, Nationalist Theory, and the Foundations of Black America* (New York, 1987), 3-98 and Benjamin Peter Hunt, *Remarks on Hayti* (Philadelphia, 1860), 4-14 for a description of the emigration.

28. See especially Herbert Aptheker, *Negro Slave Revolts in the United States, 1526-1860* (New York, 1939), 219-26; Arna Bontemp's fictionalization of the event, *Black Thunder* (1936; Boston, 1986 reprint ed.); Gerald W. Mullin, *Flight and Rebellion: Slave Resistance in Eighteenth Century Virginia* (New York, 1972), 140-61; Paula Giddings, *When and Where I Enter* (New York, 1984), 40.

29. Hunt, *Hayti's Influence on Antebellum America,* 152.

30. Jesse Torrey, *A Portrait of Domestic Slavery in the United States and a Project of a Colonial Asylum for Free Persons of Color* (Philadelphia, 1817), 22-23.

31. Prince Hall, *A Charge Delivered to the African Lodge, June 24th, 1797, at Menotomy,* as reproduced in William Cooper Nell, *Colored Patriots of the American Revolution* (Boston, 1855), 62.

32. John Brown Russwurm (1799-1851) was born in Jamaica to a free white father and a slave mother, although he was treated as a free person during his Jamaican boyhood. Russwurm was sent to Quebec in 1807 and there received his primary education, joining his father and (white) stepmother in Portland, Maine when he was a teenager. Russwurm graduated from Bowdoin College in 1826, moved to New York City, and, in partnership with Samuel E. Cornish, became the co-founder and co-editor of the first African-American newspaper in the United States, *Freedom's Journal.* Cornish and Russwurm first published David Walker's fiery *Appeal* in the pages of their newspaper. Although initially opposed to colonization, by 1829 Russwurm had come to believe that African Americans could never enjoy the rights and privileges of full and unconditional citizenship in the United States and in the pages of *Freedom's Journal* announced his intention to emigrate to Liberia. In Liberia he entered fully into civic life, publishing the widely read and respected *Liberia Herald* from 1835 to 1840, holding a number of administrative positions in the government, and guiding the colony to independence and national autonomy in 1847. See: William M. Brewer, "John B. Russwurm," *Journal of Negro History* 13 (October 1928), 413-22; Philip S. Foner, "John B. Russwurm, A Document," *Journal of Negro History* 54 (October 1969), 393-397.

33. *Freedom's Journal,* March 16, 1827.

34. Foner, "John B. Russwurm," *Journal of Negro History;* David Walker, *Walker's Appeal, in four Articles* (Boston, 1829); *Minutes of the Fourth Annual Convention, for the improvement of the free people of colour* (New York, 1834); Henry

Highland Garnet, "An Address to the Slaves of the United States" in *Negro Orators and Their Orations,* ed. Carter G. Woodson (Washington, D.C., 1925), 157; John S. Rock, "I Will Sink or Swim With My Race," *The Liberator,* March 12, 1858, as reproduced in Aptheker, *A Documentary History,* 403.

CHAPTER FOUR

1. American Colonization Society, *Fourth Annual Report* (Washington, D.C., 1821), Appendix, 3.
2. *Mercury,* New Bedford, Massachusetts, January 28, 1814, 4.
3. The correspondence with Cuffe: Womsbey to Cuffe, n.d., Folder 6; Morse to Cuffe, April 14, 1815, Folder 4; Peckhama to Cuffe, November 7, 1815, Folder 4; Saunders to Cuffe, March 27, 1815, Folder 5, Series A, *Paul Cuffe Papers,* Old Dartmouth Historical Society, Fall River, Massachusetts. Daniel Coker, *Journal of Daniel Coker, A Descendant of Africa, From the Time of Leaving New York, in the Ship Elizabeth, on a Voyage for Sherbro, In Africa* (Baltimore, 1820), 21.
4. See especially: Sister M. Reginald Gerdes, OSP, "To Educate and Evangelize: Black Catholic Schools of the Oblate Sisters of Providence (1820-1880)," *U.S. Catholic Historian* 7 (spring/summer 1988):183-200; Julie Winch, *Philadelphia's Black Elite. Activism, Accommodation, and the Struggle for Autonomy, 1787-1848* (Philadelphia, 1988), 49-69.
5. Archibald Alexander, *A History of Colonization on the Western Coast of Africa* (Philadelphia, 1846), Chapter 2, "Origins of the Colony at Sierra Leone," 39-48.
6. John Matthews, *A Voyage to the River Sierra-Leone in the Years 1785, 1786, and 1787* (London, 1788), 22.
7. *Substance of the Report of the Court of Directors of the Sierra Leone Company to the General Court on the 19th of October 1791* (London, 1791), 51.
8. C. B. Wadstrom, *An Essay on Colonization, Particularly Applied to the Western Coast of Africa* (London, 1795), Part II, Chapter 11, 18-19.
9. *Substance of the Report Delivered to the Court of Directors of the Sierra Leone Company to the General Court of Proprietors* (London, 1787), 37-38.
10. Floyd J. Miller, *The Search for a Black Nationality* (Urbana, 1975), 21-52.
11. John Clarkson, *Clarkson's Mission to America, 1791-1792* (Halifax, Nova Scotia, 1971), 58-59.
12. Wadstrom, *An Essay on Colonization,* Part II: 28, 71-81; *Substance of the Report Delivered to the Court of Directors of the Sierra Leone Company to the General Court of Proprietors on March 27th, 1794* (Philadelphia, 1795).
13. *Substance of the Report Delivered to the Court of Directors of the Sierra Leone Company to the General Court of Proprietors on March 27th, 1794*; Wadstrom, *An Essay on Colonization,* 78.
14. Wadstrom, *An Essay on Colonization,* Part II: 65.

15. F. Harrison Rankin, *The White Man's Grave: A Visit to Sierra Leone in 1834,* 2 Vols. (London, 1836), 90-91; *A Residence at Sierra Leone,* ed. Mrs. Norton (London, 1849), 232-37; Wadstrom, *An Essay on Colonization,* 38-43.

16. Wadstrom, *An Essay on Colonization,* 66-69.

17. *Substance of the Report Delivered to the Court of Directors of the Sierra Leone Company to the General Court of Proprietors on March 27th, 1794,* 46-54.

18. Maroon communities, living as virtual outlaw bands, were highly skilled in guerilla warfare, maximizing the advantage afforded by harsh environments, evasive and elusive in their warfare, and without mercy in their dealings with deserters from the group and with the white Europeans who sought to reenslave them. See: Roger Bastide, *African Civilizations in the New World* (New York, 1972 translated ed.); D. Brymner, "The Jamaica Maroons: How They Came to Nova Scotia—How They Left It," *Transactions of the Royal Society of Canada* second series, 1(1895), 81-90; David Dalby, "Ashanti Survivals in the Language and Traditions of the Windward Maroons of Jamaica," *African Language Studies* 12 (January 1971), 31-51; Bryan Edwards, "Observations on the disposition, character, manners, and habits of life, of the Maroon Negroes of the island of Jamaica," in Bryan Edwards, *The History of the West Indies* (London, 1807): Vol. I, 522-76; A.E. Furness, "The Maroon War of 1795," *Jamaican Historical Review* 5 (January 1965), 30-49; Richard Hart, "Cudjoe and the First Maroon War in Jamaica," *Caribbean Historical Review* 1 (January 1950), 46-79; Orlando Patterson, "Slavery and Slave Revolts: A Socio-historical Analysis of the First Maroon War, 1655-1740," *Social and Economic Studies* 19 (April 1970), 289-325; Carey Robinson, *The Fighting Maroons of Jamaica* (Kingston, Jamaica, 1969).

19. By 1826 about half the original settlers were believed to have disappeared into the bush, and in 1834 there were only about three hundred Nova Scotians still living in the Colony, "including such as had been born during forty-two years" of residence in Sierra Leone. Rankin, *White Man's Grave,* 92-97, 102-18.

20. Miller, *The Search for a Black Nationality,* 21-52; George Washington Williams, *A History of the Negro Race in America,* 2 vols. (New York, 1882), Vol. 1, 86-88. For contemporary descriptions of Sierra Leone see especially: Anna Maria Falconbridge, *Two Voyages to Sierra Leone During the Years 1791-2-3* (London, 1795, 3rd ed.); Mrs. Norton, *A Residence at Sierra Leone* (London, 1849); Thomas Eyre Poole, *Life, Scenery, and Customs in Sierra Leone,* 2 vols. (London, 1850).

21. Lott Cary (born ca. 1780) was born into slavery around 1780 in the rural tobacco country south of Richmond, Virginia. In 1804 Cary's owner put him to work in a Richmond tobacco warehouse where he began to drink heavily and "contracted the vicious habit of swearing." In 1807 Cary was drawn into the evangelical Protestant revival, baptized and received into Richmond's First Baptist Church, and there learned to read and write through Bible study classes. He changed his habits, began to lead religious meetings of African Americans in the Richmond area, saved his money, and in 1813 bought his own freedom

and that of his two children. A widower, Cary married again in 1815, worked as a waged day laborer, and joined the African Missionary Society, making annual contributions that ranged from $100 to $150 to the African missions. He bought a small farm, but he dreamed of Africa and of settling there. In 1821 Cary used his life savings, $1800, to pay passage to Africa for his family on the ACS ship *Nautilus*. He worked for a time in Freetown as cooper and itinerant preacher and then joined other African Americans at the ACS Cape Mesurado settlement in 1822. There is no biography of Lott Cary. See: Archibald Alexander, *A History of Colonization on the Western Coast of Africa*, 2nd ed. (Philadelphia, 1846).

22. Richard West, *Back to Africa, A History of Sierra Leone and Liberia* (London, 1970), 91-95. See also: Jehudi Ashmun, *History of the American Colony in Liberia* (Washington, 1826); Frederic Bancroft, *Colonization of American Negroes* (Norman, Oklahoma, 1957); Ralph Randolph Gurley, *On the Colonization and Civilization of Africa* (London, 1841) for discussions of the organization of the American Colonization Society.

23. The idea had an enduring appeal for some. The question of a state or territory set aside for African Americans surfaced again during Reconstruction. Government officials debated the feasibility of setting aside Indian Territory for the resettlement of newly emancipated African Americans and in the West a number of African-American entrepreneurs guided the development of all-black towns: Nicodemus, Kansas (1879), Mound Bayou, Mississippi (1887), and Boley, Oklahoma (1904) are among the most well known. See: Norman L. Crockett, *The Black Towns* (Lawrence, Kansas, 1979); Kenneth Hamilton, "The Origin and Early Development of Langston, Oklahoma," *Journal of Negro History* 62 (July 1977), 270-82; Edgar R. Iles, "Boley: An Exclusively Negro Town in Oklahoma," *Opportunity: The Journal of Negro Life* 3 (April 1925), 231-35; Daniel F. Littlefield, Jr. and Lonnie E. Underhill, "Black Dreams and the Town of Mound Bayou," *Phylon* 15 (Fourth Quarter 1954), 396-401; William H. Pease and Jane H. Pease, "Organized Negro Communities: A North American Experiment," *Journal of Negro History* 47 (January 1962), 19-34.

24. William Lloyd Garrison, *Thoughts on African Colonization* (Boston, 1832), 60ff.

25. *Address to the American Society for Colonizing the Free People of Colour, as Read at a Special Meeting in the City of Washington, November 21st, 1818* (Washington, D.C., 1818); American Colonization Society, *Second Annual Report* (Washington, D.C., 1819), 24; Samuel Swan to Brothers, Atlantic Ocean, August 1811, Swan Letterbook. Peabody Museum; *Captain George Howland's Voyage to West Africa, 1816-1817,* Rhode Island Historical Society.

26. Daniel Coker, son of Susan Coker, a white indentured servant, and an African slave, was born in Maryland, initially named Isaac Wright, but took his half-brother's and his mother's name (Coker) when he migrated from Maryland to New York as a young man. Like Richard Allen, Coker was ordained a deacon in the Methodist Episcopal Church by Bishop Francis Asbury in 1808. He returned to Baltimore where he organized a school for African Americans. In

1816 Coker became the minister of the African Methodist Episcopal Bethel Society, later the African Methodist Episcopal (AME) denomination, which was organizationally linked to black Methodist congregations in Philadelphia and Attleborough, Pennsylvania, Wilmington, Delaware, and Salem, New Jersey. Coker was elected the first Bishop of the AME Church, but resigned in favor of Richard Allen almost immediately. He was expelled from the denomination in 1818 although the substance of the charges was never disclosed. There is no biography of Coker. For additional information see: Francis Asbury, *Journal and Letters of Francis Asbury* (Nashville, 1958); Carol V. R. George, *Segregated Sabbaths: Richard Allen and the Rise of Independent Black Churches* (New York, 1973); Daniel Alexander Payne, *History of the AME Church* (Nashville, 1891); James M. Wright, *The Free Negro in Maryland, 1634-1860* (New York, 1921); Charles H. Wesley, *Richard Allen, Apostle of Freedom* (Washington, 1935).

27. Elijah Johnson (ca. 1780-1849) was probably born in New Jersey, but known to be in New Jersey by 1789. He received rudimentary schooling in New Jersey and New York, served with New Jersey, New York, and Massachusetts regiments during the War of 1812, and studied for the Methodist ministry. Johnson emigrated to the African west coast on the ACS ship *Elizabeth* in February 1820, at the age of forty, and with Daniel Coker took charge of the first ACS settlement when white society agents died. Johnson generally took charge of the settlement's military defenses during the 1820s, was appointed Commissary of Stores in 1822, and served in the 1847 Liberian Constitutional Convention. Johnson's son, Hiliary Richard Johnson, served as president of Liberia and his grandson, F. E. R. Johnson, served as the nation's secretary of state. For additional information see: Alexander, *A History of Colonization*; Richard Bardolph, *Negro Vanguard* (New York, 1961); R. B. Gurley, *Life of Jehudi Ashmun* (Washington, D.C., 1835); Sir Harry Johnson, *Liberia*, 2 vols. (London, 1906); *The African Repository and Colonial Journal*, Washington, D.C., especially the August 1849 issue, which reprints Johnson's obituary from the *Liberia Herald*.

28. Alexander, *A History of Colonization*, 114.; *Journal of Daniel Coker*, 16-19.

29. *Journal of Daniel Coker*, 21, 44.

30. Ibid., 21-22.

31. Ibid., 24-5.

32. American Colonization Society, *Second Annual Report*, 35.

33. Ibid., 58-60.

34. See: Asbury, *Journal and Letters of Francis Asbury*; George, *Segregated Sabbaths*; Payne, *History of the AME Church*; Wright, *The Free Negro in Maryland, 1634-1860*; For a contemporary account see: Alexander, *A History of Colonization*, 128-138; American Colonization Society, *Fourth Annual Report*, 18.

35. Alexander, *History of Colonization*, 131.

36. Charles Henry Huberich, *The Political and Legislative History of Liberia* Vol. I (New York, 1947), 225-26.

37. American Colonization Society, *Fourth Annual Report,* 18; Appendix, 3.

38. Alexander, *A History of Colonization,* 136-37; Carlisle, *The Roots of Black Nationalism,* 31-35.

39. Alexander, *A History of Colonization,* 243-46; C.C. Boone, *Liberia As I Know It* (Richmond, 1929), 25-37. As *Nautilus* sailed, the American Colonization Society reported "one hundred black persons in the City of Philadelphia have expressed the desire to remove to Africa. . . . Seventy-nine have communicated the same request through the Auxiliary society of New-York. A considerable number have likewise offered themselves to the Society, from Richmond, Petersburg, and Norfolk." American Colonization Society, *Fifth Annual Report* (Washington, D.C., 1822), 24.

40. *Captain George Howland's Voyage to West Africa, 1822-1823.* Manuscript. Rhode Island Historical Society; Alexander, *A History of Colonization,* 246.

41. Huberich, *The Political and Legislative History of Liberia,* 226.

42. *Howland's Voyage to West Africa, 1822-1823.* Rhode Island Historical Society.

43. Alexander, *A History of Colonization,* 177-98.

44. American Colonization Society, *Sixth Annual Report,* 13; *Seventh Annual Report,* 64-65; Huberich, *The Political and Legislative History of Liberia,* 143-322; ed. Lucius E. Smith, *Heroes and Martyrs of the Modern Missionary Enterprise* (Providence, Rhode Island, 1857), 355-62.

45. Alexander, *A History of Colonization,* 207-19.

46. American Colonization Society, *Eighth Annual Report* (Washington, D.C., 1825), *Tenth Annual Report* (Washington, D.C., 1827) 32-33; Alexander, *A History of Colonization,* 223-24; *Genius of Universal Emancipation,* Vol. 5 (June 10, 1826) 42, 325.

47. Boone, *Liberia As I Knew It,* 33-34; American Colonization Society, *Seventh Annual Report* (Washington, D.C., 1824); *Census of the Colony of Liberia, July 20, 1823,* 160-61; Plymouth, Massachusetts *Old Colony Memorial,* September 22, 1827.

48. *Freedom's Journal,* April 4, 1828.

49. *Freedom's Journal,* January 11, 1828; American Colonization Society, *Ninth Annual Report* (Washington, D.C., 1826), 16-18;

50. *Freedom's Journal,* June 20, 1828.

51. Rodney Carlisle, *The Roots of Black Nationalism* (Port Washington, New York, 1975), 40.

52. American Colonization Society, *Thirteenth Annual Report* (Washington, D.C., 1830), 31.

53. *Minutes and Proceedings* (Philadelphia, 1830), 6.

CHAPTER FIVE

1. *Minutes of the Fifth Annual Convention for the Improvement of The Free People of Colour in the United States, Held by Adjournments, in the Wesley Church,*

Philadelphia, from the First to the Fifth of June, Inclusive, 1835 (Philadelphia, 1835), 30.

2. The riot and surrounding circumstances are variously described in: Charles T. Hickok, *The Negro in Ohio, 1802-1870* (Cleveland, 1896); Frank U. Quillen, *The Color Line in Ohio, A History of Race Prejudice in a Typical Northern State* (Ann Arbor, 1913); James H. Rodabaugh, "The Negro in Ohio," *Journal of Negro History* 31 (January 1946), 9-28; J. Reuben Sheeler; "The Struggle of the Negro in Ohio," *Journal of Negro History* 31 (April 1946), 208-26; Richard C. Wade, "The Negro in Cincinnati, 1800-1830," *Journal of Negro History* 39 (January 1954), 43-57.

3. See especially: *The Rights of All*, August 7, September 18, 1829. Cornish, who strongly opposed African colonization schemes in general, published *The Rights of All* from May through October 1829. While various anti-slavery newspapers also provided interpretive coverage of the events in Cincinnati and the African colonization movement, *The Rights of All* remains the only direct contemporary coverage of and from the African-American perspective.

4. For a summary of the Ohio Black Codes see especially: Charles J. Wilson, "The Negro in Early Ohio," *Ohio Archeological and Historical Society Publications* 39 (1930), 717-68.

5. *Liberty Hall*, Cincinnati, Ohio, January 28, 1825. By 1829 the Cincinnati African-American population was counted at 2,258 according to *The Cincinnati Directory for the Year 1829* (Cincinnati, 1829), n.p., or approximately 10 percent of the city's total population.

6. Wade, "The Negro in Cincinnati, 1800-1830," 49.

7. Daniel Drake, *Natural and Statistical View, or Picture of Cincinnati* (Cincinnati, 1815) provides a particularly complete ethno-economic description of Cincinnati during the early decades of the nineteenth century.

8. The legislation requiring all African Americans moving into Ohio to post a surety bond of $500 and present evidence of their free status had been on the books since 1807, but never had been enforced locally. Not all black Cincinnatians agreed with Malvin. Some two hundred members of the Methodist Episcopal Church denied any support for the protest, stating that they sought no changes in the state's legal codes and asked only for a "continuation of the smiles of the white people as we have hitherto enjoyed." Carter G. Woodson, "Negroes of Cincinnati Prior to the Civil War," *Journal of Negro History* 1 (January 1916), 1-22.

9. John Malvin, *Autobiography of John Malvin* (Cleveland, 1879); Harry E. Davis, "John Malvin, A Western Reserve Pioneer," *Journal of Negro History* 23 (October 1938), 426-34.

10. By the 1840s this strategy for mobilizing economic resources had become institutionalized as the "begging system," a scheme routinely employed by a number of African-American Canadian refugees settlements to supplement their meager economic resources. See especially: Robin Winks, *Blacks in Canada* (Montreal, 1971).

11. In due time, other black Cincinnatians would follow, and this group would establish the Wilberforce Colony in Upper Canada. See chapter 6 for additional discussion of the Canadian refugee settlements.

12. For discussions of the circumstances surrounding the 1829 Cincinnati Crisis see: Wendell P. Dabney, *Colored Citizens of Cincinnati* (Cincinnati, 1926), 30-35; B. Drake and E. D. Mansfield, "Cincinnati," in *Sketches of a Journey Through the Western States* (London, 1827), 27ff; *The Rights of All*, August 7, 1829; *Report on the Conditions of the Free People of Color* (Columbus, Ohio, 1830), 3-4; Woodson, "Negroes of Cincinnati Prior to the Civil War"; "Banishment of the People of Color from Cincinnati, A Document" *Journal of Negro History* 7 (April 1923), 331-33.

13. *Freedom's Journal*, April 20, 1827 and June 1, 1827, offered suggestive comparative data for the 800 African Americans living in New Haven, the 900 in Portland, Maine, the 2,000 in Boston, and the 20,000 in Philadelphia.

14. Michael Lipsky, "Protest as a Political Resource," *American Political Science Review* 62 (December 1968), 1114-58. For a reanalysis of the Birmingham confrontation see: Aldon D. Morris, "Birmingham Reconsidered: An Analysis of the Dynamics and Tactics of Mobilization," *American Sociological Review,* 58 (October 1993), 621-36. For broader discussions of the 1960s civil rights protests see: David J. Garrow, *Bearing the Cross* (New York, 1986); Aldon D. Morris, *The Origins of the Civil Rights Movement: Black Communities Organizing for Change* (New York, 1984);

15. *The Colored American,* October 7, 1837; "The First Colored Convention," *The Anglo-African Magazine* 1 (October, 1859) 10, 305-10; Carol V. R. George, *Segregated Sabbaths, Richard Allen and the Rise of Independent Black Churches, 1760-1840* (New York, 1973), 122ff; Julie Winch, *Philadelphia's Black Elite* (Philadelphia: Temple University Press, 1988), 91-93.

16. *Freedom's Journal*, March 16, 1827; David Walker, *Walker's Appeal in Four Articles: Together with a Preamble, to the Coloured Citizens of the World, but in particular and very expressly, to those of the United States of America, written in Boston, State of Massachusetts, September 28, 1829* (Boston, 1829); Henry Highland Garnet, *Walker's Appeal, With A Brief Sketch of His Life. By Henry Highland Garnet. And Also Garnet's Address to the Slaves* (New York, 1848).

17. *Freedom's Journal*, May 4, 11, 18, 1827; *The Rights of All*, September 18, October 9, 1829; *The Colored American,* March 11, 18, July 1, August 5, 1837; March 3, 5, 22, April 5, 12, June 30, August 4, 25, September 15, 22, October 20, November 3, 18, 1838; January 19, February 2, 23, March 9, September 28, November 23, 1830; January 23, May 1, August 7, 21, September 18, 1841.

18. *Freedom's Journal*, August 3, December 7, 1827; *The Rights of All*, August 7, 1829; *The Colored American,* October 20, 1828, April 25, May 30, 1840; February 27, March 13, April 10, August 14, 1841.

19. See "Report on the Conditions of the People of Color in the State of Ohio," *Proceedings of the Ohio Anti-Slavery Convention* (Columbus, Ohio, 1835) for the abolitionist analysis. See also: Dabney, *Cincinnati's Colored Citizens;*

Hickok, *The Negro in Ohio;* Quillin, *The Color Line in Ohio;* Wilson, "The Negro in Early Ohio."

20. See especially: Bella Gross, "The First National Negro Convention," *Journal of Negro History* 31 (October 1946), 435-43; ed. Howard H. Bell, *Minutes and Proceedings of the National Negro Conventions, 1830-1864* (New York, 1969).

21. Howard Bell, "National Negro Conventions," *Journal of Negro History* 42 (April 1957), 247-60; Bella Gross, "The First National Convention"; Bella Gross, *Clarion Call: The History and Development of the Negro Convention Movement in the United States* (New York, 1947); Charles Wesley, "Negroes of New York, Early Convention Movements," *Journal of Negro History* 24 (January 1939), 72-80.

22. See especially: George, *Segregated Sabbaths;* Winch, *Philadelphia's Black Elite.*

23. David Walker, *Walker's Appeal in Four Articles, Together with a Preamble to the Coloured Citizens of the World, Third and Last Edition* (Boston, 1830).

24. William Lloyd Garrison, *Thoughts on Colonization,* Part II (Boston, 1832), 10-23; *The Liberator,* April 2, 1831, 54. See especially: Leonard I. Sweet, *Black Images of America, 1784-1920* (Unpublished Ph.D. dissertation, University of Rochester, 1974) for a detailed analysis of African-American responses to various American national and political events that were reconstituted as *lieux de memoire.*

25. *Frederick Douglass' Paper,* 4 January 4, 1855.

26. See *The Liberator,* April 9, May 14, 1831 for commentary on Allen's life and the vacuum his death left in contemporary African-American leadership circles.

27. *Proceedings of the First Annual Convention of the People of Colour, Held by Adjournment in the City of Philadelphia, From the Sixth to the Eleventh of June, Inclusive, 1831* (Philadelphia, 1831).

28. *The Anglo-African Magazine* 1 (1859); Elizabeth Rauh Bethel, "Images of Hayti, The Construction of an Afro-American *Lieu de Memoire,*" *Callaloo* 15 (October 1992), 827-41.

29. See especially: *Proceedings of the American Convention of Abolition Societies* (1794 & 1795); *Joseph Lancaster and the Monitorial School Movement,* ed. Carl F. Kaestle, (New York, 1973); Diane Ravitch, *The Great School Wars, New York City, 1805-1973* (Basic Books, 1974), 12-19; Carter G. Woodson, *Education of the Negro Prior to 1861* (New York, 1915), 72ff.

30. *Proceedings of the First Annual Convention of the People of Colour* (1831).

31. Ibid.

32. Ibid.

33. G. B. Stebbins, *Facts and Opinions Touching the Real Origin, Character, and Influence of the American Colonization Society* (Boston, 1853), 194-210.

34. See: *William Styron's Nat Turner; Ten Black Writers Respond,* ed. John Henrik Clarke, (Boston, 1968); Stephen B. Oates, *Our Fiery Trial: Abraham Lincoln, John Brown, and the Civil War Era* (Amherst, 1979).

35. *Minutes and Proceedings of the Second Annual Convention, for the Improvement of the Free People of Color in these United States, Held by Adjournment in the City*

of Philadelphia, from the 4th to the 13th of June inclusive, 1831 (Philadelphia, 1832).

36. Ibid.

37. Ibid.

38. *Minutes and Proceedings of the Third Annual Convention, for the Improvement of Free People of Colour, Held by Adjournment, in the City of Philadelphia, from the 3rd to the 13th of June Inclusive, 1833* (Philadelphia, 1833); *Minutes and Proceedings of the Fifth Annual (National) Convention for the Improvement of the Free People of Colour in the United States* (Philadelphia, 1836); Bella Gross, *Clarion Call.*

INTRODUCTION TO PART III

1. The ideological schism between the emigrationists and those whose identity and politics remained anchored in the United States is easily traced through the state conventions that met irregularly from 1840-1865. Primary source documents are easily accessed through *Proceedings of the Black State Conventions, 1840-1865,* eds. Philip S. Foner and George E. Walker, 2 vols. (Philadelphia, 1979).

2. Rodney Carlisle, *The Roots of Black Nationalism* (Port Washington, New York, 1975); Theodore Draper, *The Rediscovery of Black Nationalism* (New York, 1970), 14-47.

3. Frederick Douglass, "Review of *The Black Man, His Antecedents, His Genius and His Achievements.*" *Douglass' Monthly* (January 1863), 10.

4. William Wells Brown, *The Black Man, His Antecedents, His Genius and His Achievement* (1863, Miami, Florida, 1969 reprint ed.), 1.

CHAPTER SIX

1. Benjamin Drew, *The Refugee: or the Narratives of Fugitive Slaves in Canada* (Boston, 1856), 279.

2. Theodore Draper, *The Roots of Black Nationalism* (Port Washington, New York, 1975), 14-47.

3. See especially: Robin Winks, *Blacks in Canada* (Montreal, 1971), 145; *Genius of Universal Emancipation* (Baltimore), November 18, 1826; *Freedom's Journal* (New York), August 3, 1827; January 9, 1829.

4. William Wells Brown, *The Black Man, His Antecedents, His Genius and His Achievement* (1863, Miami, Florida, 1969 reprint ed.), 1.

5. Joseph A. Carroll, *Slave Insurrections in the United States* (Boston, 1938), 43-44; Rayford Logan, *The Diplomatic Relations of the United States with Hayti, 1776-1891* (Chapel Hill, North Carolina, 1941), 29-35. See chapter 3 for a discussion of Gabriel's Rebellion.

6. See especially: Sister M. Reginald Gerdes, OSP, "To Educate and Evangelize: Black Catholic Schools of the Oblate Sisters of Providence (1828-1880)," *U.S. Catholic Historian*, 7 (spring/summer 1988), 183-200; Julie Winch, *Philadelphia's Black Elite. Activism, Accommodation, and the Struggle for Autonomy, 1787-1848* (Philadelphia: Temple University Press, 1988), 49-69.

7. Henri Christophe served in a St. Domingue slave regiment that fought with the Americans at the Battle of Savannah, served during the Haytian Revolution as one of Toussaint's generals, and was crowned King of Hayti with Dessalines's assassination in 1806.

8. C. L. R. James, *Black Jacobins* (New York, 1963); H. P. Davis, *Black Democracy* (New York, 1936 revised ed.); Selden Rodman, *Hayti: The Black Republic* (New York, 1954). See chapter 4 for a discussion of Wilberforce's role in colonizing Sierra Leone.

9. Winch, *Philadelphia's Black Elite*, 50-52; Miller, *Search for a Black Nationality*, 74-81; Carlisle, *The Roots of Black Nationalism*, 50-54.

10. Prince Saunders, *Haytien Papers. A Collection of the Very Interesting Proclamations and Other Official Documents of the Kingdom of Hayti* (London, 1816; Boston, 1818), iii, v, ix.

11. Saunders, *Haytien* Papers, 24.

12. Prince Saunders, *A Memoire Presented to the American Convention for Promoting the Abolition of Slavery* (Philadelphia, 1818); Prince Saunders, *An Address Delivered at Bethel Church, Philadelphia, on the 30th of September, Before the Pennsylvania Augustine Society for the Education of People of Colour* (Philadelphia, 1818); *Henri Christophe and Thomas Clarkson: A Correspondence,* Earl Leslie Griggs and Clifford H. Prator, eds.(Berkeley, 1952).

13. Davis, *Black Democracy,* 99-114.

14. Formal United States recognition of Hayti did not occur until 1862. For an extensive discussion see: Rayford Logan, *The Diplomatic Relations of the United States with Hayti, 1776-1891* (Chapel Hill, 1941).

15. Loring Daniel Dewey to Jean Pierre Boyer, March 4, 1824, Boyer to Dewey, March 4, April 30, 1824, *Correspondence Relative to the Emigration to Hayti of Free People of Colour in the United States* (New York, 1824).

16. Boyer to Dewey, April 30, 1824, *Correspondence Relative to the Emigration to Hayti,* 6-11.

17. Inginac to Dewey, May 7, 1824, Boyer to Dewey, May 24, 1824, *Correspondence Relative to the Emigration to Hayti,* 12-14.

18. Boyer to Charles Collins, May 25, 1824, *Correspondence Relative to the Emigration to Hayti,* 15-17.

19. Jean Pierre Boyer, Instructions to the Citizen Jr. Granville, *Correspondence Relative to the Emigration to Hayti,* 19.

20. See especially: *The Genius of Universal Emancipation,* Vol. III Supplement (June 1824), 193, 194.

21. As cited in Winch, *Philadelphia's Black Elite,* 55.

22. *Correspondence Relative to the Emigration to Hayti,* 31.

23. *Columbian Sentinel* (Athens, Georgia), July 3, 1824, as reprinted in *Correspondence Relative to the Emigration to Hayti.*

24. General Inginac to Richard Allen, n.d., *Genius of Universal Emancipation,* Vol. IV, No. 4 (January 1825).

25. Loring D. Dewey to The Editor, February 3, 1825, *Genius of Universal Emancipation,* Vol. IV, No. 49 (March 1825), 88; Winch, *Philadelphia's Black Elite,* 56-57.

26. *Genius of Universal Emancipation,* George Flower to Lundy, June 23, 1824; Arthur Jones and George Jann to George Flower, as received by Lundy June 26, 1824, Vol. IV, No. 44 (October 1824), 9, 10; Charles W. Fisher to his Father, February 13, 1825; Daniel Copeland to Rev. Richard Allen, May 10, 1825; Francis Wright to Lundy, March 7, 1830; Jeremie to Lundy, December 6, 1824; George Mayes to Lundy, February 6, 1825; Margaret Patterson to Lundy, April 12, 1825, Vol. IV, No. 47 (January 1825), 58; No. 49 (March 1825), 91; No. 50 (April 1825), 99; No. 53 (July 1825), 103, 152; No. 54 (August 1825), 175; Vol. X, No. 231 (October 1829), 38; Vol. XI, No. 253 (April 1830), 16.

27. Benjamin Peter Hunt, *Remarks on Hayti* (Philadelphia, 1860) , 4-14.

28. Loring Daniel Dewey, *Correspondence Relative to the Emigration to Hayti,* 30.

29. See: *Freedom's Journal,* July 20, December 7, 1827; June 20, October 10, 1828.

30. See: *Freedom's Journal,* August 24, September 28, October 12, November 9, 1827; January 25, February 29, June 20, July 18, November 7, 1828.

31. *Freedom's Journal,* April 27, May 4, 11, June 15, 29, October 12, 1827.

32. Ibid.

33. *Freedom's Journal,* May 4, 11, 1827.

34. *Freedom's Journal,* December 21, 1827.

35. *Freedom's Journal,* January 18, 25, February 8, 15, 1828.

36. Austin Steward, *Twenty-Two Years a Slave and Forty Years a Freeman* (Rochester, 1861, 3rd ed.), 176-79.

37. Ibid., 182.

38. Utica, New York *Friend of Man,* Hiram Wilson to William Goodell, 14 March 14, 1838:150; July 24, 1839:22; *The Liberator,* November 23, 1833; Steward, *Twenty-Two Years a Slave,* 281-83; *The Diary of Benjamin Lundy, written during his journey through Upper Canada, January, 1832,* Ontario Historical Society Papers and Records 19 (1922).

39. Winks, *Blacks in Canada,* 178-80

40. Reverend Josiah Henson, *The Life of Josiah Henson* (London: 1851), 92.

41. *An Autobiography of the Reverend Josiah Henson, With a Preface by Mrs. Harriet Beecher Stowe* (London, 1876), 127-30, 164-75. See also: *The Liberator,* Hiram Wilson to Rev. Charles Torry, May 17, 1839:77; Hiram Wilson to William Lloyd Garrison, August 26, 1841:207, April 7, 1848:55, December 13, 1850:198, June 6, 1851:92; (Philadelphia) *Pennsylvania Freeman,* Hiram Wilson to Goodell, October 24, 1839:3.

42. Benjamin Drew, *The Refugee: or the Narratives of Fugitive Slaves in Canada* (Boston, 1856), 234-39; *Frederick Douglass' Paper,* August 11, 18, 1854.

43. Drew, *The Refugee,* 291-98; Daniel G. Hill, *The Freedom-Seekers* (Agincourt, Canada, 1981), 76-89; Winks, *Blacks in Canada,* 208-18.

44. Refugee Home Society, *Thirty Thousand Refugees* (Detroit, 1852).

45. Fred Landon, "Henry Bibb, The Colonizer," *Journal of Negro History* 5 (October 1920), 437-47; Donald G. Simpson, *Negroes in Ontario from Early Times to 1870* (Unpublished Ph.D. Thesis, University of Western Ontario, London, 1970):596; Winks, *Blacks in Canada,* 204-08.

46. See especially: *The Liberator,* June 25, 1847, December 13, 1850, February 4, 1853; Drew, *The Refugee,* 327-28.

47. *The Liberator,* October 4, 1850, April 25, 1851; *Voice of the Fugitive,* July 29, 1852; Siebert, *The Underground Railroad,* 249.

48. *The (New York)Weekly Anglo-African,* August 20, 1859; Drew, *The Refugee,* 307ff; Annie Strath Jameson, *William King, Friend and Champion of Slaves* (Toronto: Mission of Evangelism, 1925), 114; Fred Landon, "Negro Migration to Canada After the Passing of the Fugitive Slave Act," *Journal of Negro History* 5 (January 1920), 22-36.

49. *Frederick Douglass' Paper,* August 25, 1854; Victor Ullman, *Look to the North Star* (Boston, 1969), 178-206.

50. Ullman, *Look to the North Star,* 270-88.

51. Martin Robinson Delany (1812-1885) the son of a slave father and a free-born mother, produced the first full-length statement of black nationalism, which incorporated a recommendation for emigration into an indictment of American racism: *The Condition, Elevation, Emigration and Destiny of the Colored People of the United States, Politically Considered* (Philadelphia, 1852). In 1854 Delany convened the National Emigration Convention in Cleveland where he continued to promote emigration as a viable option for African Americans seeking to escape racism. Delany joined the migration to Canada, where he lived in Chatham. In 1859 Delany and Robert Campbell, a young science teacher, traveled in Liberia and the Niger Valley, seeking a site for African Americans to settle and established an autonomous colony. For a biographical summary and an interpretation of Delany's philosophy see Nell Irvin Painter, "Martin R. Delany: Elitism and Black Nationalism," in *Black Leaders of the Nineteenth Century,* eds. Leon Litwack and August Meier (Urbana, 1988), 149-71.

52. Joseph Cinque and the *Amistad* case are initially chronicled in John W. Barber, *A History of the Amistad Captives* (New Haven, 1840). See also: Mary Cable, *Black Odyssey: The Case of the Slave Ship Amistad* (New York, 1971); Edwin Palmer Hoyt, *The Amistad Affair* (New York, 1970). Donald DeFreeze's use of "Cinque" during the 1974 Symbionese Liberation Army's kidnapping of Patricia Hearst reflects the enduring nature of memory and representations of resistance to oppression.

CHAPTER SEVEN

1. Malcolm X, *Malcolm X at the Audubon,* as reproduced in *Malcolm X Speaks* (New York, 1965), 116.

2. Both C. Wright Mills, *The Sociological Imagination* (New York, 1959) and Herbert G. Gutman, "Historical Consciousness in Contemporary America," in *Power and Culture,* Ira Berlin, ed. (New York, 1987), 395-412 identify historical consciousness as the insight and understanding that lie at the intersection of personal troubles and public issues. It is in that sense that I use the phrase "historical consciousness," as an awareness of the ways in which sociohistorical forces shape individual biography. For discussions of the relationship between historical consciousness and political agency see especially: David Thelen, "Memory and American History," *The Journal of American History* (March, 1898), 1117-29; Leonard Thompson, *The Political Mythology of Apartheid* (New Haven, 1985); Sterling Stucky, *Slave Culture: Nationalist Theory and the Foundations of Black America* (New York, 1987).

3. Some may accurately note that Brown's three female entries grossly underrepresented the public presence of African-American women in the political arenas of the anti-slavery and Convention movements. That numerical slight aside, Brown's choices—Wheatly, Watkins, and Forten—typify the nexus of class and politics for African-American women in the antebellum North. John D'Emilio and Estelle B. Freedman, in *Intimate Matters, A History of Sexuality in America* (New York, 1988), 85-108 provide a particularly lucid discussion of the conflicting definitions of morality and gender-specific behaviors that differentiated the white middle class and peoples of color in mid-nineteenth-century America.

4. See: *The Interesting Narrative of the Life of Olaudah Equiano, or Gustavus Vassa the African, Written by Himself* (London, 1798); *Equiano's Travels,* Paul Edwards, ed. (London, 1977 rev. ed.); G. I. Jones, "Olaudah Equiano of the Niger Ibo," in *Africa Remembered, Narratives by West Africans from the Era of the Slave Trade,* Philip D. Curtin, ed. (Madison, Wisconsin, 1967), 60-98; Lemuel Haynes, *Universal Salvation, A Very Ancient Doctrine With Some Account of the Life and Character of the Author. A Sermon Delivered at Rutland, Vermont, in the Year 1805* (New Haven, 1806); *The Life and Religious Experience of Jarena Lee, A Colored Lady, Giving An Account of her Call to Preach the Gospel. Revised and Corrected from the Original Manuscript, Written by Herself* (Philadelphia, 1836); John Marrant, *An Interesting Narrative in the Life of John Marrant, (a man of colour), Compiled Originally by the Rev. J. Aldridge* (Brighton, England, 1829).

5. See: Prince Hall, *A Charge Delivered to the Brethren of the African in Lodge in Charlestowne* (Boston, 1792); *A Charge Delivered to the African Lodge at Menotomy* (Boston, 1797); Jupiter Hammon, *An Evening's Improvement, Shewing the Necessity of Beholding the Lamb of God, to which is added A Dialogue Entitled The Kind Master and Dutiful Servant* (Hartford, 1783): Absalom Jones

and Richard Allen, *A Short Account of the Proceedings of the Black People During the Awful Calamity in Philadelphia in the Year 1793* (Philadelphia, 1794); Absalom Jones, *A Thanksgiving Sermon, Preached January 1, 1808, in St. Thomas's, or the African Episcopal Church, Philadelphia, On Account of the Abolition of the Slave Trade* (Philadelphia, 1808); Peter Williams, Jr., *A Discourse Delivered on the Death of Captain Paul Cuffee in the African Methodist Episcopal Zion Church of New-York City* (New York, 1817).

6. Jupiter Hammon, *An Address to the Negroes in the State of New-York* (New York African Society, 1787); "Prince Hall to Dear Brethren of the African Society, Boston, September 16, 1789," in *The Proceedings of the Free African Union Society and the African Benevolent Society. Newport, Rhode Island, 1780-1824,* William H. Robinson, ed. (Providence, 1976), 25-26.

7. See Samuel E. Cornish and Theodore S. Wright, *The Colonization Plan Considered in its Rejection by the Colored People—In Its Tendency to Uphold Caste—In Its Unfitness for Christianizing and Civilizing Aborigines of Africa and for Putting a Stop to the African Slave Trade* (Newark, 1840).

8. All biographical details here and elsewhere are taken from Herman Edward Thomas, *An Analysis of the Life and Work of James W.C. Pennington, A Black Churchman and Abolitionist.* (Unpublished Ph.D. dissertation, Hartford Seminary, 1978).

9. See Howard Jones, *Mutiny on the Amistad* (New York, 1987) for a description and legal analysis of the Amistad case. *The Colored American* provided contemporary coverage from an African-American perspective, including a description of Pennington's role in the care of the captives, which Jones neglected. John W. Barber, *A History of the Amistad Captives* (New Haven, 1840) also provides a contemporary narrative of the Amistad case and the Africans' sojourn in the United States.

10. There is no biography for William Cooper Nell. See prologue, note 7 for sources on Nell. All spatial information was extrapolated from annual volumes of the Boston *City Directory,* 1820-1830.

11. Howard Schuman and Jacqueline Scott, "Generations and Collective Memories," *American Sociological Review,* 54 (April 1989), 359-81 offers evidence suggesting that the most resonant political memories derive from events experienced during adolescence. The generalization certainly illuminates the factors that influenced not only Nell's adult political beliefs but those of William Wells Brown, William Still, and Frances Ellen Watkins Harper, as well.

12. William E. Farrison, *William Wells Brown: Author and Reformer* (Chicago, 1969).

13. James P. Boyd, "William Still: His Life and Work to this Time," *Still's Underground Rail Road Records* (Philadelphia, 1886 revised ed.).

14. Gross, *Clarion Call,* 40-41.

15. "Triumph of Equal School Rights in Boston," in *Proceedings of the Presentation Meeting Held in Boston: December 17, 1855* (Boston, 1855).

16. Boyd, "William Still: His Life," xiff.

17. Still, *Still's Undergroud Rail Road Records* , 9.

18. "New York State Free Suffrage Convention, September 8, 1845" in *Proceedings of the Black State Conventions, 1840-1865,* eds., Philip S. Foner and George E. Walker, Vol. I (Philadelphia, 1979), 37-41.

19. Nell, *Colored Patriots,* 325; Samuel Ringgold Ward to Frederick Douglass, January 1855, in *Black Abolitionist Papers,* Vol. I, 412-14; *Proceedings of the State Convention of Colored Men of the State of Ohio held in Cleveland on the January 21st, 22nd, & 23rd, 1857* (Columbus, 1857).

20. "Convention of the Colored Citizens of Massachusetts, August 1, 1858," in Foner and Walker, *Proceedings,* Vol. II:96-105; *A Brief Narrative of the Struggle for the Rights of the Colored People of Philadelphia in the City Railway Cars,* ed. Maxwell Whiteman, Afro-American History Series, Historic Publication No. 240, n.d.

21. *Proceedings of a Convention of the Colored Men of Ohio. Held in the City of Cincinnati, on the 23rd, 24th, 25th, and 26th Days of November, 1858* in Foner and Walker, *Proceedings of the Black State Conventions, 1840-1865,* 332-41.

22. Louis Agassiz, "The Diversity of Origin of the Human Races," *Christian Examiner,* 49, 4th series (July 1850), 110-45.

23. William Wells Brown, *The Black Man, His Antecedents, His Genius, and His Achievements* (Boston, 1865), 6. Anticipating subsequent re-rememberings of the Civil War, Brown revised the biographical dictionary and appended it to an ambitious narrative history in *The Rising Son: or, The Antecedents and Advancements of the Colored Race* (Boston, 1874), deleting many of the African and Caribbean entries and adding a number of women and men who rose to political and civic prominence during the Civil War and Reconstruction. On those re-rememberings, see David W. Blight, "'For Something Beyond the Battlefield'" Frederick Douglass and the Struggle for the Memory of the Civil War," Journal of American History 75 (March 1989), 1156-78.

24. Nell, *Colored Patriots,* 10.

EPILOGUE

1. William Still, *The Underground Rail Road* (1872; Chicago, 1970 reprint ed.), i.

2. Ibid., x.

3. William Still to Dr. J. Holmes, June 5, 1873; Still to Mrs. Carey, September 9, 1873; Still to William Wells Brown, September 9, October 23, 1783; Still to William Wells Brown, September 9, October 23, 1783. William Still Letterbook. Historical Society of Pennsylvania. I am indebted to Philip Lapsansky for directing my attention to this and other manuscript material related to William Still.

4. Oliver Johnson to Still, October 17, 1871. Box 8G, Leon Gardiner Collection, American Negro Historical Society Papers (ANHSP). Historical Society of Pennsylvania (hereafter, HSP).

5. John Hunn to Still, October 19, November 21, 1871, Leon Gardiner Collection, ANHSP. HSP.

6. J. A. Tappan to Still, October 20, 1871, Box 8G, ANHSP. HSP. In the end, Tappan's material appears in *The Underground Rail Road* (Philadelphia, 1886 revised ed.), 704-11.

7. Philip Lapsansky, "William Still's *The Underground Rail Road*: A Bibliographic Artifact of Negro Americana" (typescript, 1973); Memorandum of Agreement, Between Porter and Coates, Publishers and Booksellers, and William Still, January 29, 1872; Memorandum of Agreement Supplemental to an Agreement dated January 29, 1872, between Porter and Coates, Publishers and Booksellers, and William Still, March 5, 1873. William Still Correspondence, Gardiner Collection, ANHSP. HSP.

8. Lucy McKim Garrison to Still, December 8, 1871; James Miller McKim to Still, December 23, 1871. Box 8G, Gardiner Collection, ANHSP. HSP.

9. McKim to Still, February 29, 1872, January 2, 1873; Johnson to Still, April 11, 1873. Box 9G, Gardiner Collection, ANHSP; Still to Philip A. Bell, September 9, 1873, Still Letterbook. HSP.

10. Bleby to Still, July 27, 1871; Sarah J. Tappan to Still, May 13, 1872; (Illegible), from Fort Ellis, Montana to Still, n.d. Box 9G, f12, Gardiner Collection, ANHSP. HSP.

11. Craft to Still, June 13, 1873; Marshall to Still, April 30, 1874; Filley to Still, February 9, 1876; Stanton to Still, January 15, 1878. Box 9G, f14, Gardiner Collection, ANHSP. Still to Jones, June 5, 1873. Still Letterbook. HSP.

12. Still to Jones, June 5, 1873; Marshall to Still, April 30, 1874; Filley to Still, February 9, 1876; Stanton to Still, January 15, 1878. Box 9G, f14, Gardiner Collection, ANHSP. Still to Jones, 5 June 1873. Still Letterbook. HSP.

13. Still to Tiester, June 3, 1873; Still to Leonard, June 13, 1873; Still to Joiner, June 14, 1873; Still to Steward, June 17, 1873. Still Letterbook. HSP.

14. Still to Tate, August 14, 16, 1873; Still to Price, June 23, 30, 1873. Still Letterbook. HSP.

15. Still to Price, June 3, 1873. Still Letterbook. HSP.

16. Still to Carey, September 9, 1873; Still to Holmes, June 5, 1873; Still to Brown, September 9, October 23, November 7, 1873; Still to Jones, July 7, 1873; Still to Steward, 17 June 1873. Still Letterbook. HSP.

17. Still to Brown, August 12, 1873. Still Letterbook; Brown to Still, May 27, 1874. Box 9G, f18, Gardiner Collection, ANGSP. HSP.

18. While it is not my intention to directly discuss the role African Americans played in Reconstruction, the following sources provide preliminary description and analysis of this historical period: W. E. B. DuBois, *Black Reconstruction in America* (1935; New York, 1973 reprint ed.); Eric Foner, *Reconstruction, America's Unfinished Revolution* (New York, 1988); James M. McPherson, *Battle Cry of Freedom, The Civil War Era* (New York, 1988); Willie Lee Rose, *Rehearsal for Reconstruction* (Indianapolis, 1964); Louis S. Gerteis, *From*

Contraband to Freedman (Westport, 1973); Claude F. Oubre, Forty Acres and a Mule (Baton Rouge, 1978).

19. William Still, "Introduction," in Frances Ellen Watkins Harper, Iola Leroy, or Shadows Uplifted (1893; New York, 1988 reprint ed.), 1-3.

20. Still, Underground Rail Road, 797-98.

21. Harper, Iola Leroy (1988 revised ed.), 34.

22. Ibid., 115-16.

23. Ibid., 144-48; 179-81.

24. Life and Times of Frederick Douglass, Written by Himself. His Early Life as a Slave, His Escape from Bondage, and His Complete History to the Present Time (Hartford, 1882), 224-26.

25. Harper, Iola Leroy, 130-31.

26. DuBois, Black Reconstruction ; Harper, Iola Leroy, 152 ff; Carol R. Bleser, The Promised Land, A History of the South Carolina Land Commission (Columbia, SC, 1969) chronicles the statewide land redistribution program in South Carolina and Elizabeth Rauh Bethel, Promiseland, A Century of Life in a Negro Community (1981; Columbia, South Carolina, 1997) documents and examines the creation of one South Carolina community that resulted from that land redistribution program.

INDEX